'A book that will enable you to think differently about people who think differently. An incredibly insightful read that perfectly brings together why organizations should value neurodiverse talent and how they can best provide an environment for that talent to shine. It takes you on an incredible journey from understanding why neurodiversity is important, all the way to the successes that organizations can hope for – stopping off on the way to deliver impactful, practical and real-life advice for anyone whose role it is to hire, develop or retain talent.'
Alan Walker, Co-founder, Udder, and Co-founder and Editor-in-chief, ChatTalent

'The book is packed with great case studies, examples and important messaging to take away, plus insights and explanations of the spiky profiles we all have (some more than others). In the authors' words, "True change requires commitment – sustained and anticipatory". This book will help any reader on that journey – it's one of the most detailed texts I have encountered on the subject.'
Jean Hewitt, Senior Inclusive Design Consultant, BuroHappold Engineering

'A compelling look into how we can leverage neurodiversity strengths into our workplace. It is truly a must-read for all as it provides practical ways for inclusivity of neurodiversity to drive innovation and growth!'
Christine Ramsay, CDP (Certified Diversity Professional), Global Senior Diversity, Equity, Inclusion and Engagement Leader, Jazz Pharmaceuticals

'Neurodiversity is an important area of Diversity, Equity and Inclusion (DE&I) that has only really come into our consciences over the last few years. We know it impacts a wide range of people either in the workforce or finding insurmountable challenges to enter it. I applaud both authors for their honesty in sharing their own lived experience of work, and for collecting so many stories to share. This is a real almanac for making difference. Reading over, let the hard work start.'
Bill Boorman, strategic HR tech adviser and Founder, #tru

'Neurodiversity is one of the most important and untapped opportunities in business today. This book clearly explains the issue and honours the necessity to pay close attention to every employee's individual needs and leverage everyone's extra-special capabilities in unique and powerful ways.'
Josh Bersin, Principal and Founder, Bersin by Deloitte

'I want to give huge credit to Amanda Kirby and Theo Smith who have brought their whole selves, personal and professional, to create an up-to-date guide on neurodiversity in the workplace. They provide a comprehensive review the current perspectives of the neurodiversity paradigm, good practice in the workplace and real-world examples of innovative programmes and strategies. There is no such thing as a "degree in Neurodiversity" for HR and D&I professionals, but for anyone looking to expand their knowledge in this field, this book is as close as you are going to get to it!'
Aidan Healy, Chief Executive Officer, Lexxic

Neurodiversity at Work

*Drive innovation, performance and productivity
with a neurodiverse workforce*

Theo Smith
Amanda Kirby

KoganPage

First published in Great Britain and the United States in 2021 by Kogan Page Limited

2nd Floor, 45 Gee Street	122 W 27th St, 10th Floor	4737/23 Ansari Road
London	New York, NY 10001	Daryaganj
EC1V 3RS	USA	New Delhi 110002
United Kingdom		India
www.koganpage.com		

Kogan Page books are printed on paper from sustainable forests.

ISBNs

Hardback   978 1 3986 0026 3
Paperback   978 1 3986 0024 9
Ebook   978 1 3986 0025 6

British Library Cataloguing-in-Publication Data

A CIP record for this book is available from the British Library.

Library of Congress Cataloging-in-Publication Data

Names: Smith, Theo (Theo A.), author. | Kirby, Amanda, editor.
Title: Neurodiversity at work : drive innovation, performance and
   productivity with a neurodiverse workforce / Theo Smith, Amanda Kirby.
Description: London, United Kingdom ; New York, NY : Kogan Page Limited,
   2021. | Includes bibliographical references and index.
Identifiers: LCCN 2021022714 (print) | LCCN 2021022715 (ebook) | ISBN
   9781398600249 (paperback) | ISBN 9781398600263 (hardback) | ISBN
   9781398600256 (ebook)
Subjects: LCSH: Diversity in the workplace. | Neurodiversity.
Classification: LCC HF5549.5.M5 S595 2021 (print) | LCC HF5549.5.M5
   (ebook) | DDC 658.30087/4–dc23
LC record available at https://lccn.loc.gov/2021022714
LC ebook record available at https://lccn.loc.gov/2021022715

Typeset by Hong Kong FIVE Workshop, Hong Kong
Print production managed by Jellyfish
Printed and bound by CPI Group (UK) Ltd, Croydon CR0 4YY

We have written this book through a global pandemic, for our families, children, and all those who each and every day get up and swim against the tide. This book is for you. May you no longer have to swim so hard so often, with so little support and recognition for how truly brilliant you are. Together, we shall overcome...

CONTENTS

ABOUT THE AUTHORS

Theo Smith

Theo has worn many hats in his life, from fairground operator to actor, from salesperson to poet and from failure to success many times over.

More recently he has been a Talent Acquisition leader and a member of the Resourcing Leaders 100, working with other recruitment leaders to improve the in-house recruitment industry for all, and of course a passionate advocate for the neurodiversity movement.

Theo led recruitment strategy at NICE: The National Institute for Health and Care Excellence. He is also neurodiverse; dyslexic, personally associates with ADHD, and has a child and relatives who also identify as neurodiverse.

Theo didn't find out he was dyslexic until he attended university with no formal qualifications as a mature student at the age of 21. He often found himself either on the wrong side of trouble as a boy or being revered for an outstanding performance, or obscure piece of work; sometimes he fell between the two.

In primary school in Barry Town, South Wales, he was on one of many occasions caught not concentrating in class, or at least not concentrating on what the teacher expected him to be focused on.

When the teacher challenged him on why he wasn't listening, he replied, 'because I've been watching those girls practising that welsh poem "Y Lein Ddillad" (Welsh for "the washing line") in the other partition.'

Theo then went on to say, 'and now I can recite it too!'

The teacher, thinking he was being clever, asked him to recite it there and then.

And so he did.

When Theo's parents got the call to explain their son hadn't been concentrating in class, they didn't expect to be told, 'but whilst not listening in class he's learned a poem that he'll be reciting to the whole school during assembly tomorrow morning.'

So it is with some irony that it has taken him over 15 years of work experience within recruitment and the birth of his son and daughter for Theo to realize that he also identifies as ADHD and who knows what else! The brain is after all, unique.

It is no surprise then that Theo is highly creative and adaptive to change and loves the challenge life has thrown at him.

It was with this new-found knowledge and energy that he explored what information and support was available on the subject of neurodiversity at work. Unfortunately he couldn't find enough information and guidance as a point of reference to help him on his journey.

That's why Theo set out on a mission to influence the world of work to make the required changes to support the inclusion of those who think and act differently and do not fit the current rigid paradigm of the education and employment system.

He now produces a podcast 'Neurodiversity: Eliminating Kryptonite and Enabling Superheroes' and also writes regularly for various publications and is often invited to speak with global in-house recruitment teams on the subject of neurodiversity in the workplace.

He also felt impassioned to create a legacy for his kids and for the children of all the parents who have struggled, like he has, to connect the dots between their children's incredible abilities versus what's being asked of them and expected of them throughout academia and into employment.

The real change must start here; it must start now. If not for the sake of our own sanity, for the sake of future generations, who'll hopefully love and lead the new world to becoming a more inclusive place for all.

Professor Amanda Kirby

Professor Amanda Kirby is unusual, as she is a GP, experienced researcher, clinician and most importantly has many family members who are neuro-divergent. This provides her with an understanding of neurodiversity and co-occurrence from differing perspectives and a drive to raise awareness and champion best practices.

While writing this book she started thinking a lot about herself and her family. She often describes herself as an 'oddball'. In school, she never quite fitted in. She didn't always feel she belonged and was never in the 'in crowd' or wanted to be! She was quite mature compared to some of her peers and often found older friends to be better companions. Her hobbies were a little out of sync with others and she could never remember lyrics to any songs being sung, or know who the artist was apart from Simon and Garfunkel and Elton John despite everyone else being seemingly able to do this so eas-ily! She was super organized for future planning but also very disorganized in the present. Amanda was better at playing one-to-one sports, such as table tennis or doing gymnastics and swimming, but found it much harder in big teams and tended to be put in goals!

One thing she was able to do was talk and as long as she talked about ideas she was fine and would come up with some whacky connections! But she found it much harder to get thoughts down onto paper. She was often told her exam results were disappointing. She fidgeted in class and would be the first to get up to help (being a helper has always been a strategy to be able to move around) and an endless doodler!

As she grew up, she knew she wanted to be a doctor, but had to work very, very hard in medical school to remember endless facts and found lectures a very hard way to absorb information. She would have to work all hours instead of going out to drink and party with her friends. She loved being on the wards in the hospital and as soon as she was with patients, she was off and away and could remember every patient and their lives. Real-life engagement for her was 100 times easier than trying to learn abstract information. Listening to someone telling their 'story' has always been humbling for her in that someone is sharing this with her and feeling they are in a safe space to do so.

Why is this important in the context of this book? She has a very spiky profile and only has put the pieces together as an adult. In her late teens, she had an eating disorder and was very anxious about exams, and had an overwhelming fear of failure. But as a female no one suggested that this could be a part of neurodiversity or her traits could be associated with ADHD at all. She thinks at her age and stage she has coping mechanisms in place but it seems a real shame that it has taken 30 years working in the field of neurodiversity for this to happen.

As a consequence of her personal experiences, more than 20 years ago she set up The Dyscovery Centre, an interdisciplinary centre of health and educational professionals. As a result of her research and clinical work she became a professor at the University of South Wales and has lectured to more than 100,000 individuals worldwide, written over 100 research papers and nine books which have been translated into more than five languages. Her books include: *How to Succeed in Employment with Dyslexia, Dyspraxia, Autism and ADHD* and *How to Succeed in College and University with Dyslexia, Dyspraxia, Autism and ADHD*.

During this time Amanda has been an adviser to the Department of Work and Pensions on neurodiversity, is the chairperson for Movement Matters (the UK umbrella organization for DCD/Dyspraxia) and became a Disability

Confident Leader, trying to raise awareness among employers about the importance of reducing the disability employment gap and why this was good for business. She also is an adviser to a number of organizations supporting people with autism spectrum conditions, ADHD, dyslexia and DCD in the UK and New Zealand.

Amanda is CEO of Do-IT Solutions, a tech-for-good company. The company has developed a unique person-centred computer profiling system used to help map strengths and challenges and map out other people's spiky profiles and highlight their strengths. It is used in schools, universities, apprenticeships, colleges, employment, offending and into-work and employment settings in the UK and internationally (www.doitprofiler.com (archived at https://perma.cc/CG8B-P8RN)). She launched the neurodiversity work tools and apps to help adults to gain practical guidance to maximize their talents and minimize challenges. Amanda has won a number of accolades over the years including in the past being voted the UK GP of the year. In 2019 she was a runner up for a lifetime achievement award at the UK Inclusive Awards and was voted one of LinkedIn 2020 UK Top Voices.

PREFACE

Why have we created this book?

Although neurodiversity has been discussed and debated across a range of platforms more recently, many people within the neurodiverse community remain with limited opportunities to translate and amplify their messages to a mainstream audience. We saw an opportunity to bring together these disparate discussions, ideas, case studies, research, and evidence in one place with the central theme of 'Neurodiversity at Work'.

We see the workplace as an important and influential arena of change. It is our belief that organizations can play a pivotal role in changing society's paradigm of the 'ideal employee' and bring about wider societal reform and acceptance for those who are neurodiverse. This task assumes great importance given that education systems, health systems, political systems and our built environments are often too complex and slow to change to accommodate those who do not fit into the defined norm.

In an ideal world, educational reform would be brought about for 'its own sake' as 'intrinsically worthwhile' and 'for the greater good'. Sadly, this is often not the case. Government systems and agendas are transient and politically expedient; hence, not committed to the level of influence and long-term change required to transform our education systems to be more inclusive and to give those who are neurodiverse an equal opportunity to learn and work.

In this book, we seek to highlight how organizations can improve business outcomes, employee satisfaction and brand impact by recruiting, supporting, and valuing neurodiversity in the workplace. Thereby, we postulate how this 'modus operandi' could be used on a macro level, when considering how we educate and train our children and build our social structures.

By coming together and writing this book we bring different parts of our professional and personal lives together, allowing us to challenge our own perspectives and, we hope, yours.

Who is it for?

We hope many people will find value in what we discuss in this book, including:

- Parents and employees
- Human Resources (HR) managers
- Diversity and Inclusion (D&I) leaders
- Recruitment professionals
- Employers
- People working in Further (FE) and Higher education (HE)
- Apprenticeship providers
- Employment agencies
- Occupational psychologists
- Workplace assessors

Introduction

In 2018 Theo wrote an article for #ChatTalent called 'Leading From Da Back of Da Class'. It was the first article on Neurodiversity to be shared by Hung Lee's #RecruitingBrainfood and it was the beginning of a journey that led both Amanda and Theo to write this book.

The article begins with:

> A western society that has built an academic prison for the 20 per cent of the working population whose brains engage and respond differently, are not broken, they don't need fixing and contrary to popular belief, it is not a disability!
>
> These particular dynamic and highly interesting creative brains have been disabled or confined by the constructs and constraints of our education system and furthermore by our built environments and the fabrications, processes and leadership styles of our businesses.
>
> We've also not helped matters by allowing the 80 per cent to create the assessment and selection process that very rarely likes or appreciates the needs and capabilities of the 20 per cent.[1]

That article came off the back of Theo visiting a recruitment leaders' summit in Whitstable, which he was invited to by Jamie Leonard, founder and CEO of The Recruitment Events Co, who's also an advocate for neurodiversity. The event was part of the Resourcing Leaders 100 (RL100), a think tank of thought leaders and practitioners from within the in-house recruitment industry. This was where he heard for the first time the term 'Neurodiversity' and in the context of people who are dyslexic, ADHD, autistic, dyspraxic… and/or all of the above.

Kirstie Kelly and Ed Thompson were presenting part of the day on the concept of what neurodiversity is and how we as recruitment leaders could get involved in making our workplaces more inclusive.

Ed is the founder of 'Uptimize', who support organizations like JPMorgan Chase, helping to educate them and their employees about neurodiversity in the context of the workplace. They do this via a combination of approaches including online learning and development tools and technology.

Kirstie Kelly helps businesses and individuals to develop their wellbeing, satisfaction and growth, through leadership coaching, counselling and therapy, people and culture change, and team development.

They came together to deliver this interactive and engaging presentation and round table discussion, which gave Theo his first taste of what neurodiversity could mean to him.

Throughout the following chapters, we will explore further what neurodiversity means to different people and we'll give you what is considered the 'correct' terminology. We'll also share different perspectives from candidates, hiring managers, parents and advocates to provide real contexts for what we're discussing.

But first we need to consider this!

The word neurodiversity means everyone's brains are different: with 100 billion brain cells connecting in various ways, it's no surprise that we are all so different. Sometimes we forget this. Neurodiversity is a term that describes the fact that we are all neurologically different, but as noted in the previous quotation, it also highlights the reality that due to the way society is set up, there are some people who experience unfair barriers that can limit their access to society, education and, significantly, to work.

That doesn't mean people who have brains that are wired to think and act differently from others will never get a job, but some may just struggle to find work they enjoy or work that is structured in such a way that it will get the best out of them. Many people are already in jobs at all levels too. However, we can see that for many it remains harder to apply for jobs and find something that fits their talents or supports their experience. For some it may be harder to be successful in a traditional interview setting, even though they may have some amazing talents. For some people it may be harder to work day to day if support has not been put in place or adjustments made in a timely manner. We will talk more about this in later chapters.

We want to give you the facts in this book, but more importantly we also want to give you the individual viewpoints and experiences that go way beyond the words and what they mean. We want to go right to the heart of what neurodiversity is (or how we understand it at this point in time). We want to share our thinking with those who have embraced this ideology, or have recently been introduced to it, and why it matters so much to us and to those that champion the cause.

We will also show you that superhuman efforts and superhuman powers are not all about flying through the sky and cutting through metal with lasers from your eyes! Actually, the ability to complete a task within a team that nobody else within the team has the motivation or skill to achieve, is in our eyes a superpower in itself. It is the efforts taken by so many people to overcome social and employment barriers that are 'superhuman'. This should not have to be something someone has to do.

We are all neurodiverse

As mentioned previously, everyone's brains are wired differently, with millions and millions of connections firing off and connecting in different ways. People you work with will all think differently, see things differently, sense things differently, move differently and do things differently from others. No way is right or wrong, but we sometimes assume that most people see, do and act like us, and we don't always consider that someone may be sensing the world differently. It's often not a case of purposely miscommunicating but an ignorance that this is taking place.

As Sun Tzu said in *The Art of War*:

> There are not more than five primary colours, yet in combination they produce more hues than can ever be seen. There are not more than five cardinal tastes, yet combinations of them yield more flavours than can ever be tasted.[2]

Allowing a mix of skills and talents will provide new thinking and new solutions. However, some people hold negative perceptions in that someone with cognitive differences can be seen to lack ability or capability or require more support from others. Sometimes this is about stereotyping people or fixed thinking. This thinking results in creating barriers to education and employment and has a human and societal cost.

We need to understand the opportunity that valuing a neurodiverse society offers, especially when it comes to employment, new ideas, work productivity, wellbeing and maximizing the talents of all.

In 2015, the United Nations international community constructed a 2030 Agenda for Sustainable Development[3] that includes 17 goals to transform the world for persons with disabilities; four of these goals are very pertinent to the context of this book.

Goal 3 is ensuring healthy lives and promoting wellbeing for all persons with disabilities; Goal 5 focuses on gender equality; Goal 8 is to promote sustained, inclusive and sustainable economic growth, full and productive employment and decent work for all and by 2030 to achieve full and productive employment and decent work for all women and men, including for young people and persons with disabilities, and equal pay for work of equal value; and Goal 10 is to reduce inequality.

To even consider implementing any of these goals requires stepped changes. We need to put in place some processes, policies and actions to do this. There is a need for employers (and educators) to allow people to have the confidence to feel they can be the person they are and ask for support at any stage of their careers. In some workplaces globally we are starting to see the setting up of Equality, Diversity and Inclusion (EDI) teams. In the UK this may be in part because of the implementation of the Equality Act 2010, which despite being more than 10 years old, has not been fully enacted. Though awareness days and networking events, newsletters and 'lunch and learns' can all be starters, they cannot be seen as one-offs or this year's activities. The reality is that the cost-effective way to reach all is to provide systemic solutions that are woven into the fabric of all organizations, and we will discuss the details of this in later chapters.

For inclusion to be truly enacted we need to realize that intersectionality is a reality. We are all complex. Some of us will be female, gay, Black, Asian or another ethnic minority grouping as well as neurodivergent. We certainly don't fit into one box. We often recruit in our own likeness or in the likeness of our best teammate. Using a sporting analogy, a good football team needs different players with different skill sets to be successful. If we inadvertently create a team of strikers or defenders, it will leave us weak in several other areas.

Creating an efficient and effective working team can take time and effort, but the reward at the end is that we have something that works. The sum of the parts can be greater than the whole.

For us that's the power of having a neurodiverse world. It is in fact the diversity that crosses all diversities and if we can crack the cognitive enigma code, we can truly and positively transform the world of work for the better, enable true inclusivity and all live and prosper in a world where we can have a sense of belonging.

People with neurological differences are not incomplete versions of 'typical' people or flawed. People with neurological differences are not broken and certainly don't need fixing! The built environment, systems, processes and organizations are more likely to be broken, or there are hurdles in place that limit progress.

At no time in the past 50 years have there been the changes that have been seen in recent times. We are seeing forced change on a global scale that will alter the way we see the world of work. This is a rapid change that should and could have taken a decade or more to occur but has happened in months. The Industrial Revolution was huge, but the Digital Revolution and what this means to be 'at work' has been accelerated even more by Covid-19, which has already shaken the world and the way we work and will change how we will operate forever.

So in writing this book about Neurodiversity in the Workplace, let us hear from the person who is the originator of the term, because it was her early research relating to neurodiversity, and her passion for the subject, that allowed us to even have this debate and explore what neurodiversity means to us. Judy Singer is an Australian sociologist and comes from a family of neurodivergent people. It was her vision of considering the concepts of biodiversity and relating this to the (neuro)cognitive variability that exists in humans. She coined the term neurodiversity in the late 1990s when she was studying for her master's degree.

Judy Singer writes in her book *NeuroDiversity: The birth of an idea*[4] that the term neurodiversity 'came out of a lifetime of personal experiences of exclusion and invalidation as a person struggling in a family affected by "hidden disability" that neither we nor society recognised for what it was'. She goes on to say her focus was primarily relating to autism as that had also been her personal and family experiences, but she and Harvey Blume were talking to each other at this time and both realized that neurodiversity as a concept was important. Judy was coming from an important perspective with an interest in disability politics and activism, and Harvey Blume as a journalist and writer could write incisively and objectively about the topic they were discussing, which started off as 'neurological differences' but became neurodiversity. Blume wrote in the late 1990s in *The Atlantic*:

> Neurodiversity may be every bit as crucial for the human race as biodiversity is for life in general. Who can say what form of wiring will prove best at any given moment?[5]

We recognize that in the last 20 years since the start of this term being used there has been an evolving language relating to its meaning and increasing interest in how we conceptualize it and use it practically in everyday working practices. In future chapters, we will discuss terms such as neurodiversity, neurodivergence and neurominority, and why language is constantly changing and being challenged. We will use a variety of framing that sometimes may be inconsistent. There is a reason for this. We see that each person describes themselves the way they want and this may change over time.

Some people want to be known as autistic and others as someone with autism. Some people describe themselves as having dyslexia or being dyslexic. We don't believe we have the right to say which is correct or not. Terms such as neurodivergent may be comfortable for some people and allow them to feel a part of a group (or, as some people describe, as a tribe) but may sound divisive and categorical to others and used as separatist, eg the neurodivergents and the neuorotypicals. As T S Eliot said in *Four Quartets* very pertinently, 'For last year's words belong to last year's language, And next year's words await another voice.'[6]

We have included a glossary as a starting point for discussion, with an understanding that the meanings will change with time, usage and different contexts.

Throughout this book we will have a mix of case studies, quotes, and facts to help stimulate further discussion. We will offer some practical ideas and tips to use and also share many wonderful examples of not just how organizations are adapting their processes to be more inclusive, but how they are adapting their environments to also meet the needs of the rapidly adapting workforce.

Reducing stigma makes a real difference

Theo still has vivid memories of how teachers and the kids treated those who were diagnosed with dyslexia when he was at school. The view which we still hear from some parents is that it means they are less than, or they lack academic ability, they struggle with learning or are 'different'. Words are powerful and stay with you for a long time. The 'clumsy' child in school was not chosen for the school team and was often laughed at when last in the running race on sports day or tripping over and falling in the three-legged race despite perhaps having great maths skills. When specific skills are valued more than others in society it presents a sense of being valued less. It's taking a long time for us to not stigmatize left-handed people!

Now we all know being 'different' at school was generally a challenge for the child who was deemed different by peers or teachers. This is especially true in the teen years where for many young people being like your peers becomes very important. Different, difficult or terms such as 'special' were labels used to describe some children and gaining these labels sometimes came with some support, but generally they defined the child as 'other' and this wasn't always a positive framing. It was never usually celebrated and was a way of separating the child from the mainstream population.

Many parents do not see dyslexia, dyspraxia or autism for example as disabilities and certainly not as 'something wrong' with their child, but because of responses from others it evokes negative feelings and a sense of shame or something that should be hidden or not spoken about. It is not so long ago that terms such as 'idiot', 'imbecile' and 'moron' were terms in common use and were used in a pejorative manner.[7] So we can see that language can be powerful in creating either an exclusive or more preferably an inclusive society.

Being different to others in an educational setting doesn't just impact the child, it impacts the way the parents feel and act, and rightly or wrongly perceive their child, but more impactfully how others perceive the child and the parents of that child.

This goes way beyond just the education setting, it also spills into the home environment, the workplace and beyond. Conversations are not had or if they are, parents are worried about what others may think. There remain myths and the need to dispel the myths is important if we are going to break down the stigma.

Part of Theo's path to understanding neurodiversity and what it means to him has been a journey of self-discovery but also an acceptance that there still is a stigma with having ADHD and being dyslexic. But the only way to break down the stigma and positively change the way people see ADHD, dyslexia and other neurodiverse labels, for example, was for Theo to stand up and be counted. He started to own his labels and the narrative around them, to hopefully help empower others to feel positive about themselves.

Not everybody is in the position both from a psychological perspective and/or a professional perspective to do so. But for him there was an immediate urgency to find that voice and platform so that he could shift the narrative from a negative perception to a positive one.

Even today he can sift through guides on neurodiversity in the workplace created by organizations and universities, and still they highlight 10 negative points to every positive. They highlight them as challenges, but for him this still plays into the hands of perceived areas for improvement.

Amanda's experiences come from personal and professional settings and her knowledge of meeting many people working in a wide range of work settings. She has seen some really talented people not gain jobs because the recruitment processes generated such high levels of anxiety, often amplified by low self-esteem and bad past experiences. In many cases individuals have ended up not being able to show what they can do. These poor experiences have then resulted in driving even higher levels of anxiety the next time that person goes to an interview as they expect failure again. A lack of feedback after an interview can also often mean the person doesn't know how they can do better next time, and thus the cycle becomes harder to break. The interview becomes a performance failure and not a stage that allows skills to be seen.

Theo and Amanda both want to see a world where we focus on individual strengths. For those with 'spikier profiles' (which we'll talk more about later in the book), if we keep focusing on deficits we get distracted from seeing the incredible abilities. This is about opportunity to find out what your strengths are and an opportunity to develop them.

In this book you will hear from people who have gained success, what led to this happening and what challenges they had to overcome. However, we need also to understand the reality relating to the real barriers that remain in place and consider what these are so that more people have their potential fulfilled. When considering the workplace we don't only mean those in executive positions but valuing all who can contribute to workplaces. Seeing through different lenses provides us all with new opportunities for solutions in all parts of our worlds.

This book is a result of the work Theo and Amanda do in their everyday life, listening to the voices of individuals, gathering experiences from the workplace and exploring what works. We aim to share this with you and take you on our exciting and emerging journey of discovery.

The following chapters are:

Chapter 1: Why neurodiversity is important

Chapter 2: Labels: what do they mean?

Chapter 3: Categories and spiky profiles

Notes

1   Smith, Theo (2018) Leading from Da back of Da Class, #ChatTalent,
    21 October, https://www.chattalent.com/recruitment-hiring/leading-from-da-
    back-of-da-class/ (archived at https://perma.cc/7FX5-55DE)
2   Tzu, S (2007) *The Art of War*, El Paso Norte Press, Texas, p 67
3   United Nations (2015) #Envision2030: 17 goals to transform the world for
    persons with disabilities, Department of Economic and Social Affairs, Disability,
    September, https://www.un.org/development/desa/disabilities/envision2030.html
    (archived at https://perma.cc/8NQC-BLPK)
4   Singer, J (2016) *NeuroDiversity: The birth of an idea*, Kindle eBook
5   Blume, H (1998) Neurodiversity: On the neurological underpinnings of geekdom,
    The Atlantic, September, https://www.theatlantic.com/magazine/archive/
    1998/09/neurodiversity/305909/ (archived at https://perma.cc/M2ES-W4KC)
6   Howard, K (2018) One Great Moment, *Nieman News*, 3 January,
    https://nieman.harvard.edu/stories/for-last-years-words-belong-to-last-years-
    language-and-next-years-words-await-another-voice/ (archived at
    https://perma.cc/H46A-PKA2)
7   Burke Huey, E (2019; originally published 1912) *Backward and Feeble-Minded
    Children*, Wentworth Press, London

01

Why neurodiversity is important

Introduction

In this chapter we will consider the rationale for employers to consider the concept of neurodiversity.

Without cognitive diversity we would have limited variations in music, in art, science or mathematics; therefore, potentially the development of new forms of electronics, computers, AI, and who knows what else in our futures could be limited.

It's important, therefore, to recognize that in all elements of society, we need representation. This is the true meaning of inclusivity. If we don't get the opportunity to have representation of views, ideas and experiences, how can we ever be able to know what we are potentially missing? It often feels easier and more familiar to recruit 'in our own likeness'; to recruit people who have more in common with us. Communication is less effortful. But when we do so, those that offer different solutions, or communicate differently, remain excluded.

Inclusion is essential across society and starts in school. We are at the beginning of developing neuro-inclusive processes and procedures in some bigger companies where they have in place Equality, Diversity and Inclusion initiatives. We see some companies have focused in past years on LGBTQ+, BAME or gender. More companies are starting to consider neurodiversity as well; they can see that diversity of thought and of cultural and life experiences!

At the present time there is a lack of representation and opportunity for neurodivergent thinkers to progress and especially reach the C-suite. Too many people from the same gender, ethnicity and academic backgrounds end up in the top jobs and so the stories we hear remain the same and the viewpoint then remains narrow. Often the person who does reach the top who becomes interested in neurodiversity has a neurodiverse family member and understands the challenges from a personal perspective.

We are often still thinking in silos: while specific campaigns such as those for gender equality are crucial, there also needs to be focus on intersectional campaigns. We don't all fit into one category or another. There is no one-size approach. It is impossible to understand the development and training needs of each person without fully understanding the opinions and experiences of people who are working in variable settings. Unique skills and experiences bring different perspectives. Context is everything. A different work setting and culture will require a different understanding of needs, expectations and support.

Why do we exclude some people from the conversation?

That's complicated. There are myriad social reasons why some people get a voice at the table and others don't get a look in at all despite having similar qualifications and experiences. We can use business metaphors such as 'groupthink' and misuse ideas like 'culture fit' to maintain a status quo of recruiting using a narrow range of characteristics. Thousands of years of racism, sexism and of privilege make it harder in the modern world to be suddenly representative of all those you serve. Unless of course you, your team and your organizations are as diverse as the communities you repre-sent and become disruptive in the way you think. Power has a part to play. If you are concerned about your job you may be reticent to ask for help or point out any challenges you may be having in that work setting. Often conversations happen as part of a performance review when things have 'gone wrong'.

A true change requires commitment that is more than tokenistic as it needs to be sustained and anticipatory. The only way we can really do this is to measure what we do. We also need to ensure that diversity and inclu-sion is a part of all our processes and not a policy that is written and then stuck in a drawer. This requires a commitment to see through different eyes and accept at times our ignorance and the need to open up honest conversations. It requires revision and review and is not static. Change can happen when we see enough value in doing so. Progress depends on how effectively we work to change people's thinking and never happens overnight. But let's be clear, the path is not always an easy one and it takes dedication and a focus to make change. But the rewards and impact for the organization and society are great.

With studies and research from the likes of McKinsey[1] and Deloitte[2] to name just two, we can clearly see that diversity correlates with better financial performance and diversity of thinking is the new frontier. Let's face it, sometimes the only way to encourage businesses to shift their thinking is to help them see how it affects the bottom line. However, for a lot of organizations and their leaders, these reports are ethereal, and they struggle to see the tangible difference it will make today.

In 2011, Deloitte recognized the challenges in encouraging organizations to take actionable steps, as shown in a report on the business case for diversity published in 2011:

> How deep does the message go? Is it understood from the factory floor to
> the boardroom and with the weight of firm conviction? Truth be told – there
> appears to be more head nodding about the business case than a rolling up of
> the sleeves to take action.[3]

When considering where we are at with neurodiversity, we can take some evidence from past experience from Diversity and Inclusion initiatives. To accelerate the change and adoption we desperately need, we should move from high-level statistics and figures to actionable hints and tips that can help organizations really start to get to grips with how they can fully embrace neurodiversity within the workforce. It's not enough to agree with the concept and empathize with the cause; action must be taken.

We hope to give those tangible actionable steps, through case studies and personal experiences throughout this book.

Why should employers be more neuro-inclusive?

Ethical, moral and legal responsibilities

If we examine official measures of employment and unemployment, between 2013 and 2019, the disability employment gap in the UK had reduced, with the data showing roughly half of disabled people were in employment (53.2 per cent) compared with just over four out of five non-disabled people (81.8 per cent). This data came from The Labour Force Survey (LFS) and Annual Population Survey (APS) and forms part of the Office for National Statistics series of bulletins, which have explored outcomes for disabled people across a number of areas of life.[4] A real concern is that the impact of the Covid-19 pandemic will reverse this trend unless a spotlight is put on action. This is an ethical and moral responsibility for society otherwise it will potentially turn back time.

This gap is much wider for some than for others and also worsens with age. How the statistics are gathered also means you can only be counted as in one category or another. For example, the number of disabled people in work aged 16 to 64 years in 2019 in the UK who are categorized as having depression, bad nerves or anxiety was 17.9 per cent compared to those grouped as having severe or specific learning difficulties where the percentage was only 0.8 per cent. This means the true level is unclear, as many people who are autistic, for example, will also have some mental health challenges.

There are some concerns, however, that the impact of Covid-19 in 2020 and beyond will have a longer-term effect on many global employment settings and that we may see that the gap widens rather than contracts. The ethical and moral responsibility for organizations is to maintain a spotlight on this.

Equality provision

Equality affirms that all human beings are born free and equal. It presupposes that all individuals have the same rights and deserve the same level of respect and have the right to be treated equally. This means that laws, policies and programmes should not be discriminatory. How this is enacted may vary from country to country.

In the UK we have the Equality Act 2010, which followed on from the Disability Discrimination Act. All European Union Member States have designated a specialized body for the promotion of equal treatment irrespective of racial or ethnic origin, as required by Article 13 of the Racial Equality Directive, but implementation may vary from country to country. In the United States, the Equality Act was passed by the US House of Representatives in 2019. However, since then the US Senate has received the bill, but it has not been fully ratified.

Different countries globally are at different stages of operationalizing and determining what equality really means. In the context of neurodiversity in the workplace, having a legal framework encourages organizations to need to comply. Tribunal cases in the UK provide examples of non-compliance and encourage other organizations to do better.

Attracting new talent

Attracting talent is more than an advert with a 'cookie cutter' job description of a job in another department that is similar (but not quite the same) and which doesn't describe at all the elements of the job you need to do and what is expected of you. It may lack the exciting information that draws someone in because it misses out on key information that is important to that person such as presenting the values or ethos of the organization. If the advert doesn't provide an obvious means of engaging with all people then valuable talent may be lost. We never know who doesn't apply for the job; there may be different reasons. The words and phrases used in an advert may put someone off; a lack of information about how to ask for adjustments, and the application process itself, can all mean the organization appears less inclusive.

In this book we will explore the ways you can ensure more neuro-inclusive hiring processes and we will take you through this step by step to show how you may encourage someone to apply. This will include considering your website, the job description, application process, pre-interview materials for the applicant and your interview panel, the interview process (virtual or face to face) and the follow-up after the event.

Maintaining the talent that you have

It costs a lot to lose good people and optimizing the talent you have makes a lot of sense. Recruiting and training a new employee requires staff time and money. A US study in 2016 by the Society for Human Resource Management (SHRM)[5] estimated that the average cost per hire is $4,129. In terms of employee retention, the average employee tenure is eight years, and the annual turnover rate is 19 per cent. The average replacement cost of a salaried employee is estimated to be six to nine months' salary. For an employee earning $60,000 per year, that totals approximately $30,000 to $45,000 in recruiting and training costs.

Key factors for retention include good hiring and onboarding processes with good initial training in place as well as maintaining productivity.

There may be an assumption that training and support costs will be far greater for neurodivergent team members, but this is not exactly true. Most adjustments made by employers are low-cost or even free. The average cost of reasonable adjustments is about £75 per person and there are government schemes in the UK such as Access to Work that provide some or all of the funding depending on the size of the organization.

What can be costly for organizations is not being compliant under each country's equality legislation and this will be discussed further along with the implications of this for the person and organization.

Not missing potential

We all know a young person who went on to be successful in business or is an entrepreneur who looks back and remembers the lack of belief that the teachers had in them when in school. They proved them wrong. You will also hear of success that will be pinpointed to a time when someone gave them a chance and the opportunity to thrive in a safe environment. It made all the difference. You will read in this book examples of both these experiences. We cannot underestimate the impact that a person who sees potential and provides support or mentoring can have on someone's future. This could be a family member, a teacher, a youth worker or someone they have met by chance. The results can have a life-changing impact.

But how many people are being missed? We know that about one in three people in prison are neurodivergent and we will discuss this in more detail in further chapters in the book: why some people are missed and therefore miss the opportunities to excel.[6]

Wasting opportunity

There is growing evidence of many successful entrepreneurs who are neurodivergent and some are speaking openly about this: loud and proud! There are also many international companies that are realizing the untapped potential of neurodiverse talent. These include internationally recognized companies such as the BBC, SAP, Hewlett Packard Enterprise (HPE), Microsoft, Willis Towers Watson, Ford, and EY. There are many others, including Caterpillar, Dell Technologies, Deloitte, IBM, JPMorgan Chase, and UBS. [7]

However, it is less clear the exact numbers on boards and in leadership positions and the percentage of those disclosing at all levels of business. As Peter Drucker is credited with saying, 'what gets measured, gets managed',[8] thus providing the potential for improvement. While there are gender equality measures and percentages of people from BAME communities working in different roles, measuring neurodiversity quotients of any sort seems to be a rarer phenomenon.

In later chapters we will be discussing ways to change this and techniques that can be used to permeate a process throughout companies. At the moment recruitment tends to be focused mainly on autistic people rather than encompassing neurodiversity as a whole. Some companies are embracing reverse mentoring, having sponsors and using coaching approaches to focus specifically on increasing representation at all levels of the company.

Developing creative and innovative solutions and having more effective neuro-complementary teams

Now more than ever we need innovative solutions for complex world problems. Bringing together teams to work better together has to be a positive for everyone. Until relatively recently we have tended to ask people to behave and communicate in a way that was common for most (but not for all). Sitting in a room of people in a meeting required turn-taking, focus, and communication skills. Interjection or interruption can be seen as forcefulness or irritating for some. The transition to large-scale working from home and video conferencing that occurred as a result of the Covid-19 pandemic has made alternative ways of working and communicating be considered in a way we could never have imagined.

What neurodiversity as a concept means to different people

There appear to be a lot of opinions about defining who someone is and how they describe themselves and anger if this is wrongly stated. In a book like this we open ourselves up for criticism. We either got it right or we got it very wrong. What we are hoping to do is open up dialogue and allow individual conversations to happen that ask about each person and their input and viewpoint.

As William H Whyte remarked in 1950, 'The great enemy of communication, we find, is the illusion of it'.[9] The worst thing we can do is assume we've had the conversation or indeed not even care to listen to the answer.

During the research and creation of this book we went out to the neurodiversity community and asked them what neurodiversity means to them; here are a selection of their replies:

'Neurodiversity is seeing the value in the different ways people work best. Advancement in technology and science has greatly improved understanding of our brains' functionalities, particularly how these can differ, yet there is still an extreme gap in translating the importance and relevance of these to the working world.'

'Neurodiversity remains a bit of an uncharted territory for most of us, but you won't require a degree in neuroscience for either you or your team to see the benefits, instead only a willingness to revisit the ways in which we assess the capabilities of those around us is needed. Neurodiversity highlights the hefty cost burden placed on business growth by the limitations of these deep-seated beliefs, and the scale of opportunity right in front of us when we are instead all able to work to the best of our abilities' (Amy O'Shea, 2020).

'Neurodiversity for me is the recognition of and appreciation for individual human cognition; how each of us experience our reality and how we interact with that reality. It is important because it offers us a profound opportunity to consider both a physical and metaphysical diversity of humanity, beyond those social constructs by which current society inadequately measures or judges people. Neurodiversity offers us an opportunity to reframe concepts like 'normal', introducing instead a new perspective of ability and it provides us a framework which explains the dividend from the wider Diversity & Inclusion agenda (Sean Gilroy, 2020).

'Human beings organize themselves into societies and the ultimate social building blocks are based on consensus. With consensus comes rules and with the practice of rules we get norms and normative behaviour. We then work and provide work rules that work to the middle and that means that at least 20–30 per cent of people think, work and act differently but have to do the same as the middle 70 per cent. It's a bit like only stocking certain sizes of clothes in a shop…' (Mike Emery, 2020).

'Neurodiversity is the idea that people have different brains and thought processes. Importantly, it encompasses the full spectrum of human experiences and perceptions. Neurodiversity is the realization of organizations seeking 'diversity of thought' within their groups. It is the pinnacle of true acceptance of every person as they are – true inclusivity. Without neurodiversity, humanity would never advance through adversity' (Gee Abraham, 2020).

'Neurodiversity helps us to see neurological and brain differences as edges of talent, ability and sometimes even exceptional superpower. From a macro perspective, it presents the whole philosophy that reimagines our vision of society not as a building created from square bricks, but more like a complicated puzzle that involves various shapes. As you can imagine, for many it's a serious challenge to create a building where every shape is included. But it still matters. And here is why...'

'If ability is correctly aligned with opportunity and an inclusive ecosystem, the neurodiversity approach expands and turns the whole concept of "diversity" into the mainstream and an invaluable source of underrepresented talent. More importantly, it can be interpolated into technologies, ecosystems and services far beyond this particular niche. Over recent years, we have seen various emerging products focused on neurodiversity, including social robotics (Robokind, LuxAi), neurodiverse workforce (Daivergent, Ultranauts), reading, learning and social adoption solutions driven by AI, smart glasses that help to learn emotions (Brain Power). Thus, neurodiversity becomes a powerful engine for other areas, including mental health, personality disorders, disability and minority inclusion, dramatically impacting social mobility, workforce, education and our vision of the creative economy across sectors and niches' (Jonah Welker, 2020).

'Neurodiversity is the idea that people have different ways of thinking, different viewpoints and different skill sets. Specifically, neurodiversity refers to people with conditions such as autism, ADHD, dyslexia, dyspraxia, Tourette's etc. The implication behind neurodiversity, and why it is important to consider, is that these conditions should not always be thought of as disabilities or disorders. In the right context, these differences mean people can offer unique perspectives and powerful competitive advantages' (Michael Barton, 2020).

'You don't have to consider neurodiversity. It just is. The question is whether you want to understand it, work with it and use it as a tool to progress the human race or thwart it' (Caroline Turner, 2020).

And two more we have included from past works:

'If society were to get to a point where all ways of experiencing and interacting with the world were treated equitably, then simply all would be typical or divergent under the umbrella of human neurodiversity – dependent on if you are a "glass half full" or "glass half empty" kind of philosopher.'[10]

'Neurodiversity is the diversity of human minds, the infinite variation in neurocognitive functioning within our species.'[11]

KEY POINTS

Why neurodiversity is important for organizations

- Ethical and moral and legal responsibility.
- Attracting, optimizing and maintaining talent.
- Creating novel solutions.
- Good for business.
- Maintaining the talent you have.
- Good for customer relations and business.

Notes

1 McKinsey & Company (2015) Diversity Matters, https://www.insurance.ca.gov/diversity/41-ISDGBD/GBDExternal/upload/McKinseyDivmatters-201501.pdf (archived at https://perma.cc/3NT6-3VYJ)

2 Deloitte (2018) The Diversity and Inclusion Revolution, *Deloitte Review*, 22, https://www2.deloitte.com/content/dam/insights/us/articles/4209_Diversity-and-inclusion-revolution/DI_Diversity-and-inclusion-revolution.pdf (archived at https://perma.cc/P8PP-9QSQ)

3 Deloitte (2011) Only Skin Deep? Re-examining the business case for diversity, https://www2.deloitte.com/content/dam/Deloitte/au/Documents/human-capital/

deloitte-au-hc-diversity-skin-deep-2011.pdf (archived at https://perma.cc/VAH7-GNLD)

4 Office for National Statistics (2019) Disability and Employment, UK: 2019, https://www.ons.gov.uk/peoplepopulationandcommunity/healthandsocialcare/disability/bulletins/disabilityandemploymentuk/2019#employment-by-disability (archived at https://perma.cc/F8JH-K32R)

5 The Society for Human Resource Management (2016) Average Cost-per-Hire for Companies Is $4,129, SHRM Survey Finds, 3 August, https://www.shrm.org/about-shrm/press-room/press-releases/pages/human-capital-benchmarking-report.aspx (archived at https://perma.cc/RZC7-8P49)

6 Kirby, A and Saunders, L (2015) A case study of an embedded system in prison to support individuals with learning difficulties and disabilities in the criminal justice system, *Journal of Intellectual Disabilities and Offending Behaviour*, 6, (2), pp 112–24

7 Annabi, H (2019) Autism @Work Playbook, https://s3.amazonaws.com/disabilityin-bulk/2019/Autism_At_Work_Playbook_Final_02112019.pdf (archived at https://perma.cc/3HL7-JXDX)

8 Prusak, L (2010) What can't be measured, *Harvard Business Review*, 7 October, hbr.org/2010/10/what-cant-be-measured (archived at https://perma.cc/DQ6T-25SN)

9 Llopis, G (2017) The greatest enemy of teamwork is the illusion that it has happened, *Forbes*, 5 December, https://www.forbes.com/sites/glennllopis/2017/12/05/the-greatest-enemy-of-teamwork-is-the-illusion-it-has-happened/?sh=691ddc7d37b0 (archived at https://perma.cc/RC9L-URY8)

10 Farahar, C and Bishopp-Ford, L (2020) Stigmaphrenia: Reducing mental health stigma with a script about neurodiversity, in D Milton (ed), *The Neurodiversity Reader: Exploring concepts, lived experience and implications for practice*, pp 48–66, Pavilion Publishing & Media, Shoreham by Sea

11 Walker, N (2014) Neurodiversity: Some basic terms & definitions, *Neurocosmopolitanism*, 27 September, http://neurocosmopolitanism.com/neurodiversity-some-basic-terms-definitions/ (archived at https://perma.cc/8GRM-RGHT)

02

Labels: what do they mean?

Introduction

Throughout this book you'll hear Amanda and Theo talk in the third person, as we're doing now! This is important; Theo is not an academic, Amanda is. Amanda doesn't have more than a decade in recruitment at the coal face of engaging and attracting talent, Theo does. Theo is not a GP, researcher or an academic and would never in a million years have achieved that accolade, while Amanda has worked clinically and in research for more than 25 years. But we do have a lot in common. We are passionate about ensuring neurodiversity is a subject that everyone's talking about and also hearing how the language we use can engender real emotion. We also come from neurodivergent families and have a lot of shared experiences.

There is no single truth or single voice around the topic of neurodiversity. We all have unique brains like thumbprints, and we need to embrace difference as the new normal. For this reason, we want our voices to be combined. Sometimes if you know Theo or Amanda you might hear one of their voices more than the other as you read a paragraph, and that's OK, but not something we are seeking. We are not teaching or preaching; we want to excite, delight and open up the discussion around neurodiversity. This chapter has been one of the hardest to write as it will probably provoke more discussion and debate than any of the others. We hope it does.

The English language is complex and often feels contradictory. So, it's OK not to be a wordsmith and it is definitely OK not to feel comfortable with words and labels. It's probably better to feel like you don't have all the answers, because none of us can say we do! But also consider the F Scott Fitzgerald quote:

> To **be kind** is more important than to **be right**. Many times, what people need is not a brilliant mind that speaks but a special heart that listens.[1]

What is important is that we empower people at all levels of employment to have a voice and to receive appropriate support so that they can succeed. Enabling a conversation is key to ensuring the right help is available. Sometimes we close the conversation down or don't even get started because we are worried that we may make a mistake. Our fear of getting it wrong and the consequences of that stop us even trying. This is crucial to developing a neuro-inclusive workplace where dialogue can happen.

Dialogue, by definition, is a two-way street and no one person can be the expert in everything. You would not as an employer be expected to know everything about migraine or diabetes for example, so why do we think we need to know everything about dyslexia or autism? The person who has bravely decided on that day to tell you that they are dyslexic may also have been the same person having several sleepless nights and pacing up and down outside your door. You may be the first person they have decided to tell. Shutting down the conversation may mean it is 100 per cent harder to re-open it.

We will talk about the debate of 'to label or not to label'. However, at this time, it's important to acknowledge that sometimes without a label it can be difficult to access the support we need. This is especially true when moving through educational systems and for acceptance of need also in employment. Many children will be overlooked without gaining a diagnosis that defines their special educational needs, and even then, it can still be a tough and winding long road to gain the help they need (and truly exhausting and an anguishing experience for parents).

Despite wanting to operate a more social model we still mainly operate a medical model to determine if support is given or not. It is also a categorical one – based on a hard stop. You either have 'it' or not. There is extensive published evidence to challenge this and to see that co-occurrence or overlap between neurodiverse traits is very common. The diagnosis someone may have obtained is more often related to the professional they have happened to see.

Alongside neurodiversity being a mesh of different strengths and challenges we also see an overlap with physical and psychological conditions. We have included in this chapter some references, published in the last 20 years or more, which demonstrate this time and time again. See Further Reading at the end of the chapter.

Getting the words right or wrong

It's inevitable that we will all get the terminology wrong from time to time, and what is right for one person may not be right for another. So just as we think we've cracked it, we inadvertently cause a social media storm by using the term neurodiverse to describe ourselves instead of neurodivergent. But the fact we are having the debate and positively challenging one another is important and helps further the conversation. Language changes over time and the meanings we ascribe to words do too. This is discussed in Amanda's paper with Dr Mary Cleaton which emphasizes that different organizations such as education, health and justice often use different terms and phrases to describe the same person.[2]

We need to be honest and accept we won't get it right all the time and each person describes themselves differently and that's OK. Labels can be divisive and create negative viewpoints and trigger associations, so we should never seek to label someone else and certainly not enforce a label just to convince ourselves that we are doing the right thing. We can come with a set of biases relating to specific labels that may have been garnered from experiences in school, within the family and from what we read in the papers and see on the TV. In the late 1940s Dr Leo Kanner, an Austrian child psychiatrist who moved from Vienna to the United States, suggested that autism may be related to a 'genuine lack of maternal warmth'. He noted that some children were exposed from 'the beginning to parental coldness, obsessiveness, and a mechanical type of attention to material needs only... They were left neatly in refrigerators which did not defrost.'[3] It took a long time to dispel these myths.

There have also been negative associations linked to ADHD and the thought that the condition was due to 'bad parenting'.[4] It is only relatively recently that this has changed to some extent despite much evidence to show differences in regions in the brain and a wide range of different genes associated with ADHD.

Sometimes we hear comments like someone saying, 'He's like my brother and he's autistic' or 'Everyone is a bit ADHD!' or 'We are all a bit on the spectrum!' These can effectively close down discussions, even if the person was well meaning.[5]

We'll try our best to bring as much clarity as we can to what each word and/or label means (at the moment), with as much context as possible. The more information we have the better decisions we can make and ultimately this is a journey many of us have only just begun, so we are all learning together.

Let's start with the terms neurodiversity and neurodivergence, as they are the ones being used more and we want to provide some clarity over this, at least in relation to how they are being described by some at this time. However, do remember that we cannot be overly prescriptive as each person has the right to determine how they describe themselves. There is no right or wrong.

What is neurodiversity?

Neurodiversity is not a trait that one person has: we are all diverse. Neurodiversity as a concept is about the biological and genetic variations that exist across all society and have remained and not been bred out over time. There is also a growing acceptance that there must be a sound reason in society for the different types of cognitive processing to have remained.

Neurodiversity is not one label or an exclusive club that only some people can join. It certainly should not be considered as the ability to segregate people into boxes. It doesn't represent only one set of diagnoses, ie ADHD, dyslexia, developmental coordination disorder (dyspraxia), autism spectrum disorder or condition, for example, and not include cerebral palsy. There is no logic in this as cerebral palsy and DCD can often be difficult to separate.[6] However, often it is portrayed in that way in that neurodiversity is X, Y and Z but not A, B and C.

You also don't 'have' neurodiversity or not. In an ideal world there should be no need for a specific diagnosis, or a badge or proof of why somebody requires an adjustment. This is one reason Theo doesn't like the use of 'reasonable adjustments' as a catch-all term for those who would like an adjustment, or some support put in place to a process or assessment or application. It gives the impression that you have a disability, and someone (else) determines whether supplying something is reasonable or not.

Though some people, like Theo, would never request a 'reasonable adjustment' on that basis, the concept has allowed for an important legal right and one that may be needed and wanted by many. Theo would, however, make some suggestions about how the recruitment process could be adapted to get the best out of his approach, skills and experience if he was asked. There will be more about this in later chapters.

When someone diverges from what is deemed as the dominant cognitive way of functioning/communicating/thinking we then say that this person is **neurodivergent.**

This is defined as one whose neurological development and state are atypical or diverge from the dominant neurological, cognitive and behavioural norms. The term has been thought to have been generated by the neurodiversity movement and initially focused far more on autistic people. It was seen as the opposite to 'neurotypical'.

However, using the term in this way may cause challenges of 'otherness' and sets people up as being either neurotypical OR neurodivergent, ie either sitting in one camp or another, when in reality people are far more complex and nuanced and cognition is far more than representing just one domain.

The term divergence is also defined as separating, changing into something different, or having a difference of opinion. The term neurodivergent, while being semantically correct, is not always liked by everyone. For context, Theo feels slightly uncomfortable using the term neurodivergent to describe himself and is much more comfortable saying to others he is neurodiverse. However, grammatically this is not correct and in written form could confuse some people around his understanding and meaning of the word or term.

Some people may not want to be defined at all by one specific label or condition and prefer to be defined by who they are as an individual. As we have mentioned, each person has the right to choose and overly rigid use of socially understood terms can result in argument rather than debate.

No one is 'just' neurodivergent in the same way no one is 'just' dyslexic or someone with autism spectrum disorder. The label used only describes a part of who they are. Additionally, gender, culture, where we live, our interests, the country we live in, our past experiences all influence the person we are. You may diverge away from the 'average' person in the way you communicate or the way you move, or your maths skills for example but may not for other aspects of how you function.

What is positive about embracing the term neurodiversity is the acceptance of the reality of our cognitive variability. This term acknowledges that each person cannot be subsumed into a set of simple boxes. It also reframes the narrative that in the past we focused far more on what you couldn't do, such as the use of terms like disorder (as in attention deficit hyperactivity disorder) or difficulty (as in specific learning difficulty). The reality is that not everyone is impaired by their varying cognitive profiles and often it is the demands that are placed on you, and the environment you have been placed in that disables you. This, of course, is not intended to minimize the reality that some people may have significant challenges in some areas of their life and require significant support to enable participation and independence.

When you are in school, being different can bring unwanted attention and suffering from bullying. It can have a long-term negative impact on one's mental health, wellbeing and self-confidence. The past trauma can be replayed in the workplace if your skills are challenged as it can replay feelings of shame from many years ago.

Ironically, later in life when you're trying to make your mark in the working world, the ability to provide a different perspective should be empowering and differentiate you from the crowd and help raise your voice above the noise. Theo has had positive experiences of his cognitive differences helping him stand out. However, some people may lack confidence and have lowered self-esteem. This may make it even harder to demonstrate their skills. It can take one person providing an opportunity and seeing the potential to change a person's whole life trajectory.

For Theo's podcast *Neurodiversity: Eliminating Kryptonite and Enabling Superheroes*,[7] he interviewed 'High Contrast', a leading electronic music producer and DJ, which we will hear about in more detail in Chapter 4. High Contrast produced the music for the entrance of the athletes at the London Olympics, which was watched by over 900 million people across the world. He has been nominated for a Grammy, regularly plays at some of the coolest venues and has definitely been instrumental in shifting the global sound of Drum & Bass.

He said on the podcast that his neurological difference has been at the heart of his success. He was a bit of a self-confessed loner at school and doesn't like being in busy places like shops, but put him in front of a computer and ask him to create incredible sounds and he produces brilliant work like no other.

Another interesting fact is that he doesn't dislike *all* crowded spaces; he in fact has to play to large audiences at music venues across the world. So, we cannot assume that because somebody is affected by light or sound, that all light and all sound will affect them negatively. There are other factors that can play into this. Each person will have their specific strengths and challenges and they may differ from place to place and time to time, depending on the task's demands and the environment they are being placed in. Nothing is the same all the time, and there aren't single solutions that are the right fit for everyone. We have to take a holistic person-centred approach to help each individual reach their potential.

So neurodiversity is… the beautiful reality that all our brains are unique and we should start to celebrate and embrace that fact more often, and not allow language or labels to determine what's normal and what's not! Amanda's normal is living in a very varied neurodivergent family – this is her neurotypical!

In the end we want to have the tools and confidence to empower each of us to be our best selves.

Warning: words have different meanings to different people at different times

Human evolution, the distinction between us and our pets at home, is the fact we use language and words to communicate like no other being on this planet.

Is getting the words right and the terminology accurate the most important thing? Well, if you're Theo, dyslexic, ADHD, dyspraxic, dyscalculic… then language is a little bit tricky. Not only will he struggle to remember the rules around language and the use of specific words and terminology, but he'll also often confuse one word or term with another. His wife often lovingly jokes how he uses words like 'cacophony' sometimes perfectly and beautifully presented just at the right time and in the correct context and other times wildly out of context and for completely the wrong meaning.

The fun and creative element to this is sometimes he will use it just on the margins of error, but every now and then it creates a divergent meaning that may be just about acceptable or challenge the status quo.

But like his father always taught him: 'Theo, always speak with conviction and if you do that, even if you use a word in the wrong way or out of context, people will very rarely challenge your use of the word.'

This is where it becomes interesting, because where the truth lies in what Theo's father told him is that only part of people's understanding of what you say is in the words you use. It is also in your physiological response, the way your eyes and mouth move, and in the way you inflect your voice up and down the octaves with differing levels of volume and intensity.

Sometimes the words really don't matter because you're expressing yourself in so many other ways. Who really cares if you write Fcuk instead of… or use the letter d instead b? The reality is one word does not make a sentence and one sentence does not make a book. We are all full of contradictions, including texts that have contributed to so much of our understanding.

If we insist that labels and language are at the forefront of meaning, we then immediately cut off a large proportion of those we are looking to encourage and support. It's not to say that language isn't important; it is clearly an integral part of human communication and evolution. But we need to understand that we do not all have the capacity and capability to get the language right and that should not exclude us from the conversation.

In fact, challenging so-called correct terminology like 'neurodivergent' can be a good way for us to explore different words and meanings to help us all feel involved and included and less marginalized. This is particularly true when words and their meaning have a negative impact on our mental health and wellbeing and the way we see ourselves. Who gets to choose that 'divergent' or 'deficit' or 'disorder' is a good way to explain differences in human cognition and processing of information? We can do so much better if only we try and break the mould of correctness over and above what is human.

That being said, we also have to work with what is current parlance, and there is no point throwing the baby out with the bathwater.

A common understanding is helpful and empowering each and every one with the ability to make sense of themselves and others is important. So let's try and be mindful that we are all unique and complex, therefore what works and is right for one, may not work for another and that words and their meanings can change over time.

As Stephen Covey said in 7 Habits of Highly Effective People, 'Let us seek first to understand, then to be understood'.[8]

Why do we like labels?

Categorization and classification allow humans to organize things, objects, and ideas that exist around them and simplify their understanding of the world, especially when there are too many factors to take on board; we then want to group them to be able to try to understand this.

Classifying it fills a human need in ourselves to impose order on nature and find hidden relationships. This is very useful when we have tried to sort lots of different information, and we want to catalogue it and be able to retrieve it.

Diagnosis of a specific condition associated with being neurodivergent is often described with one word or phrase, but we sometimes need to question a diagnosis we have been given such as dyslexia, and how valid and useful it is. That's a BIG one, a bit like challenging the meaning of life. We are not completely saying get rid of diagnoses, but we need to question if the words we use are of their time.

The word 'valid' is derived from the Latin *validus*, meaning strong, and it is defined as 'well-founded and applicable; sound and to the point; against which no objection can fairly be brought.'[9] What we mean by using this is that there isn't a single, agreed-upon definition of some of the diagnostic neurominority groupings that we describe, although there has been a general acceptance of what we refer to when we use a term such as ADHD. Despite the definition (there are agreed international descriptors) there isn't one single test that scores you and says if you have ADHD or not. The descriptor can be interpreted in a number of ways. This can result in the same person being given a diagnosis by one professional and not by another.

It is amazing that we often describe people with cognitive differences by using a collection of seven or eight commonly used descriptors such as autism, ADHD, dyslexia, dyspraxia. We gain a label and for some we take on that persona. We can instantly forget the many other parts of us and be subsumed by being autistic or dyslexic. We seem to forget at times how intersectionality plays into a lot of who we all are. We are each the sum of a lot of different parts.

A label can represent a short-hand descriptor to a 'club' we want to join or alternatively a group we don't want to belong to. It may be either beneficial for us or may be limiting in terms of how others can see us or how we may even see ourselves. It can result in feelings of 'otherness' or difference or result in others considering you having fewer skills or talents as a consequence of that specific label. Or alternatively, the feeling of otherness may have been something we have felt in our past and gaining a diagnosis can be hugely positive and allows us to see we are no longer alone. Some people say they have found their 'tribe'. It may be the first time having an explanation of why you were (or are) having challenges in a neurotypical world and it provides the means of articulating this to others in a positive way. However, a 'tribe' can be seen by some as separatist.

Changing perceptions

What is important is that the language we use and what it stands for can change over time. Ian Hacking, a Canadian philosopher, describes a 'looping' effect in how we generate categories.[10] He describes that sometimes scientists can categorize by providing a name for a set of attributes and then this group comes into existence.

Amanda has been working as a researcher and clinician for more than 25 years and has seen how terms such as specific learning difficulties, developmental disorders and even terms like minimal brain dysfunction and atypical brain disorder have been used to describe a group of people who are cognitively diverse.

In the past we have seen specific groups of people 'pathologized'. One example of changing perspectives and categorizations is how society used to view left-handed people. Abram Blau, a psychiatrist from New York City, wrote what was an influential book in the 1940s: *The Master Hand: A study of the origin and meaning of left and right sidedness*.[11] He warned that, unless retrained, left-handed children risked severe and life-long mental and cognitive deficits.

This negative view is astounding to read today when we consider 10–15 per cent of any population is left-handed. It also feels quite close to home as Amanda's grandson and husband are both left-handed. Her mother-in-law was also left-handed and was forced to write with her right hand in school and ridiculed for being a left-hander. One person also told Amanda that when they were in school in the 1960s they were regularly hit with a ruler if they wrote with their left hand, and another man told her he was made to wear a sock on his left hand in school in the 1980s.

The words we use and how they are interpreted are important in how others perceive you. Though today we don't see a left-handed person as being bad or good, some of the earliest negative associations with being left-handed date from the 14th century and also relate to some measure of evil, foreboding, or malevolence. Also, the words for left are *sinister* in Latin, and *gauche* in French. Meanwhile, 'right' was always more positively associated with, for example, being 'righteous'. However, it wasn't all bad; the Bible mentions the higher numbers of left-handers from the tribe of Benjamin and this was seen as potentially conferring a strategic advantage in battle, somewhat like a left-handed tennis player or footballer today playing against right-handed or footed opponent. We also know of many famous and successful left-handers including Leonardo Da Vinci, Whoopi Goldberg, Lewis Carroll, David Bowie, Albert Einstein and Aristotle!

What we are trying to show is that wrong framing around labels and people's perception of what is in reality part of human variability has real consequences for many.

Changing labels over time

There has been much criticism for medicalizing patterns of our traits, behaviour and mood which for some are seen as part of the diversity of all humans. We have called this the 'medical model'. Most resources have been decided upon by someone being categorized as having one 'difficulty, disorder or disability'. It has been the 'golden ticket'. You needed to prove to others that the strengths and challenges you had were aligned to one condition or another. If they were, and it was one that was recognized by others, then this generally led to support, money or resources.

We think it is worth spending a short time understanding how international medical diagnostic systems work and the power of what happens when they make a decision over changing terminology too.

Two diagnostic categorization tools that are used across the world are the Diagnostic Statistical Manual (DSM),[12] published by the American Psychiatric Association, and the International Classification of Diseases (ICD),[13] published by the World Health Organization. These are classification systems used for diagnosis and research purposes. DSM was created to enable mental health professionals to communicate using a common diagnostic language. Its forerunner was published in 1917, primarily for gathering statistics across mental hospitals. It had the politically incorrect title *Statistical Manual for the Use of Institutions for the Insane* and included just 22 diagnoses. The DSM was first published in 1952 when the US armed forces wanted a guide on the diagnosis of servicemen. There was also an increasing push against the idea of treating people in institutions.

The first version of DSM had many concepts and suggestions that would be shocking to us today. Infamously, homosexuality was listed as a 'sociopathic personality disorder' and remained so until 1973. Autistic spectrum disorders were also thought to be a type of childhood schizophrenia.

Due to our greater understanding of mental health today and how genes and environment impact and interact with each other, the DSM is periodically updated. In each revision, mental health conditions that are no longer considered valid are removed, while newly defined conditions are added. This is clear evidence once again that views and terms change over time.

This change is really relevant with regard to the topic of neurodiversity. In the latest and fifth version of DSM published in 2013, Asperger's syndrome was removed. Asperger's syndrome was named after Hans Asperger, a Viennese psychiatrist who decided to group some children he was seeing and called them 'autistic psychopaths' in 1938.

Before the removal of the diagnosis there had been a lot of debate among clinicians about how those who were diagnosing Asperger's syndrome were doing so. In 2013 the latest iteration of the DSM Asperger's syndrome was removed and it was incorporated under the umbrella of autism spectrum disorder. This generated, as you could imagine, a lot of strong debate and discussion among scientists and clinicians. The change was especially difficult for people who had already been diagnosed with Asperger's syndrome and what that meant to them. While some may have seen this change as positive, some people who have been diagnosed as having Asperger's syndrome also refer to themselves as 'Aspies' or use other similar terms that represent their unique attributes and characteristics. It had become part of their understanding of themselves, and so removing it would have had consequences for them. This goes back to our discussions earlier in this chapter about what a name means to a person.

There has also been a potential secondary reason for moving away from having diagnostic conditions named after a person. In the case of Hans Asperger there has been some ambivalent discussion about his alignment with National Socialism in Vienna during the Second World War and his stance regarding eugenics. A research paper published in 2018 by Herwig Czech reviews this association in more detail.[14]

So... is it a good thing or not to have a label?

We clearly think this is personal but also has social biases, as we will discuss in other chapters about why some people don't get diagnosed at all or have the opportunity to do so. Some people want to belong to a group, and it feels welcoming to find a home to be with others, especially if your feelings of difference have also led to feeling isolated from others a lot of your life.

However, the other side of this is that it can lead to stereotyping people and we hear tropes or clichéd thinking such as 'all autistic people are good at IT' or 'all dyslexic people are creative', which are both untrue. While some autistic people are good at IT, clearly not all are, and though some dyslexic people are amazingly creative, again this is not true of all.

Some people like to be in an 'in group' of neurodivergent people especially if it has a perceived value such as being 'high functioning' or creative or analytical. It has kudos that may have some value in society. It can also be used as a shorthand to describe some skills. However, some labels may have less 'social currency' or understanding and so a diagnosis such as being clumsy may be avoided more.

Another potential downside of labels is that when we turn people into statistics and convert continuous measures into discrete categories, we lose valuable information about the complexity of each person. Humans are so much more than being autistic or dyslexic, outgoing or reserved, scientific or creative, disabled or 'abled', or high functioning or not. The reality is that every single person across the world has their own unique combination of traits and life experiences and it is very different from categorizing objects.

If we are to understand each individual it is essential that we move away from narrow medical models to a more biopsychosocial model. A key person who described this was Urie Bronfenbrenner 30 years ago.[15] His theory was based on an ecological system, where the person was in the middle, but other parts of that person's life, now and in the past, were also part of the whole picture. This included where they lived, with whom they mixed, their families, and the place and country in which they live.

The World Health Organization also has a framework, called the International Classification of Disability, Functioning and Health (ICF).[16] This framework is used internationally as a way of describing both challenges and strengths in the context of a person's life and is much more about seeing people as whole individuals rather than a narrow set of traits.

There is no right or wrong in someone gaining or wanting a diagnosis. It may lead to specific help or support to maximize talents. There is wrong, though, if not gaining one means your support needs are not met. For some adults the experience of only finding out why they had challenges in childhood comes late (and for some not at all). It can be a relief and it may generate feelings of anger and frustration in terms of what might have been. Many adults Amanda has met over the years have come to the realization they are neurodivergent because of a child or other family member gaining a diagnosis. In her experience some people wanted to have a 'label' and others just wanted explanations to gain understanding and be provided with guidance where it was appropriate.

THE IMPACT OF A LATER DIAGNOSIS

Finally, let's hear from Keith Fraser and his experience of gaining a diagnosis of dyslexia in adult life and what that meant for him.

'I am Keith Fraser and I am dyslexic. I would like to share my journey of discovery with you and also my journey post being diagnosed.

'As a child growing up going through infant school, junior school and secondary school I always knew I was different. I used to wonder why my spelling was awful, my handwriting wasn't the best (no matter how much money I spent on buying a pen) and I was usually the last one to finish reading something. I also noticed that when I read, I would often lose and still do lose my way on the page. I find myself a few lines down or even missing out just a few words and wondering how I got there after I realized what had happened.

'It's an odd feeling being dyslexic, at times. I suppose the best way to describe it is when you're writing something, you have a block sometimes and the shortest paragraph could take you 15 minutes to write. The best analogy I can use is like you're walking down the road and suddenly you stop, you try to move forward and you know where to go, but there is this invisible wind which you can't feel, but it is holding you back and making your journey slower. Then, for no apparent reason, this invisible wind, it suddenly subsides and you carry on with your journey. Then without warning the wind picks up again and stops you in your tracks. This happens arbitrarily and you do not know when this invisible wind that you cannot feel will stop you.

'Despite these challenges I had a happy and productive childhood. You may think listening to the above that I was extremely miserable as a result of these challenges, but I wasn't. I just thought I had to work a little bit harder (which I did) and then I would succeed. As a child I was always very visionary and that has continued into adulthood. My visions for the future are often the things that drive me and keep me going and I'm passionate about what I do get involved in.

'As a young child at about seven or eight I decided that I wanted to be a police officer and that passion has never left me. Therefore, everything I did from an educational perspective and to a certain extent in my private life was geared around fulfilling that ambition. I even completed an application form when I was 14 and wrote to the Home Office; fortunately some caring, unknown civil servant wrote back to me with a letter of encouragement and more information about joining the police. I finished school with five grade C or above O-level passes and a number of CSEs. The one that surprised my teachers and me the most was when I retook my English language and I rose from a CSE grade 3 to an O-level grade B. I remember the shock on the face of my strict but caring English teacher as a result. I did go on to do A-levels, but I didn't complete them and that was more to do with my desire to become a police officer and taking my foot off the pedal as soon as I knew I had got the job.

'Whilst in full-time work, I completed a degree in business studies (human resource management pathway) and I was awarded a 2:1. Again that shocked me, but I had to work extremely hard. A senior member of staff in the HR directorate was extremely interested in my dissertation on flexible organizations. I remember her asking if she could see the outcome of my research. I checked my dissertation after it had been marked and I had been praised, and to my horror, I noticed a number of spelling mistakes. As a result of that I ignored the request and probably missed an opportunity to progress in my work as a police officer and help change the organization.

'Despite this, I was successful as a police officer, becoming a senior cop and having to do a number of presentations and reports et cetera et cetera, both of which I hated doing but they were part of the job. I remember that if I was reading a speech, I would often lose my way, but I became quite skilful – and still am – at ad-libbing until I had found my place on the page. I do remember some of the first times that I lost my way in a briefing or presentation and the tummy-churning feeling that I felt inside. The thoughts buzzed around my head frantically like bees trying to get into a hive. But in a split second or two, which felt like hours, I'd managed to ad-lib and also find my way back into my briefing or presentation.

'I remember the first time that I was tested for dyslexia after marking some promotion papers; one of the executives thought that I might be and I was referred to an individual for testing. The person who tested me was extremely thorough and explained that I was above average intelligence and there was nothing wrong with me. I carried on thinking that I just had to work a little bit harder to manage and deal with the blocks and challenges I'd had as a child.

'In my mid-40s and as a senior officer I was allocated a coach to support my development. This coach said to me, "Keith, I think you might be dyslexic". I dismissed his observations and said I'd been tested already, but agreed to do three free online tests over the weekend. To my shock, every one of those tests stated that there was a strong likelihood of me being dyslexic.

'I approached my line manager and HR department and sought their support for another test to see if I was dyslexic. I went through another thorough, but different test and it concluded, to my surprise and to a certain extent dismay, that I was dyslexic. I wasn't upset at being diagnosed as dyslexic, I just wondered why it hadn't been picked up throughout school and I was also a little confused about the future, now that I knew I had a disability.

'I then had to go through the process of "coming out" and deciding who I was going to tell. My initial experience with my line manager, who is a fellow senior officer, was not very good. This individual challenged my operational credibility and my wish to take on a senior command function because I was now dyslexic. I must say though, all my line managers and the HR department after that individual were extremely supportive, as have my family and friends.

'When I was initially diagnosed, I did try to brush it under the carpet, thinking if I've got this far without doing anything about it and without people knowing, why should I do anything now or make an issue? My coach said to me, if you don't take it seriously then nobody else will. Those were extremely wise words, which have stood me in good stead for the future.

'Fast forward a few years and although still daunted by the thought of writing, reading and speaking out loud, I know that with the reasonable adjustments and the coping strategies I have been given, I am able to cope better and perform better. I also realize that I'm part of a club which has some famous and intelligent individuals. I've also met many people with dyslexia and that has given me the confidence to try and understand what I am able to do and the benefits of living with dyslexia. Some of those have stood out, like Professor Amanda Kirby. She has helped me to understand the strengths and also the challenges I have, but this knowledge has enabled me to focus more on my strengths, instead of the things I can't do.

'I'm currently the chair of the Youth Justice Board for England and Wales and a Commissioner for the UK Prime Minister. I am also involved in supporting a number of charities. I'm motoring ahead and enjoying living with dyslexia. I have decided that I will not atrophy behind the bars which society has created.'

What an experience and journey Keith has had! We leave the debate open about labelling, medicalizing or describing who we are and we will watch the language changing and with it the meaning, as it has always done.

KEY POINTS

Why use labels and what do they mean?

- Language changes over time, as does its meaning.

- Neurodiversity is about individuals and encapsulates strengths as well as challenges.

- The words someone uses to describe themselves are personal; there are no rights and wrongs and they can change as our perception of ourselves changes.

- Labels can be a shorthand way of finding common ground and a starting point for a conversation. They never describe a person.

Note: We have provided a glossary of terms at the end of the book to help you understand some of the acronyms and words used. We also recognize that at some time these may change.

Notes

1   Fitzgerald, F Scott (1920) *Racconti dell'età del jazz*, https://www.goodreads.com/quotes/10215670-to-be-kind-is-more-important-than-to-be-right (archived at https://perma.cc/TG9U-S4JX)

2   Cleaton, M and Kirby, A (2018) Why Do We Find it so Hard to Calculate the Burden of Neurodevelopmental Disorders? *Journal of Childhood and Development Disorders*, https://childhood-developmental-disorders.imedpub.com/why-do-we-find-it-so-hard-to-calculate-the-burden-of-neurodevelopmental-disorders.pdf (archived at https://perma.cc/N2U9-VTRL)

3   Kanner, L (1949) Problems of nosology and psychodynamics in early childhood autism, *American Journal of Orthopsychiatry*, https://onlinelibrary.wiley.com/doi/abs/10.1111/j.1939-0025.1949.tb05441.x (archived at https://perma.cc/JNJ9-LR44)

4   Archer, T, Oscar-Berman, M and Blum, K (2011) Epigenetics in developmental disorder: ADHD and endophenotypes, *Journal of Genetic Syndromes & Gene Therapy*, https://www.longdom.org/open-access/epigenetics-in-developmental-disorder-adhd-and-endophenotypes-2157-7412.1000104.pdf (archived at https://perma.cc/2X68-H4J7)

5 Doyle, N (2021) Is Everyone a Little Autistic? *Forbes*, 16 January, https://www.forbes.com/sites/drnancydoyle/2021/01/16/is-everyone-a-little-autistic/?sh=649e04d15666 (archived at https://perma.cc/KU94-Y8AR)

6 Pearsall-Jones, J G, Piek, J P and Levy, F (2010) Developmental coordination disorder and cerebral palsy: categories or a continuum? *Human Movement Science*, https://doi.org/10.1016/j.humov.2010.04.006 (archived at https://perma.cc/NU7Y-AD2M)

7 Smith, T (2020) Neurodiversity: Eliminating Kryptonite, Enabling Superheroes [Podcast] 21 May, https://anchor.fm/neurodiversity/episodes/Ep-19-High-Contrast---Leading-Global-Drum--Bass-Producer-and-Remixer-ebnbvp (archived at https://perma.cc/35V8-JPBB)

8 Covey, S (2019) Habit 5: Seek first to understand, then to be understood, Franklin Covey website, https://www.franklincovey.com/the-7-habits/habit-5/ (archived at https://perma.cc/PF3R-N65V)

9 *The Shorter Oxford English Dictionary* (1978) 3rd ed, Clarendon Press, Oxford

10 Hacking, I (2004) Between Michel Foucault and Erving Goffman: Between discourse in the abstract and face-to-face interaction, *Economy and Society*, 333, pp 277–302

11 Blau, A (1946) *The Master Hand: A study of the origin and meaning of left and right sidedness and its relation to personality and language*, American Psychological Association, Washington

12 American Psychiatric Association (2013) *Diagnostic and Statistical Manual of Mental Disorders (DSM-5)*, American Psychiatric Association, Washington

13 World Health Organization (2019) ICD-11 International Classification of Diseases, 11th Revision, https://icd.who.int/en (archived at https://perma.cc/B5PQ-G2KZ)

14 Czech, H (2018) Hans Asperger, National Socialism, and 'race hygiene' in Nazi-era Vienna, *Molecular Autism*, https://molecularautism.biomedcentral.com/articles/10.1186/s13229-018-0208-6 (archived at https://perma.cc/V2RA-J5GA)

15 Bronfenbrenner, U (1992) Ecological systems theory, in R Vasta (ed), *Six Theories of child Development: Revised formulations and current issues* (pp 187–249). Jessica Kingsley Publishers, London

16 World Health Organization (2001) International Classification of Functioning, Disability and Health, https://www.who.int/standards/classifications/international-classification-of-functioning-disability-and-health (archived at https://perma.cc/T8N2-KG2C)

Further reading

Germanò, E and Gagliano, A (2010) Comorbidity of ADHD and dyslexia, *Developmental Neuropsychology*, **35**, pp 475–93

Kadesjö, B and Gillberg, C (2001) The comorbidity of ADHD in the general population of Swedish school-age children, *Journal of Child Psychology & Psychiatry Allied Disciplines*, **42**, pp 487–92

Kirby, A and Judge, D (2018) Addressing the inverse care law in developmental coordination disorder and related neurodevelopmental disorders, *Current Developmental Disorders Reports*, **5**, pp 18–25

Freeman, R D *et al* (2000) An international perspective on Tourette syndrome: selected findings from 3500 individuals in 22 countries, *Developmental Medicine & Child Neurology*, **42**, pp 436–47

Kaplan, B J *et al* (2001) The term comorbidity is of questionable value in reference to developmental disorders: data and theory, *Journal of Learning Disabilities*, **34**, pp 555–65

Thapar, A and Cooper, M (2016) Attention deficit hyperactivity disorder, *Lancet*, 19 March, **387** (10024) pp 1240–50

Williams, E *et al* (2008) Prevalence and characteristics of autistic spectrum disorders in the ALSPAC cohort, *Developmental Medicine & Child Neurology*, **50**, pp 672–77

03

Categories and spiky profiles

Introduction

For some time now we've been trying to crack the 'Neurodiversity Enigma Code' on how to help organizations attract candidates with greater diversity of thought. But specifically, we want to focus on those with *very* spiky profiles. What is a spiky profile? We use this term as it encapsulates both strengths and challenges and the variability of this for each of us. Those with very spiky profiles often have peaks in skills and talents but also have some dips that can impact on their ability to showcase their talents.

In this chapter we will explore this more and discuss why we like as humans to categorize, and speculate on the reasons for this.

Categories

Why do we love a category? As Dorothy L Sayers wrote:

> We are much too much inclined in these days to divide people into permanent categories, forgetting that a category only exists for its special purpose and must be forgotten as soon as that purpose is served.[1]

At the present time we may be seeing neurodiversity as a new form of categorization conceptually rather than considering that every brain is different, and society is diverse. We will mention this several times throughout this book.

Our approach as human beings has always been to categorize despite recognizing the dimensional nature of humans. The contexts of each person (now and in the past) are also important considerations and mean that each person with a diagnosis of dyslexia, DCD or ADHD for example will be very different too.

The categorizing also becomes a common language and a sense of rigidity. It gives us a way to describe groups of items, actions, symptoms and signs to others in a shorthand. It gives us a way to group our thoughts and group people but also to view people in a specific way. We can become fixed in our vision of who that person is and what they can and can't do.

The challenge comes with humans in that we are 'messy' and in reality don't fit into one neat box or another. We never fit into one group alone even though people are often given one diagnosis in isolation. This only represents the parts that have been assessed or asked about.

There is not a single test for dyslexia that in reality says you are dyslexic or not. This is determined by varying measures and is an interpretation of these with an arbitrary cut-off that someone (human) has applied. Who determines that dyslexia is a score below the 15th percentile on one test or the 5th percentile on another? Who agrees that all tests are equal and equally used and available for all, when we know that they are not? This is down to human interpretation. If the professional knows that the individual at the end of the assessment will gain provision by the report findings, they will be encouraged to lean towards the diagnosis.

We are far more diverse than ever being 'just' autistic. Amanda for example has several family members who are autistic. One is learning disabled, tall, non-verbal, epileptic, and loves everything about cars. Another one is a concert pianist, and another is gay and has a degree as an accountant. They come from very different upbringings and different family settings. They could not be classified as one 'type'. One of them reads classical texts but is not very good at maths at all. One is an amazing musician and the other tone deaf but can look at a spreadsheet and spot an error at 50 metres. The third family member can't read fluently at all. All different, but nevertheless wonderful people.

By grouping people together into diagnostic boxes, we had hoped we could take meaning from random data so we could catalogue and deliver appropriate services. In some ways it may remain true that understanding the profile of a person may allow for more tailored provision. For example, it may be useful to know that a child with ADHD also has a language difficulty and has difficulty decoding spoken information. This may be very important when designing support for the child. In adulthood it may be important to know that someone who is autistic has challenges with organizational skills relating to ADHD, in order to support them in education or the workplace.

Service options can become restricted to the taxonomies that have been devised and can be separated geographically from one another. However, we are now seeing interdisciplinary teams working together successfully in some areas of the UK. It becomes very difficult and costly in time and money for families to cope when they or their children are straddle between services. At the time of writing this, waiting times for children to have ADHD assessments through the NHS CAMHS service in some areas of the UK are around 28 months and getting longer.

These waiting times are not just impacting the health and wellbeing of our children, they are also affecting the parents, which is something we often do not consider within our organizations. In this instance, a category 'potentially' provides access to support, but it also creates additional challenges around waiting times, and it's those periods of uncertainty that can create a lot of stress and anxiety that can feed into the education system, the workplace, and homelife. We need to consider better all-round and practical support for not just those in our workplaces challenged by their working environment and working practices, but also the challenges individuals are facing at home balancing their family life too. Many neurodivergent adults will also have neurodivergent children.

Opportunity to be supported is important

Embracing neurodiversity represents a part of a changing picture of moving to a strengths and challenges viewpoint that each of us can also evolve over time, and are dependent on varying factors. One person with dyslexia may get identified as having challenges with reading and spelling at six years of age, and gain intervention strategies in school to support them. They may also have the tools and family support to assist in their development and end up moving from education to employment with confidence.

Another person never gains a diagnosis. They find navigating school impossibly difficult, avoid attending and end up dropping out early. They have a talent for maths, and this ends up being channelled into a 'successful' way of utilizing it, gaining a criminal record for drug dealing.

Classification fills a human need to impose order on nature and find relationships, links and associations that may not be immediately obvious.

There is extensive evidence that conditions that have been associated with 'neurodivergence' co-occur and these marked areas are far less tangible than was considered 10–15 years ago.

Over the past 50 years or more we have tried to conceptualize the 'messiness' of individuals in a number of ways. We have used terms such as Minimal Brain Dysfunction ('a term often employed in child psychiatry and developmental paediatrics from the 1950s to the early 1980s'),[2] Deficits in Attention, Motor Control and Perception (DAMP – this never gained popularity among parents who didn't want to refer to their children as being DAMP!)[3] and more recently, Early Symptomatic Syndromes Eliciting Neurodevelopmental Clinical Examinations (ESSENCE).[4] The latter two acronyms were coined by Gillberg, a Swedish child and adolescent psychiatrist, to attempt to group symptoms and signs together that didn't really fit into one condition. In many research papers you will read the term heterogeneous describing groups of people under one label such as dyslexia or dyspraxia. This term means consisting of different, distinguishable parts or elements and reflects that when we study a group of people we see differences between them, even when they have the same diagnosis.

Two recent papers in the past few years have exemplified the need to consider how services are delivered and are really saying we need to move away from the strict categorization and medical model of psychiatry and paediatrics. The recent consensus paper on identification and treatment of ADHD and ASD[5] and the seminal paper from Thapar, Cooper and Rutter[6] both highlight the real clinical conundrum of 'the complexity of clinical phenotypes and the importance of the social context'. A phenotype means the challenges or strengths that someone can observe in someone. They go on to argue 'the importance of viewing neurodevelopmental disorders as traits but highlight that this is not the only approach to use'.

Moving away from the medical model approach to a more social model produces real emotions in both parents and adults, with some people wanting to be known as autistic and being defined as such and others not wanting a diagnosis or to be defined by one label. For parents it can be a two-edged sword, where they may not want a diagnosis but recognize that without one their child may not receive support or recognition of their hidden strengths. While intervention is based on a diagnosis this fear and need will remain. For some a diagnosis really provides a lot. It can provide meaning, a sense of relief, a place to find people with a common language, and understanding and support for starters.

The flipside of this is that categorization creates stereotypes such as that all people who are autistic are good at computer programming and people who are dyslexic are all creative. The converse may be right, in that in some areas of work you may find higher rates of neurodivergence, but it is not true that all people who have certain neurodivergent characteristics are good at specific roles. There may be other factors in their success as well, including resilience and opportunity.

As James McGrath rightly said in relation to autistic people (people with autism): 'These stereotypes matter because they are misrepresenting what people with autism are actually like. They often present autistics to be "a certain way", a loner or socially awkward – when in fact this varies person to person (autistic or not).'[7]

We have all heard phrases spoken such as 'How can you be good at X and autistic?' or 'You don't seem to look or act autistic!' These stereotypes are then further portrayed in the press and by representative organizations that repeat the same thing again and again.

It can also mean we see what is sometimes called the 'benevolence barrier' where someone doesn't get advancement in their job as others think that the person may not be able to deal with the pressures or will be liable to take excessive sick leave or disability-related absences; or adjustments will be more expensive as they climb higher in the organization.

We can see from some studies that neurodivergent people may have spiky profiles with peaks of strengths in some areas and dips in others. Hong and Milgram in 2010 studied the relationships between general and domain creativity in a sample of 130 university students, about half of whom had a learning difficulty.[8] This turned out not to affect their general creative thinking. However, the students performed worse in academic problem-solving, but better than controls in the visual and intuitive aspects of creative thinking. In a more recent study from Italy, they showed that the creative thinking that is spoken of may not be subject-specific but about seeing relationships between different or opposite elements and being able to find alternative solutions.[9] However, the reason for this may be because the strategies that others may be teaching or using with them haven't worked and this leads them to find alternative ways to problem-solve and apply these original strategies.

This study and similar ones open up the debate that rather than saying autistic people are good at IT and dyslexic people are creative, instead we celebrate people's skills, interests and motivations and harness them in the settings where they want to be, not constrain them by stereotyping.

Spiky profiles

What are Spiky Profiles?

We all have spiky profiles.[10] This means that none of us are good at everything or bad at everything. We each have our own pattern of strengths and challenges. Some challenges may be related to navigating a world with specific expectations to conform in certain ways. Some may be down to our current built environment and work structures and practices.

The reality is that people who recognize themselves as autistic, dyslexic or have ADHD for example usually have a *spikier* profile. This can result in a greater contrast between the peak of an individual strength versus the dips of particular cognitive challenges. The difference between the two can impact on day-to-day lives. An example is shown in Figure 3.1.

FIGURE 3.1   An example of spiky profiles

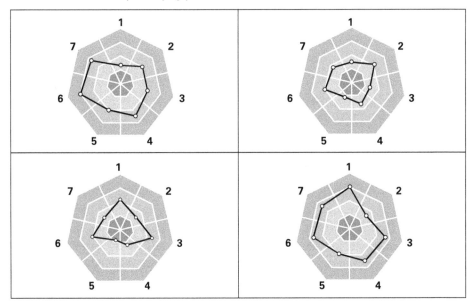

1 Emotion and Feelings
2 Attention, organizing and time management
3 Speaking, listening and understanding
4 Literacy

5 Memory, vision, auditory skills, senses
6 Physical and coordination
7 Numeracy Skills

SOURCE Do-IT Neurodiversity Profiler

If you see these four spiky profiles taken from the Do-IT Neurodiversity Profiler that Amanda and her team have designed you can see that the pictures are all wonderfully different.

What does this mean practically?

Well, we can have MAD skills in very specific areas, but it can be at the cost of other abilities.

Most people, or dare we say the 'average' person (we haven't met that person yet!), don't have these significant dips and strengths and have a more even profile. But for people who are neurodiverse it is often recognized that their cognitive abilities can be off the chart, either significantly above or below the average in one or more areas.

So why is this important and what should we consider when thinking of how we get the best out of these MAD abilities?

MAD abilities

Theo has coined this term – MAD: **M**oving **A**ttitudes towards **D**iverse abilities.

We are going to look at Theo's as an example, but you too can go and check your spiky profile if you want. So, this is where we get personal.

Figures 3.2–3.4 show three images, each showing diagrams for some of Theo's cognitive abilities and challenges. There are seven levels available, but for the purpose of what we are discussing here, we have selected three to focus on.

The first (Figure 3.2) shows Theo's spiky profile for speaking, listening and understanding.

So, something to pick up on is that Theo has significant strength in conversing with others and that he is a 'people person'. On the other end, he has some challenges around listening to others, which is to do with noisy environments or where many people are speaking at once; it isn't that he does not like to listen to others, which would clearly conflict with being a 'people person'.

He also struggles with social nuances, like understanding jokes; he never really did get comedians! However, it doesn't mean he doesn't 'get' people; his ability to read people's emotions based on their facial expressions is very high. For example, he scored 100 per cent for this via a gamified psychometric assessment.

FIGURE 3.2 Spiky profile for speaking, listening and understanding

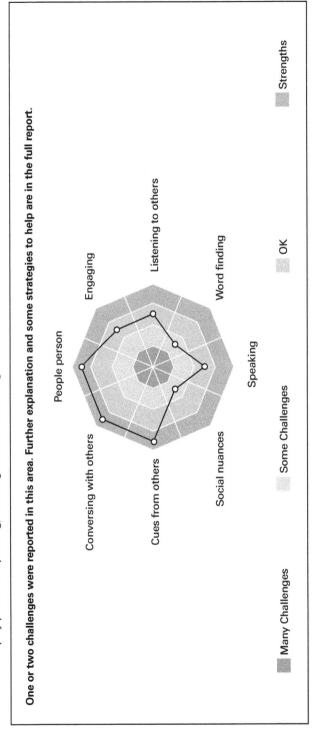

One or two challenges were reported in this area. Further explanation and some strategies to help are in the full report.

As we'll discuss later, technology and assessments broadly aren't the single problem, we just need to get them working for those who have spiky profiles. After all, technology is built by humans, so the secret to making technology inclusive and accessible is there!

Next, in Figure 3.3 you'll see a much spikier profile. Theo's happy (positive), manages change well and he's empathic.

The flip side of that is that he's very rarely relaxed (very energetic), believe it or not his confidence isn't always as high as you'd think, and he can be quite impulsive. We also see this in many actors and comedians. They perform on stage, on film and attend large events, but actually they struggle socially and are not as confident as you'd expect. They are just brilliant at their job and love what they do, in the moments they do it.

The risk here as we've seen with actors like Robin Williams, who was believed to have undiagnosed ADHD, is that they can hyper focus, on camera they are exceptional, but they struggle with the highs and lows of life – the balance between their incredible unique strengths and their extreme challenges. This is something that often is associated with ADHD.

Theo's Dad once met Robin Williams at a NATO meeting in a military camp in Afghanistan, and he tells the story of how Williams walked around the table introducing himself to many of the attendees from across the globe in their own language and managing to make each one laugh. His Dad to this day doesn't know what he said to each individual, but he was shocked when he spoke to him in Welsh, which as you can imagine is not a widely spoken language. His ability to make people laugh using languages he'd never spoken himself was incredible. Williams then stayed on afterwards to personally meet every soldier in the camp to recognize the work they were doing, and there were thousands of them!

This is what 'MAD' abilities can look like, acting or working in a way that may seem off the scale to others, but unfortunately it can come with challenges, which is why it's so important that we focus on individual strengths.

Knowing these things about yourself can be key to having a successful life and career. Not knowing these things can lead to challenges with mental health and wellbeing and questionable career choices: in extreme sports risking life and limb… or prison!

Extensive studies have shown that around one in three people in prison have ADHD and other related neurodiverse traits.[11] Studies in prisons across the world including in Texas, in Nordic countries, and one at Chelmsford prison in the UK, amongst many others, have shown around 50 per cent of

FIGURE 3.3   Spiky profiles for emotions and feelings

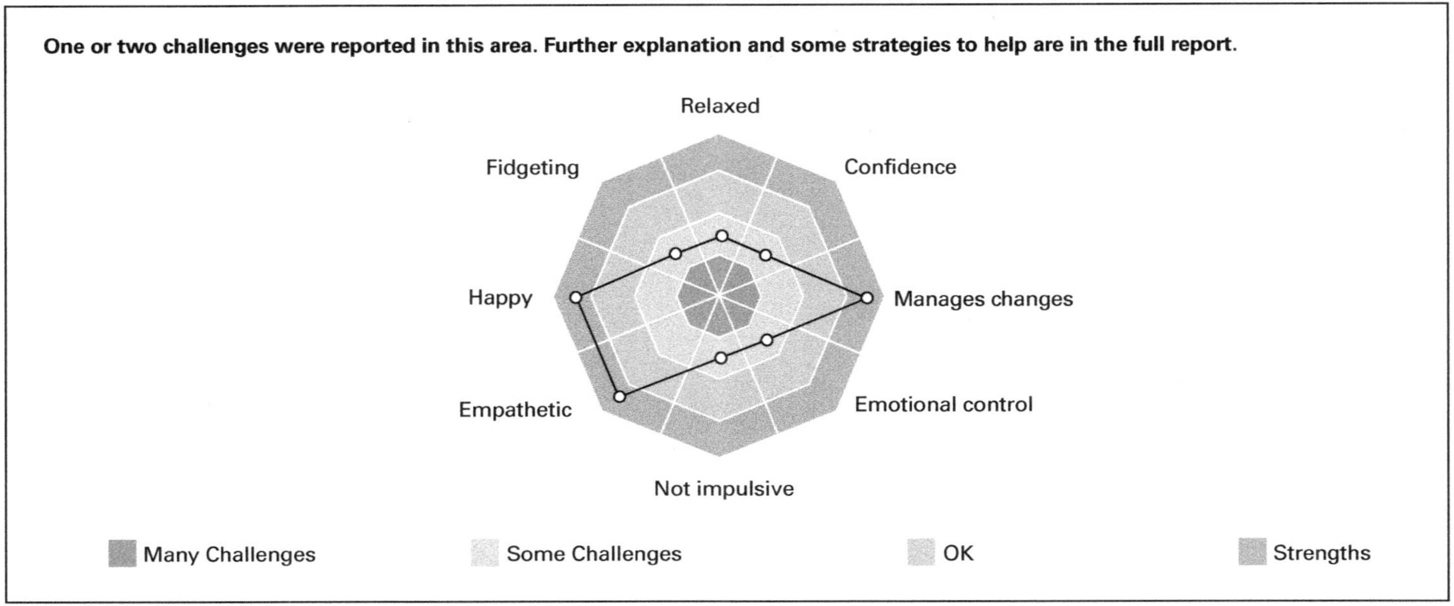

One or two challenges were reported in this area. Further explanation and some strategies to help are in the full report.

Confidence

Relaxed

Manages changes

Emotional control

Fidgeting

Not impulsive

Happy

Empathetic

Many Challenges

Some Challenges

OK

Strengths

the prisoners were identified as being dyslexic or have significant literacy difficulties.[12]

In a speech relating to young offenders sentenced to custody made by the then UK Lord Chancellor and Secretary of State for Justice, Chris Grayling, on 13 June 2013 at Civitas, he said:

> They are something like ten times more likely to have learning disabilities (23–32 per cent v 2–4 per cent). A high proportion of them – maybe more than half – will have dyslexia (43–57 per cent). That compares with just 10 per cent in the population as a whole.[13]

There has been some debate over the years relating to chicken or egg, ie have some people missed school because they were excluded or opted out of education and thus didn't learn to read, or alternatively were they dyslexic and inattentive and fell out of school as they found it harder to engage and learn? Increasing understanding is leading us to find it is often in reality a mix of the two.[14]

Increasingly there is an understanding of the intersection between low literacy skills and a number of other factors including lack of opportunity to have needs met, relating also to poverty. People's perceived self-efficacy (according to psychologist Albert Bandura) is essential to academic success.[15] For people in prison, many of whom will also have been in care as a child, been homeless and/or excluded from education, some studies indicate that academic self-efficacy is a contributor to educational participation, which in turn can increase their academic self-efficacy. It is a complex mix.

Either way, understanding your brain as early as possible and having the right support network at home, in school and beyond is vitally important for all so that skills can be optimized. Having a parent, teacher, partner, manager who understands your skills/strengths can be the difference between being understood and supported in life and in the workplace, rather than being misunderstood and placed at risk, because you are forced to 'play' to your challenges, rather than to your significant strengths.

We have sadly seen the negative side of this in some specialist residential settings where individuals who are on the autism spectrum have been treated with excessive force, because staff have misunderstood the person trying to communicate a need. The interactions can result in high levels of distress and sometimes violent responses that could have potentially been diverted if they had been better understood.

FIGURE 3.4 Spiky profile of memory, vision, auditory skills, senses

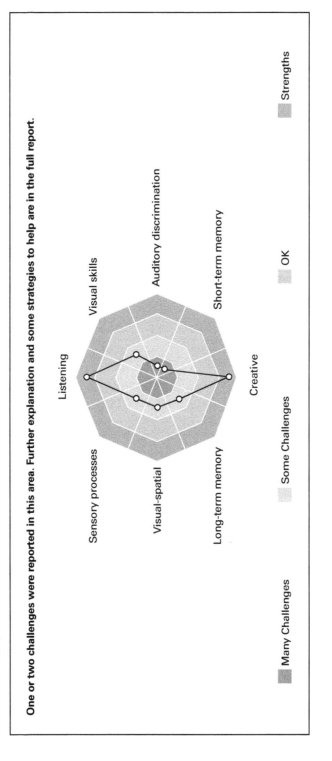

One or two challenges were reported in this area. Further explanation and some strategies to help are in the full report.

This is no different to people in the work setting, in that communication is two-way. Not being understood is frustrating for all of us, especially when you are trying hard but it is being wrongly received.

The final image in Figure 3.4 is the spikiest of the three, and therefore it's really important to harness this strength, because if it's not utilized effectively, it is surrounded by so many potential challenges.

If harnessed correctly and given the space to be used, 'creativity' at a spiky level is a powerful ace card to have in any team or organization. It is the ability to see around corners and to combat 'groupthink'.

So, let's analyse the above. Clearly, Theo has many challenges, as do other people who are neurodiverse and/or who have spiky profiles. However, he has several areas that are positively spiky. These are: Empathic, Positive (happy), Creative, Problem-Solving and Managing Change.

What are all organizations currently going through?
Change!

What do organizations need in times of change?
Creativity, problem-solvers and change agents!

What do teams and customers need during times of change?
Empathic and positive team members/leaders!

You can see where we are going with this.

The reality is that people with MAD abilities have an incredible amount to offer, but unfortunately, we very rarely tease out these super abilities. Instead, we often allow the challenges to come to the forefront of our minds or we don't put in place workplace support quickly enough to enable that person's MAD abilities to be shown to others.

How are we ever going to enable neurologically diverse minds to apply and then succeed within our organizations if we don't significantly change the way we approach attracting, assessing, and importantly supporting those who think differently?

That is without even considering that a higher proportion of people with neurodiverse minds could be ending up in prison or facing significant challenges in academia, which then goes on to create additional barriers when they try to gain entry to the workplace.

Now Theo is one of the lucky few, through the work he's doing to promote neurodiversity and his ability to focus and harness his own super abilities – he's not the one we really need to focus on here! But we can all learn from his laser focus on personal strengths. If nothing else it gives you a sense of self-worth and improves your psychological wellbeing, which we all need a bit of in today's ever-changing and evolving world.

Why aren't we always hiring people with very spiky profiles?

Part of the challenge is that the traditional process for attracting and selecting candidates is inconsistent, or at the very least entrenched in archaic evidence-based approaches that are being challenged. More on actionable steps you can take through the recruitment process later in the book.

So, what are we talking about?

Some systems still use only psychometric assessments, rigid interview structures, lengthy, wordy job descriptions, and inaccessible adverts... we could go on.

Let us just take some psychometric assessments as one example. Over-use of any single measure has limitations, and potentially can be discriminatory to those who have neurodivergent traits.

It's great to offer adjustments for interviews but it is not enough to allow candidates a bit more time or the use of a screen reader etc... The assessment and interview process can provide plenty of opportunity for biases around a person's capabilities. It also flags areas of risk/weakness but without the context of what's actually really going on in the individual's brain. The reason for poor performance on the test may be related to anxiety rather than lack of skill. It could also be the fact the test has been taken in a room with a lot of external noise, or the person has to record information by hand and they have poor fine motor skills so someone can't read their writing. They get scored badly because of their writing and not the responses. These are just some examples of where interpretation of results can fall down.

Assumptions are often based on research and data that has been built broadly around a system that is trying to recruit an average person (but do remember there is no average person). This results in doors not even being opened to up to 20 per cent of those who do not conform to this.

Theo has had this happen to him at least twice in his career, where he was told at a leading communications company after graduating that he was too empathetic, based on the results of a psychometric test, for a customer service job he was already employed to do for them. They were testing new psychometric tools on their current employees and his manager said he would not have employed him based on his psychometric results.

Needless to say, it didn't turn out to be his calling in life.

His other experience was during a gruelling three-hour third-stage interview, where the human resource director (HRD) had as much as given him 'the wink' that the job was his. Two managers in the interview used the psychometrics results to show him why he wasn't a good fit for the job, rather than using the results to understand how he could best be supported to play to his significant strengths.

But hey, this isn't about bashing any one form of assessment. We think we're getting it wrong across the table and small specific changes could make a real difference to being inclusive. There must be better ways and solutions that meet the needs of all and not some.

For example, Theo recently did some work with a gamified assessment company and we think this could potentially be one good option to consider for some people. However, we have to consider the implications of the results of those who are neurodivergent and how they would be interpreted. We must also consider that just because it works well for one person who happens to be autistic and/or ADHD, doesn't mean it works for all.

We already know that a computer and/or AI making decisions is currently doing so based on the information it's been fed, and if that information is the same information that feeds into traditional psychometrics, then we are just digitizing an assessment method that's broken.

The most important thing is, where possible, to provide as many options as possible so that we are not all forced through a funnel where dolphins, monkeys, rats and turtles are all asked to complete the same assessment task, when all have unique skills they could bring to the job, if only we provide them with the most appropriate platform to show off those skills.

If we look at a series of spiky profiles as in Figure 3.1 we can see that each one is very different. Recognizing the different strengths is what it's all about.

Time for change; time to change

We need to rethink the whole piece and we need to provide the time for ourselves, hiring managers and candidates to be able to solve this conundrum. Bill Boorman and Theo had this exact discussion on his podcast

Neurodiversity: Eliminating Kryptonite and Enabling Superheroes.[16] They agreed that time is what is required more than anything else.

The time for change; the time to change.

Time is after all a social construct; within reason, we can recreate it in any way we like. We can and should find the time for the much-needed change we require!

Ultimately, if we do so then the results will mean better access to education, to work and to our environment for the many! Which will result in better outcomes for all.

We need simpler solutions to complex problems

It is enough already that the problems around diversity and specifically around neurodiversity seem so complex and so challenging that the mountain is just too high to climb.

Or is it?

Eat an apatosaurus one spoonful at a time! Maybe we are just over-complicating matters.

We have two specific user groups that we need to consider:

1 Hiring managers and/or recruiters/human resources in companies;

2 Candidates.

HIRING MANAGERS AND/OR RECRUITERS/HR

What do hiring managers need to know to support those with spiky profiles? They need to know what MAD abilities each person has.

Now they could find this out via the interview; maybe the candidate is empowered enough to know and share with them what their MAD abilities are, but perhaps not. Furthermore (as a result of pre-interview testing methods) the interview could focus solely on the candidate's perceived 'weaknesses', thereby giving them no forum in which to show their strengths.

So how can we help hiring managers and recruiters help themselves? How can we ensure they see the best in people and get the right person for the job? And how do we do it simply and at scale? As job applications are going through the roof, this is going to make it even more challenging for neurodiverse candidates.

We will focus more on this in following chapters on the practical elements of recruitment, assessment, onboarding and line management.

CANDIDATES

The reality is that candidates unfortunately often don't know or don't get the opportunity to express or be aware that they have a spiky profile. They may be less confident selling their significant strengths and abilities. Either they never make it through the recruitment/hiring process, or when they do, they join an organization that has little understanding or appreciation of their strengths and dismisses the need to support their challenges.

Past experience drives current behaviour and some candidates can suffer from a lack of confidence due to the way the recruitment process and feedback works or the negative experiences they have had. It can leave them with a lot of anxiety and confusion around their abilities and result in them feeling less capable. This can drive a spiral of increasing anxiety. Poor experiences can lead to further poor experiences.

How to fix it?

Well, it would be amazing for every candidate to come fully prepared with the knowledge of their MAD abilities.

So maybe if everyone just went and did the Do-IT Neurodiversity Profiler, that would help to have a language of strengths as well as discussing support needs. But we need to be realistic and also identify the solution at the point of need: at the application, interview and onboarding stages.

THE ASSESSMENT PARADIGM

People don't always present 'typically' and we can have stereotypes of what we expect. Assessments are only one part of understanding a person and context is important too. We can compensate and camouflage. Someone with dyslexia can have made huge efforts with their writing and ensuring its accuracy through fear of being 'found out', building mechanisms to help with their challenges around spelling. These may work well (but can be effortful). So dyslexia doesn't necessarily always mean for everyone continuing poor grammar and spelling as the person may have developed strategies to support them. Each person will have a pattern of different strengths and challenges. If an assessment for dyslexia focuses predominantly on spelling but the person has weaker reading comprehension the results could miss this information. If information is gathered from others such as a past manager or lecturer they may describe the person as 'detail oriented' as they may not have seen the effort and adjustments they had put in place. In the end there will never be a single assessment that determines a person. We are all far more complex!

Now arguably you could say, 'Wow we want to work with that person who has overcome their challenges around their spelling, as that's a real positive'. Unfortunately, some people, if they get a sniff through assessment feedback of spelling or other literacy difficulties, may be put off employing the person as they may think they require more effort to support them. As a consequence they miss out on the talents that person could have offered.

Remember Amazon and its AI (artificial intelligence) that had a 'dislike' for women? In effect, Amazon's system taught itself that male candidates were preferable, because the 10 years of data they used as part of the algorithm told it that men were preferable, in what is a male-dominated tech industry. 'It penalized CVs that, amongst other things, included the word "women's", as in "women's netball team captain".'[17]

Creating a machine that digs for gold but throws away diamonds and platinum on its journey isn't the best use of any technology for anybody, certainly not the candidates who are needlessly thrown away.

We need to find ways that encapsulate skills. According to the National Autistic Society, a recent Office for National Statistics report shows just 22 per cent of autistic adults are in any kind of employment. Furthermore, one could argue that those in work are not necessarily in meaningful work.[18] The barriers are too high, and the assessment processes are too limited, expensive or antiquated in their approach.

It's for these reasons we desperately feel we need to look at alternative ways to solve age-old problems around bias and misguided tests and assessments. A combination of tech and people skills could be the answer!

We've got to start trialling and testing new methods; we cannot sit and wait, debate, discuss and hope governments or charities or academia will make the difference. So we will explore how understanding a spiky profile can translate into success in sharing your cognitive skills.

Terms that have been used with negative connotations, such as 'disorder' and 'difficulties', could in fact be reframed with the correct support and platform to be seen as someone's greatest ability, and 'difference' and 'diversity' as something we all value in society. Opening up conversations to understand the meaning of words being used is essential for a dialogue.

As blogger and author Rachel Wolchin said, 'Be mindful when it comes to your words. A string of some that don't mean much to you, may stick with someone else for a lifetime.' [19]

KEY POINTS
Categories and spiky profiles

- Spiky profiles are about peaks in strengths and dips in challenges.

- Not everyone has had the opportunity to gain a picture of their spiky profile and may have had the focus in the past on what they can't do rather than what they can.

- Each person has a unique picture of strengths and challenges that can change over time.

- Categorizing can sometimes divide people into boxes which can become stereotypes.

- Language and use of it can change over time.

- Each person may describe themselves differently and this needs to be considered and respected.

Notes

1 Sayers, D (2005) *Are Women Human? Astute and witty essays on the role of women in society*, William B Eerdmans Publishing Co, Michigan

2 Wood, D R, Reimherr, F W, Wender P H and Johnson, G E (1976) Diagnosis and treatment of minimal brain dysfunction in adults: a preliminary report, *Archives of Psychiatry*, https://jamanetwork.com/journals/jamapsychiatry/article-abstract/491638 (archived at https://perma.cc/E8QA-NN3W)

3 Gillberg, C (2003) Deficits in attention, motor control, and perception: A brief review, *Archives of Disease in Childhood*, https://adc.bmj.com/content/88/10/904 (archived at https://perma.cc/GX8P-LHMG)

4 Gillberg, C (2010) The ESSENCE in child psychiatry: Early Symptomatic Syndromes Eliciting Neurodevelopmental Clinical Examinations, *Research in Developmental Disabilities*, https://pubmed.ncbi.nlm.nih.gov/20634041/ (archived at https://perma.cc/RH3L-VVZ4)

5 Young, S *et al* (2020) Guidance for identification and treatment of individuals with attention deficit/hyperactivity disorder and autism spectrum disorder based upon expert consensus, *BMC Medicine*, https://bmcmedicine.biomedcentral.com/articles/10.1186/s12916-020-01585-y (archived at https://perma.cc/BK5D-VCZK)

6 Thapar, A, Cooper, M and Rutter, M (2017) Neurodevelopmental disorders, *Lancet Psychiatry*, https://pubmed.ncbi.nlm.nih.gov/27979720/ (archived at https://perma.cc/T7GW-82KH)

7 McGrath, J (2019) Not all autistic people are good at maths and science – despite the stereotypes, *The Conversation*, 3 April, https://theconversation.com/not-all-autistic-people-are-good-at-maths-and-science-despite-the-stereotypes-114128 (archived at https://perma.cc/5BVH-3XWH)

8 Hong, E and Milgram, R M (2010) Creative thinking ability: Domain generality and specificity, *Creativity Research Journal*, http://dx.doi.org/10.1080/10400419.2010.503535 (archived at https://perma.cc/5BQZ-Q2XT)

9 Cancer, A, Manzoli, S and Antonietti, A (2016) The alleged link between creativity and dyslexia: Identifying the specific process in which dyslexic students excel, *Cogent Psychology*, https://www.tandfonline.com/doi/full/10.1080/23311908.2016.1190309 (archived at https://perma.cc/2NL9-TYTH)

10 Smith, T (2020) Why Mad Abilities Matter, #*Chat Talent*, 12 October, https://www.chattalent.com/blogs/why-mad-abilities-matter/ (archived at https://perma.cc/8NZG-BAQN)

11 Young, S and Cocallis, K M (2019) Attention deficit hyperactivity disorder (ADHD) in the prison system, *Current Psychiatry Reports*, https://pubmed.ncbi.nlm.nih.gov/31037396/ (archived at https://perma.cc/S5DK-SVQF)

12 Hewitt-Main, J (2012) Dyslexia behind bars: final report of a pioneering teaching and mentoring project at Chelmsford prison – 4 years on, http://www.lexion.co.uk/download/references/dyslexiabehindbars.pdf (archived at https://perma.cc/QXZ5-7NHF)

13 Grayling, C (2013) 'Speech on Crime' – Speech made by the Lord Chancellor and Secretary of State for Justice, Chris Grayling, on 13 June 2013 at Civitas, http://www.ukpol.co.uk/chris-grayling-2013-speech-on-crime/ (archived at https://perma.cc/VA89-9YEZ)

14 Baidawi, S and Piquero, A R (2020) Neurodisability among children at the nexus of the child welfare and youth justice system, *Journal of Youth Adolescence*, https://doi.org/10.1007/s10964-020-01234-w (archived at https://perma.cc/XJ85-5N9W)

15 Bandura, A (1977) Self-efficacy: toward a unifying theory of behavioral change, *Psychological Review*, https://educational-innovation.sydney.edu.au/news/pdfs/Bandura%201977.pdf (archived at https://perma.cc/XB4G-P95C)

16 Smith, T (2020) *Neurodiversity – Eliminating the Kryptonite and Enabling Superheroes*, Ep 18: Bill Boorman – The Master of Ceremonies and hero of Superheroes [Podast] 7 May, https://anchor.fm/neurodiversity/episodes/Ep-18-Bill-Boorman---The-Master-of-Ceremonies-and-hero-of-Superheros-edo7jl (archived at https://perma.cc/4XP3-52JN)

17 Dastin, J (2018) Amazon scraps secret AI recruiting tool that showed bias against women, *Reuters*, 11 October, https://www.reuters.com/article/us-amazon-com-jobs-automation-insight-idUSKCN1MK08G (archived at https://perma.cc/56R8-4VKQ)

18 National Autistic Society (2021) New shocking data highlights the autism employment gap, 19 February, https://www.autism.org.uk/what-we-do/news/new-data-on-the-autism-employment-gap (archived at https://perma.cc/YE52-ALCJ)

19 Wolchin, R (2014) Be mindful when it comes to your words. A string of some that don't mean much to you, may stick with someone else for a lifetime [Twitter] 1 January, https://twitter.com/rachelwolchin/status/418219133138792449?lang=en (archived at https://perma.cc/PM7Y-V8VF)

04

Eliminating kryptonite and enabling superheroes

Introduction

Believe it or not, talking about superheroes and/or superhuman powers in the context of neurodiversity can be controversial. Some people just don't like it at all!

Why are these terms challenging?

For some, having a disability or being disabled by society, as some would clearly define it, and potentially having other challenges that may impede daily activities and quality of life in general, are certainly not seen as super-human or having superpowers.

There are also the impacts to consider, that these challenges may have on others, such as being a parent or carer and having to seek support and navigate the education system. It can make discussing neurodiversity as superpowers, or people as superheroes, a bit difficult to swallow. This can be especially true when their associated mental health and wellbeing challenges are present on a regular or possibly on a daily basis.

As parents with varying family needs, Theo and Amanda can certainly empathize and have traversed health and educational systems seeking support and gaining help for their own children across all ages and stages. So, it is completely fair and understandable if you or anybody else feels this way.

It is also vitally important that the individual, their parents, families and/or carers are given the correct holistic and person-centred support to ensure each person can not only cope but also live a productive life.

All too often this is not the case and as we have mentioned earlier in the book, too many people lose out through lack of or delayed support and guidance.

But that is not everyone and we all have to find ways to inspire our children and each other to feel empowered by who we are and what we can potentially achieve both in work and in life.

Part of sitting down to force our ADHD brains to write this book (and it's not been easy, as we both love the ideas and hate the commas and full stops) was the real belief that we could provide support for others and a platform to help elevate our fellow human beings onto a 'field of dreams' where we all have a chance at a successful and productive life.

Eliminating kryptonite

When we talk about eliminating kryptonite, we are not saying all lights should be dimmed and all noise should be quashed. No room shall be open plan and no stairwell should be too high to climb.

What we are instead saying is let's take down the barriers to entry! Let children see that there are successful people who are dyslexic or have autism and because of their talents, not despite them.

We can all agree that it is unacceptable to expect a person in a wheelchair to climb a set of stairs to attend an interview, let alone have to do so in their daily workplace. It is also unacceptable to insist that someone who is sensitive to light and sound can't have adjustments made to help them succeed at their work.

This is what we mean by *eliminating kryptonite* and it is as true for all areas of diversity, inclusion, equity, and creating a sense of true belonging. It surely amounts to basic and fundamental human rights.

Enabling superheroes

When we consider superheroes, we may use images of cartoon heroes and we may discuss some individual successes like having superhuman powers. But it's not all lasers from the eyes and flying through the air. What we are saying is that when someone is given the support and platform to succeed with their individual strengths and talents, you can often be surprised by what they can go on to achieve.

This may simply be plugging a defensive gap in a sports team. It may be seeing a child in school who has brilliant maths and IT skills and worrying less about challenges with handwriting (which won't affect their employment when they are grown up!). By changing the perspective on a person to see what they can do and not what they can't, we see the talents.

It could be someone who has skills helping a group of salespeople to become more efficient and successful by keeping them organized and focused on the task at hand. It may be someone who has amazing communication skills and can help and inspire others.

But most importantly, when we try to explain to our children why other children find it so easy in comparison to them, to hear clearly, to read, to understand, to embrace, to make friends, to feel self-confident... we see their self-esteem go downhill and we see them see themselves as less than.

We should be proud to tell them of their significant strengths and keep doing so. Because there will also be many, many people and opportunities where their challenges and difficulties at achieving what others find relatively easy will be highlighted to them. In big bold highlighters they will be reminded each day of their inability to do stuff! Children know they are different even without words being spoken. We still value the sporty one, the one who can read out aloud and the one who can write neatly, even though these will not be for most children the skills that they will need for future employment.

So we will not apologize for calling out our key strengths and the strengths of our children as superhuman and superheroes. Often they achieve things against the odds and in situations and circumstances that through no fault of their own are designed in a way that goes against their grain.

So it's for this reason we share a story of how a disability can become an ability given the right opportunity and environment.

Throughout the book we have stories from great people who have talents. More of these stories are important to share what's possible for us all. But it does take a society to make this possible.

One of Theo's dad's best friends as a young person was Lincoln's dad, so this story has some personal relevance. But more than that it shows that sometimes our perceived disabilities are actually our greatest abilities, given the correct support and platform.

Lincoln went on to achieve fame as one of the leading electronic music producers of our day, and the way he has achieved it is through harnessing the power of his special interests.

CASE STUDY

Lincoln Barrett AKA High Contrast: the Quentin Tarantino of drum and bass electronic music production[1]

Ever since he was a little kid, he was in love with films, and then quickly got into filmmaking when he was about 10. Everyone thought he would be a film director, and that's what he wanted to do. So when he left school he went to college when he was only 16 to study media. But somewhere along the line, he lost his passion for filmmaking, and discovered electronic music and drum and bass, and realized that to make a film, you've got to have an army of people, whereas, to make electronic music you can do it all on your own.

Lincoln's always been more comfortable on his own, working on things in an obsessive manner. Drum and bass just clicked into place and took over his life. It became this thing he did every day but he had no real kind of goals, or any thought of the future. He was just in the moment enjoying what he was doing. Then just before he graduated from university, he was offered a record deal. So he just went straight into a career as a drum and bass producer and DJ.

Until he was 16 he never even listened to the radio; he had no concept of what was going on in music. He was just into film obsessively. He describes it as being like a switch got flipped. His special interest one day was film and the next drum and bass. He went from watching 300–400 films a year growing up, to watching one or two a year; it was such a radical shift once he found his passion for making drum and bass.

Lincoln has since gone on to take some incredible sounds from the past and translate them into modern drum and bass sounds. He had all this knowledge of films and soundtracks and then when he heard drum and bass and jungle and they were sampling bits of dialogue and music from films he knew, like *Taxi Driver* or *The Usual Suspects* or *Apocalypse Now*, a lightbulb was lit.

Lincoln reflects, 'Oh wow, this is a music that is taking bits from the films I love and weaving it into this kind of tapestry of sounds and it's not so much about playing an instrument as it is building this soundscape out of existing sounds.'

When we think about neurodiversity and special interests, one thing that lots of people and organizations fail to translate is how we can maximize that incredible ability of an individual elsewhere within our personal life and within our organizations.

Lincoln has demonstrated this beautifully well, taking a deep amount of knowledge, learning and passion from one area of his interests and utilizing it incredibly well and to great effect in another. This is why he stands out amongst other global DJs and music producers. Because his approach to music production is enriched by this additional knowledge of films and the music within them, giving him a wholly unique sound.

'I was like, this is something I can get into because I know so much about movies. I know all these great lines of dialogue and great musical cues. I'm drawing from as obscure sources as I can muster you know, the films that people have never heard of, or obscure records that have been completely forgotten. I love taking these remnants of the past and weaving them together into something new for today and then having them played on huge sound systems to crowds around the world.'

Lincoln recounts how his dad was severely dyslexic, but that it was never diagnosed when he was growing up because they weren't aware of it back then. 'He was definitely neurodiverse and I am my father's son. When you put the two of us together, we'd start talking about films and it would just be like everyone else in the family would just kind of go quiet and sit there while we started talking. Not really a conversation, it was more like delivering monologues about some obscure film noir that he saw in, you know, 1950 and that I saw at some point. It would probably be fascinating to people who study neurodiversity or psychology; not a normal conversation, but things that we really enjoyed. We're both passionate about film and that's where I got my love of film from, from him.'

Lincoln's accidental journey to becoming a global electronic music sensation started because he wanted a Method Man hip hop album, but he mistakenly thought he was Goldie when he was watching on TV and so his sister bought him a Goldie CD which he slowly became obsessed with.

There was something about drum and bass music that had a neurological effect on Lincoln's brain and for this reason completely captured his mind, time and energy. 'The texture in the drums and the emotion, there's a haunting quality in a lot of drum and bass and jungle and it just created these very vivid colours in my mind, you know, and it's like a particular track will trigger a dominant colour in my mind's eye.'

He eventually realized what was happening when he was producing this music and that it was not typical of most brains; however, he describes that it is more common amongst other music producers and his contemporaries. What Lincoln experiences is synesthesia. He sees sounds as colours and some people have it to a debilitating degree, where they almost can't hear a piece of music because it overwhelms their vision.

He doesn't have it to that degree, and in fact it helps him focus on brilliant sounds. If a track really speaks to him then he can see it as a colour. He then knows the music that he's making is working or even that it's finished once he sees that dominant colour in his mind.

It is no surprise then that his first album that shot him to fame in the late '90s was called *True Colours* because that's what he was experiencing.

He describes the colour coming from the emotion of the track and then drums he sees as like machines in his head. It's almost like a car engine with the pistons going. Certain drums will have a more metallic tinny sound and that will be like a very metal machine. There are also other drums that have a more wooden and maybe more acoustic kind of sound, but it creates this machine that still has pistons and things and steam coming out but it's made of wood. That's how he sees drum beats and patterns.

Growing up in school, Lincoln didn't have any real problems; he describes himself as a bit of a loner but didn't get bullied. He just got along with the teachers, but felt he needed to get out of there. It felt like a stifling environment. He describes how he thinks he would have really struggled if he had to work in an office, or at least not thrived in the way he has.

He sees himself as one of those people that needs to be left alone to go into their head and just come out with stuff. Ironically, the flip side of being the lone producer in the studio is that you then go and DJ or perform with a band on stage in front of thousands of people. On paper this shouldn't be his cup of tea. But weirdly, and an important factor to remember around neurodiversity is that we do not fit into neat boxes and neither does Lincoln. 'I feel pretty Zen-like and tranquil when I'm hitting the festivals or clubs. It's like, I guess, as long as I'm there to perform, I think it's that thing of being kind of the calm in the centre of the storm, on the decks on stage where I'm just getting into a zone. It's like, everyone else is kind of going wild in the club, but I'm actually very still.'

So he never gets any kind of anxiety or nervousness about performing; however, going to a shopping centre is much more of a struggle for him. He really doesn't feel comfortable and certainly has some anxiety that pushes his flight senses.

Even after all his success Lincoln doesn't stop. During arguably one of the most difficult periods in modern history working and living through Covid-19, he has re-educated himself in the ways of 1990s music production and has produced some amazing future sounds from the past. He's used the old hardware and even the floppy disks from that period. There is nothing nostalgic about this; he's changing the process to create new sounds. 'After 20 years of working on a computer to now be more hands-on and tactile using physical objects, it changes the way I'm making the tracks and it changes the things I come up with. So it's kind of fascinating to me to have this new set of tools to work with really.'

High Contrast is the sound of neurodiversity; he encapsulates everything that is good and positive around neurological difference. If only everyone could find the opportunity to work towards the spiky parts of their profile.

KEY POINTS

Eliminating kryptonite and enabling superheroes

- Seek strengths and talents in all.

- Share case studies of success in all areas of education and employment to show what is possible.

- Shout out loud about those who provide support and make a difference.

- Let's take the barriers down to entry!

- Let people see that there are successful people because of their talents.

- *Eliminating kryptonite* is true for all areas of diversity, inclusion, equity, and in creating a sense of true belonging. It amounts to basic and fundamental human rights.

Note

1 Smith, T (2020) *Neurodiversity: Eliminating Kryptonite and Enabling Superheroes*, Ep 19: High Contrast – Leading Global Drum & Bass Producer and Remixer [Podcast] 21 May, https://anchor.fm/neurodiversity/episodes/Ep-19-High-Contrast---Leading-Global-Drum--Bass-Producer-and-Remixer-ebnbvp (archived at https://perma.cc/35V8-JPBB)

05

Pre-employment:
the lost demographics

Introduction

There are a number of reasons why many people are still arriving at adulthood without a diagnosis or having had support with ADHD, dyslexia or other neurodivergent traits. It can often be assumed that everyone would know and so ask for help if required. It sometimes surprises some employers that someone doesn't 'disclose' in an interview. In this chapter you will hear stories from Elizabeth and Shelley about being diagnosed later in life and how they have had to overcome social and cultural barriers to be successful women today. We will also hear from Helen, working in justice and employment, and her experiences.

We will describe the challenges for those in society who end up being at the margins or fall out of typical educational processes, and end up in the justice system despite being neurodivergent, and the potential reasons for this.

The reasons for people being missed are complex. Cumulative adversity over time is something we need to be aware of and not everyone presents as 'classically' ADHD or dyspraxic. People can also be neurodivergent and have other factors in their lives that combine to result in disadvantage. For many, a challenging start in education can impact into employment prospects too.

Why do some people miss out on getting support and where have they been?

Amanda has worked in the field of neurodiversity for more than 30 years and during this time has seen a real shift in understanding. It was generally taught that boys were autistic and girls were far less likely to have any neurodivergent traits at all.

Until relatively recently there was also an accepted belief and evidently confusion in some circles that there are big differences in the way men and women's brains work that result in some behaviours and traits in men and very different ones in women. This categorical approach provided a somewhat limited view of the world, retaining the dichotomy that 'blue is for boys and pink for girls' and that the divide was a clean one.

The diagnosis of neurodevelopmental conditions still remains far greater in males than females in childhood. For example, males are diagnosed with autism spectrum disorder (ASD) approximately four times as often as females. There is also good evidence that females are less likely to receive a diagnosis than males with similar levels of autistic traits. Additionally, those who do manage to get a diagnosis have been shown to be more likely than males to be older and have more additional needs and behavioural-emotional challenges.

Until recently this had been accepted as fact rather than considering that the research or diagnostic pathways could have had some biases. Females with ASD for example have historically been virtually absent from studies investigating it. Diagnostic criteria for ASD have been developed almost entirely using more male behavioural and symptomatic presentations. Some of the instruments or specific items used to diagnose ASD may indeed have a male bias as we have been viewing autism through a more male lens. If the criteria you are checking for only look for zebras you may miss the horses all together!

Current diagnostic criteria for ADHD were developed in predominantly more male samples. It may in fact be that some diagnostic instruments may not generalize as well to females and there needs to be greater understanding of female experiences. Certainly more work needs to be done.

There is some thought of biases in how the systems work and there is something called ascertainment bias operating. Ascertainment bias refers to males being more likely to be referred for evaluation than females with equivalent challenges. For example, more boys in school could end up being referred with reading problems as they more often openly express frustration and exhibit disruptive behaviours in the classroom. They then get noticed more and cause others problems and need to be 'dealt with'. Girls within a mixed class of children may have been quiet and not disruptive so not a nuisance to anyone. We certainly have stories where low attainment in school has been as a result of not gaining support or recognition of specific challenges. Neurodivergent traits have only been identified when the person arrives at university and is recognized as dyslexic for example.

Interestingly, there may be a gender bias in terms of how we view different behaviours in others. Female teachers may be better at spotting girls with ADHD and male teachers may be better at identifying boys. In one research study from Sweden, male participants reported ADHD characteristics in boys more accurately, and female adults reported girls with ADHD more accurately. Interestingly, women have been shown to be better at determining a character's behaviour, if the vignette (a case study that is used in the research) features a character being described is female.

We know that the behaviours that are seen (or not seen) can result in different responses by professionals. As a result of this, females have less opportunity to gain a referral for a diagnosis. More males than females demonstrate what is called externalizing behaviours (these are behaviours others can see more easily such as aggression or being disruptive), which may be one reason for gaining the attention of health professionals or therapists. Females may be missed because they are more likely to have a predominantly inattentive (dreamy type) of ADHD or have ended up in other services where the professionals have not had training relating to neurodiversity. The symptoms of inattentive ADHD are less disruptive and obvious to others than those of hyperactive/impulsive ADHD. Interestingly, in one research study of primary school teachers it was found that they frequently didn't identify inattentive ADHD.

There has also been a growing discussion that some people who self-identify as autistic may use, or have used, techniques to appear socially competent and find ways to prevent others from seeing social difficulties, working hard to 'fit in'. Masking or camouflaging the way you feel takes effort and can impact on a person having to conform to stereotypical norms. While we can all 'put on a front' in a novel social situation such as going into a work meeting where you don't know people, autistic people talk about the enormous effort of doing so and the impact on their mood and energy levels.

Biases are also seen in other conditions including developmental coordination disorder (also known as dyspraxia). A survey of teachers showed that they were more likely to report concerns about the gross motor skills performance of boys, such as playing football, than the fine motor performance of girls, such as handwriting. They also considered it more important to help the children with the gross motor problems.

It is clear from this that awareness by parents and educators, and appropriate screening tools are going to be important.

So, what does this mean for lots of adult females?

We need to better understand the potential negative consequences for females (and males) whose needs are unmet. Researchers have noted that a lack of identification can result in a cascade of impact because of the cumulative effects of under-identification over time and this can then potentially result in lowered educational attainment and reduced employment opportunities.

You can read about two wonderful people and their experiences and about their lives today in the following sections.

CASE STUDY
Elizabeth Takyi

Elizabeth Takyi is the CEO and Founder of Wandsworth-based Aspire2inspire Dyslexia CIC, a social enterprise that aims to raise awareness of dyslexia and other specific learning difficulties within the local community. Diagnosed with dyslexia, dyspraxia and Irlen Syndrome and recently diagnosed with dyscalculia, after identifying a gap in support services, she took it upon herself to support adults with dyslexia and other specific learning difficulties who want to start their own business, go back to further education or improve their employability skills.

Since then, A2i has been flourishing, gaining a number of collaborative work opportunities with prestigious institutions such Imperial College London, Roehampton University and The British Dyslexia Association to name a few, as well as giving support to dyslexic children with 1:1 tuition, and running workshops surrounding employment, mental health and wellbeing and reaching your full potential.

Elizabeth has also achieved the following qualifications: Professional Graduate Certificate in Education (Lifelong Learning) (post 16), BA Hons Human Resource Management/Sociology, PTLLS-Level 4 Award in Preparing to Teach in the Life Long Learning Sector, and NVQ Level 3 A1 Assessor, whilst continuing to further her knowledge surrounding dyslexia and other SpLDs.

We asked Elizabeth why she thinks her dyslexia was missed.

'I feel the cultural barriers and stigmas surrounding "learning difficulties/differences" within my West African culture was the main factor as to why my dyslexia was never picked up until much later in my adult life. There is a lack of education and understanding when it comes to dyslexia and other SpLDs; many are led to believe that struggling in education is due to bad behaviour, being "stupid" or refusing to learn, when in fact it is a learning difference.

'There is also an understanding that being labelled with a learning "disability" will bring shame and embarrassment to the family, which often causes families to shy away from getting the individual the support they need to progress.'

We also asked what it felt like to be diagnosed later in life. 'Being diagnosed with dyslexia later on in life opened many doors for me, the main being the setting up of A2i Dyslexia. It enabled me to further my studies and gain access to the support aids I need such as assisted technology. It also enabled me to gain a deeper understanding into dyslexia and creating ways to break the negative stigma surrounding dyslexia and how to drive our community forward.'

We will hear from others in other cases within this book about the impact of being diagnosed later in life, including the very successful Keith Fraser, who is head of the Youth Justice Board.

Who else gets missed in school and what's the potential fall-out for some?

Some people have their needs missed in childhood because they may have moved around the educational system, such as being in care or in foster homes. This may result in them having less opportunity to be formally assessed even though there is evidence of higher rates of cognitive differences in these children. There is evidence of higher rates of neurodivergent traits in children in care, but lack of educational progress may be attributed erroneously to missing school, lack of parental engagement, or for emotional reasons without routine screening taking place.

Under-represented groups

Many people today are still arriving in further and higher education with no diagnosis and for some this is related to less awareness in their communities.

We have a paucity of research about levels of neurodiversity among Black, Asian and other minority ethnic groups. This crude 'clumping' of huge swathes of people misses the reality that someone from China and someone from the north or south part of India will come from very different backgrounds and environments to someone in South Africa or someone born in the UK. All will have very different educational, cultural and social experiences.

Moving around

The last group to consider who may not have been identified is those who have been or are homeless or rough sleepers. There is growing evidence that a larger proportion of autistic people are homeless but again there has been a relative lack of research. One recent study showed that 9 per cent of people screened would meet the diagnosis and another 13 per cent were borderline, ie had some autistic traits.[1] The challenge is understanding why the person became homeless in the first place; was it as a result of lack of societal understanding and/or having a means of accessible communication to gain support?

Alternative routes to recognition and support

You may have heard of the term the 'school to prison' pipeline. This is the increased risk of you going to prison if you move into alternative provision (AP) (specialist units within or outside of the school) or are excluded from school altogether. In one recent research study undertaken by Amanda and her colleagues, four out of five young men in a youth offending service had been excluded more than once from school.[2] There is an important link between this and neurodiversity.

There is repeated evidence that nearly half of the prison population have low literacy skills and high levels of undiagnosed developmental language disorder (DLD), and international and UK studies also demonstrate at least one in three have ADHD traits.[3]

Difficulties with language and communication (also known as DLD) can also act as a barrier to educational activity. There is evidence that the presence of DLD presents a considerable barrier for young adults to engage in further education and training. There is also evidence that language and communication difficulties are likely to continue into adulthood[4] and have an emotional and psychological impact.[5]

You can imagine how frustrating it must be as a child or young person if you can't say what you want or understand others, and this also makes it even harder to make friends and join in easily with conversations.

Being excluded from school results in missed learning opportunities and so when the child returns to school other young people have progressed in their learning and the excluded child has fallen even further behind, leading to even more frustration. Therefore, a delayed diagnosis or misdiagnosis (seeing behaviour rather than the reasons for the behaviour) can result in potentially limited employment outcomes. There may also be social and cultural biases in place as more people in prison will come from lower-income families and are less likely to be diagnosed: Black and other minority groups have often had less chance of gaining a diagnosis.

Amanda has heard from many people who were in trouble with the police in their teens but gained support and often had someone who saw their talents and are now successfully employed. Early support and understanding is essential, as the pathway for many could have been quite different and far less bumpy.

One person Amanda talked to said that when he was diagnosed with dyslexia as an adult, and went home to ask his parents if they knew anyone in the family with dyslexia, they dismissed it. His mother said that reading and spelling difficulties were something that was the norm in their family, for his father and grandfather too. The reality is they could have all been dyslexic!

What can we do to change this?

We need to help young people as early as possible to break the cycle of a criminal life. There are so many highly creative minds 'dying' to use their talents. Drug dealers (who may be very good at maths), gang members (who may have excellent social skills), thieves, con-artists (who could be good at sales!) and many more have potential skills and strengths that are lost to a negative cause. Across the world we are losing the talents of these young people to becoming gang members, ending up on the streets sleeping rough, or in vulnerable situations with family or carers.

Having a criminal record also leaves a legacy for the workplace. Background checks can be a double whammy for someone who is neurodivergent (but undiagnosed as well). For many companies, criminal background checks are a means to determine the safety and security risk a prospective or current employee poses on the job. There is a false assumption that the existence of a criminal record accurately predicts negative work behaviours. It is ironic that someone in a job is far less likely to commit crimes than someone unemployed and desperate for money! Providing individuals with the opportunity for stable employment lowers crime recidivism rates and thus increases public safety.

Identification and utilization of positive neurodivergent traits is the first step. If we were able to harness the talent, it could be targeted in all sorts of sectors of society including sales teams and digital teams. On this basis we have a moral obligation to reconsider how we think and act in response to a background check that shows an individual has spent time in prison or has a criminal charge. The stigma can stay with them and have a life-long impact.

In the United States they ran a campaign[6] more than a decade ago to 'ban the box', which was also followed by the UK,[7] to encourage employers not to needlessly do criminal background checks. It may be that you only take one thing away from this book and that's to implement a 'ban the box' policy on roles where you currently do a criminal check that really don't require one. That action alone is likely to positively increase the diversity of thought within those roles and actively participate in increasing opportunities for those who would otherwise be out of work and stuck in a negative cycle.

We can't change the prison system overnight, but we can change the way we see people. We can also take down barriers to entry that shouldn't be there and implement a 'ban the box' methodology.

CASE STUDY
Helen and her justice story

Helen Arnold Richardson is the managing director of Do-IT Solutions but also has had extensive experience working in prisons in the UK. She provides valuable reflections of the justice sector and what needs to be done.

'As a teacher and senior leader in youth and adult prisons for many years, I gained a great insight and understanding of the complexity of the lives and adversity faced by those I worked with. Many had faced traumatic events that some of us wouldn't even want to imagine! This could be anything from a lack of family support and a negative experience of school to substance misuse and addiction, mental health issues and homelessness or a combination of all.

'What I know now, but didn't know then, was that many of the children and adults I worked with were also neurodivergent. Some arrived through the prison gates with a diagnosis, but for many, they did not know they had challenges; and as a teacher, I didn't know and would often just see their behaviours in a negative way. This could be either aggressive or disengagement with a lesson.

'Thinking back to my time "inside", I vividly remember a young man who came into my class one day. He hated the fact that he had to come to education and needed to be in a classroom for three hours learning literacy, and as a result of his dissatisfaction he was very disruptive. What I later found out was that he had previously had negative experiences of school (excluded at 12 years for fighting) and had been in foster care as a result of his mother being a crack cocaine addict. He had been left to fend for himself and his brothers. Looking past the disruptive behaviour, I saw a young man who had great challenges with reading and difficulties concentrating on tasks that didn't interest him.

'Being in a classroom made him frustrated, angry and subsequently not wanting to learn (or allowing others to learn). Through trial and error of different strategies to engage him, I found out that he had an amazing talent that no one had ever identified, and that was his lyrical ability. He was like a modern-day Keats! I couldn't believe his wide use of metaphors and similes that brought his rap lyrics to life. When I spoke to him about his talent, he was really surprised and somewhat embarrassed that I had given him positive feedback about his ability. He didn't know how to take praise as he had always been told that he was useless and would never achieve anything in his life. Over time, both his and my confidence grew as I researched the strategies to support him with his challenges and he started to believe in himself and gained his first qualification.

'This is just one example of an all too common occurrence in prison. Please don't get me wrong, I am not excusing the fact that he (and others) had committed some heinous crimes that resulted in incarceration, or the ripple effect of this on his victims. However, this was a case of "cumulative adversity" that I was seeing on a daily basis. Each person needed time and attention to be supported to identify their strengths, manage their challenges, and enable them to gain employment on release and subsequently reduce reoffending.

'Some years on, when I was promoted into senior management, I wanted to find something to help my teams with the identification process, and this is where I came across the Do-IT Profiler. I had heard great things about the Profiler being used successfully in a prison to identify the strengths and challenges of the person whilst providing strategies where challenges were present. I was amazed by the tool and only wished that it had been available when I had been delivering education. It would not only have saved me time understanding my learners, but also would have helped me enhance my teaching practice and truly understand how to provide an inclusive learning environment. The Profiler provided my teams and I with the information and strategies we needed to understand the person's challenges and identify their strengths and talents to support them with their goals and aspirations both in custody and when they left the prison. I still think today that use of such a tool is something that should be common practice across the prison estate in the UK and could be used in other countries, as it would empower those in custody to manage their challenges and think about using their strengths for the benefit of employers. Why would we not want to utilize so much untapped talent?'

Helen's journey highlights the importance of finding ways to support those who face challenges within the prison population for when they hopefully continue their lives in civvy street.

Recognizing individual strengths and providing a platform to work to those strengths are clearly paramount if we want to help people succeed in their lives even when they have faced great adversity. They already have so many hurdles they will need to face when they leave prison, that their dyslexia or ADHD or... may only be one factor of many.

Shelley's story goes to the heart of what's possible when somebody is given a chance even when many others, institutes, organizations would have given up on her. The life she was dealt versus what she has gone on to achieve, is a lesson for us all to constantly challenge how we see others, how we assess others and ultimately why we reject others. The path of least resistance is to see a piece of paper with a criminal history and decide that's just too high a mountain to climb.

Well think again...

CASE STUDY
Shelley Winner – a winner's story[8]

Shelley Winner was formerly incarcerated. She went to prison for drugs and found out she was pregnant after her arrest. She got out of prison, turned her life around, and now she works for one of the biggest tech companies in the world.

'I think it's important to bring it back to my childhood, and that's where it stems from. The environment that one grows up in plays a huge part in the path that person will go down, and for me, both of my parents were teens. I think my mom was 17 when she got pregnant, my dad was 17, and so they were kids having kids – what do you know about parenting at 17, 18 years old? So I didn't have the best parents, growing up, or the best role models.

'My father was an addict who was in and out of prison; he basically glorified drug use, he thought it was cool. So cool that he got me drunk for the first time when I was 11 years old, me and my schoolmate. When I lived with him in high school, his rule of the house was if you get any drugs you have to bring them home and do them with me. Growing up with that environment definitely didn't set me up for success, to say the least. Statistically, they say that 76 per cent of children follow in their parents' footsteps. So, like my father, I ended up becoming an addict, and later on a drug dealer, and ended up going to prison.

'I think that had I had parents who were supportive and positive, my life would have definitely ended up a little bit different, but it didn't. So, regardless, the point is that I realized, I took responsibility for my life; I can't blame my parents. Now that I know the difference between right and wrong and I've taken responsibility for that, I've been able to turn my life around.'

Shelley was stuck in what she calls the loser's loop. Her belief is that education and knowledge is the key to breaking that cycle. Her arrest was a huge wake-up call for her; not only did she find out that she was pregnant, she was arrested by the federal government, which tends to come with much harsher sentences, where she would have to do 85 per cent of the time. She faced the prospect of 10 years in prison.

'It was a surreal moment for me. It was at that moment that I knew I had to turn my life around, whether or not I got 10 years. I had to do it for my son, I wanted to change and be a better person, I didn't want to be the same type of parent that my dad was to me to my child.'

So how did things change for Shelley?

'For me, it was going to treatment – what better place to educate yourself and learn the skills to stay sober than getting into a treatment programme? It was the best decision I ever made. So while I was out fighting my case, I enrolled myself into a programme called "Adult and Teen Challenge". It's a faith-based programme and they accepted pregnant women. Not only did I learn invaluable skills to help me stay sober, but at the same time, I was also strengthening spiritually.

'I went from this dead person to being alive and when I went in I was hoping that I wouldn't have to go to prison. I shouldn't say unfortunately, because I'm grateful for that. I ended up having to go to prison, but at least it wasn't for 10 years, it was for four years. When I went to prison, I just had this new mindset, and I was going to take advantage of that time and programme more, because I knew that they had various rehabilitative programmes there. I knew they had all kinds of different classes and I could go to college, I mean, there was all kinds of things I could do in prison to stay productive.

'What's funny is within three months of my release, I was interviewing with one of the biggest tech companies in the world, which is crazy. Until they rescinded it when they found out I had a criminal record.'

Even after all her toil and turmoil, even after the reform and education, one criminal check later and her job was rescinded! She shares how much that hurt.

'It was like being put up on a pedestal, just to be knocked down. Not only that, but I got the job offer and of course, I'm proud, I'm excited, I am fresh out of prison, now working for one of the biggest tech companies in the world. It was just unbelievable to me.

'There was no way I couldn't tell all my friends, there's no way I couldn't tell my family. There's no way I could not post it on social media. So I did, just to have them turn around after the background check say, oh sorry, we're just kidding, we're not going to hire you.

'That is the most messed up thing in the world.'

Clearly, this is a problem that probably happens a lot. Do those background checks need to take place for that job anyway? Maybe they do, maybe they don't, but then we need to really think, what is the purpose? For somebody like Shelley who has served a considerable amount of time in prison and has gone through everything that she went through to prepare herself for the workplace and then to have that taken away? How can we expect people to ever leave the 'losers loop' if once they climb the stepladder they've fought for, they find they've just climbed into another hole?

Hats off to Shelley

Shelley by her account had her life turned around because of her willingness to change, but also because she had the opportunity to learn. She has other people who went on the journey with her. She recalls one man who didn't care about the rehabilitation programme, he just wanted to reduce his time. But even he, once he was educated, and was deep into the programme, re-formed and changed his life.

The power of access to education, to mentors and support groups for those who lack the support at home they deserve is clear. Shelley is an example of somebody who had a difficult upbringing and spent considerable time behind bars, but now works for a huge technology company and has progressed within that organization.

There is still so much more to learn and to do. Our prisons all around the world are disproportionately filled with minority groups and Shelley is a wonderful example of a human being who was always far more capable than her drug-dealing skills, but just didn't have the stepladder to help her out of the hole she had found herself in.

Shelley, with the support of others, found that the law where she was living forbade discrimination in this instance and she fought the decision and won. But how many others have already fallen through the cracks?

In the UK, we have laws to protect individuals from being discriminated against. However, when it comes down to an HR manager or line manager with a criminal check report in their hands making a decision about whether or not to hire somebody, does the fear factor set in (from ignorance)? And therefore poor decisions are made that keep people in the 'losers loop' and so the cycle continues.

We share Shelley's story here because so many of the prison population are from deprived backgrounds, having had reduced access to education, limited support and based on the statistics are far more likely to be from a neuro-minority group.

Shelley is unfortunately not typical of what happens to prisoners when they enter prison; they often lack support, continue in their loop and may never leave it. The cost to the taxpayer alone is way beyond the cost of rehabilitation. One in three people in prison in the UK are neurodivergent – imagine if we got 50 per cent into employment, what a positive impact this could have on the person, their families and the economy.

Think of what Shelley has had to go through to get where she is. Think of the sacrifices she's made, and how grateful she is to have employment, to be valued and to offer value to the world herself. Imagine having somebody with her outlook, her drive, her energy in your team. What a difference she could make to your views and perspective of the world. What value she could add to your customers and to your innovations.

She and others will only get into jobs if we shift our thinking and reassess the way we assess information on candidates. We have the power and it is HR and/or recruitment that should be influencing the managers and the workforce to adapt their style and embrace the value of difference.

And it is through sharing powerful stories like Shelley's that change happens. Both in large organizations through their processes and procedures, but also through individuals on the ground who are impassioned to help others.

An incredible example of this is...

CASE STUDY
TRUFeeds

Bill Boorman is the founder of TRU (The Recruitment Unconference), and a respected adviser to the recruitment industry, Private Equity (PE) funds and startups. Partly inspired by Shelley's journey after seeing her present at a SmartRecruiters Hiring Success conference, and with an interest in employability in prisons, he went on his own journey to help others in need.

During the entire lockdown of the Covid-19 pandemic, from his home in Northampton, he, his wife and family cooked well over 6,000 meals for rough sleepers. Not the plan, but a response to a global pandemic in his local area.

What started out as a small volunteer programme supporting a homeless charity, Project 16:15, turned into their own mission, TRUFeeds, where Bill and Fran Boorman tirelessly worked to raise funds from the recruitment community and beyond to feed those in need.

This journey has gone from feeding and supporting 100 rough sleepers on the streets, to helping them connect to the key support services that can give them access to work and housing.

They now have approximately eight rough sleepers on the street. Bill says this has been a monumental effort from the charity the Hope Centre, along with government initiatives, as well as the work they have done on the street during lockdown and beyond.

When we consider the amount of vulnerable people in our local communities that lack the knowledge to access the support they need, Bill has been instrumental at plugging this gap, hand in hand with those services already available and in place. Often there are chasms in the support services, from accessing the waiting list for diagnosis to diagnosis itself as just one example.

This is a timely reminder that the required change and support we need can begin at home in our local community. We can all do our bit to make workplaces more accessible, but sometimes there is much-needed work to be done in the heart of the communities and that work is as justified and as important as any we carry out within the workplace.

What about universities?

In 2019 Theo sat in a chill-out tent at Rec Fest (a recruitment business conference in London) with Milimo Banji, CEO of TapIn, the leading disruptive creative agency for graduates in the recruitment industry. They talked about neurodiversity and the perception, understanding and appreciation of neurodiversity amongst the student population.

Now, to set the scene, Milimo has thousands of nano and micro influencers (nano = 1k followers or less, micro =1k–100k followers) embedded at all the leading universities across the UK. He has his finger on the pulse of the student population across many demographics, because he is constantly engaging with those communities across his social media channels, giving careers advice and guidance to get them into some of the most exclusive graduate programmes. His focus originally was primarily to support ethnic minority groups into organizations where they previously had little representation; however, his content is now embraced and utilized by all.

Theo asked him, wouldn't it be great if we could find out if the current student population had any idea what neurodiversity is? Milimo immediately said, 'Of course we can, they are digital natives, I can ask them via the vast social network groups I've built with followings of thousands across each group and channel.'

So that's exactly what they did and the results were fascinating!

First they asked: **Do you know what Neurodiversity is?**

Only 17 per cent of students said yes, and remember these are the most engaged students from some of the best universities, with a high level of ethnic and gender diversity across those groups. These are our future managers and leaders. The next generation!

They then got excited by the results, hungry for more; Milimo said, why don't we ask them a couple more questions? We're on a roll, how can we dig deeper?

The next question they asked was: **Would you identify as someone who is neurodivergent?**

Sixteen per cent responded with a yes, they did identify as being neurodivergent. Which is fascinating!

So, 17 per cent say they know what neurodiversity is and 16 per cent identify as being neurodivergent. So that leaves 1 per cent of the student respondents to this study who know what neurodiversity is but don't identify as being neurodivergent.

On the basis that if we take the wide variety of studies and research available on the number of those who are likely to be neurodivergent, it falls somewhere between 15 and 20 per cent of the UK population. Similar studies across the world also fall in and around those figures.

Now we may hypothesize that students may not understand fully what neurodiversity is, but they may have some understanding of dyslexia, dyspraxia, ADHD etc. However, with the level of negativity that still surrounds what are still defined as disabilities, disorders and deficits, it is unlikely there is a greater understanding from the wider student population, and if they do have some understanding, if this is positive. This is where greater awareness can have a significant impact for many.

There is a population of potentially brilliant minds waiting to be harnessed. We can certainly say the education system has yet to help properly shine a light on the potential of a neurodiverse workforce, but we have an opportunity to do exactly that.

By understanding the journey students are making and their limited understanding of the potential of neurodiversity within the workforce we can start to plan and prepare from entry level up, to ensure our future leaders are equipped with the information, evidence and support they need to help them drive productivity and high performance within our organizations. Imagine if we empower these diverse minds, and start to instil a mindset that neurodiversity is the norm and not just the gift of the 17 per cent.

So this leads us on to the final question: **Is there enough awareness and content for neurodivergent students?**

Ninety-five per cent of those who responded to the survey felt there wasn't enough awareness and content for neurodivergent students. It's clear that we need to do so much better in our schools, colleges and universities.

Some concluding thoughts

As you can see in this chapter, we are missing cognitively diverse talents at many points in the journey before employment and in society that could be harnessed if we were more aware and reduced our biases, both conscious and unconscious.

We need to consider the impact of being missed when there is intersectionality. This is the interconnected nature of social categorizations such as race, class and gender as they apply to a given individual or group, regarded as creating overlapping and interdependent systems of discrimination or disadvantage. Intersectionality as a theory was coined by the academic and campaigner Kimberlé Crenshaw in the United States. She studied how overlapping social identity categories, particularly minorities, relate to systems and structures of power and discrimination. It exemplifies the challenge of categorization by race, gender, religion, sexuality for example... or by specific cognitive conditions.

By considering intersectionality we also start to think about the potential impact of cumulative adversity, ie if you are someone who ticks more than one box and are a minority in more than one area (for example, if you are black, female and may have ADHD) are you also less likely to have gained a diagnosis in childhood or even in adulthood?

We will further explore these ideas later in the book as we start to consider what the future may look like in the context of neurodiversity.

KEY POINTS
Pre-employment: the lost demographics

- Missed, missing and misunderstood – there are a number of reasons why people don't gain support to recognize their talents and minimize challenges during childhood.

- Gender/cultural and social differences in tools, training and knowledge have resulted in misidentification or lack of support.

- Real and powerful stories describing experiences of adversity, and how this has been overcome, are presented in the chapter and allow us to consider why some people are still missed or misunderstood along the way.

Notes

1 Churchard, A *et al* (2019) The prevalence of autistic traits in a homeless population, *Autism*, https://journals.sagepub.com/doi/10.1177/1362361318768484# (archived at https://perma.cc/7AK7-UZGS)

2 Kirby, A *et al* (2020) Young men in prison with Neurodevelopmental Disorders: Missed, misdiagnosed and misinterpreted, *Prison Service Journal*, https://www.crimeandjustice.org.uk/sites/crimeandjustice.org.uk/files/PSJ%20

251%20November%202020%20%281%29.pdf (archived at https://perma.cc/
UG5V-9233)

3 Young, S and Cocallis, K M (2019) Attention deficit hyperactivity disorder
(ADHD) in the prison system, *Current Psychiatry Reports*, https://pubmed.ncbi.
nlm.nih.gov/31037396/ (archived at https://perma.cc/S5DK-SVQF)

4 Law, J *et al* (2009) Modeling developmental language difficulties from school
entry into adulthood: literacy, mental health, and employment outcomes,
Journal of Speech, Language, and Hearing Research, https://pubmed.ncbi.nlm.
nih.gov/19951922/ (archived at https://perma.cc/Q2DZ-7C9P)

5 St Clair, M C *et al* (2011) A longitudinal study of behavioral, emotional and
social difficulties in individuals with a history of specific language impairment
(SLI), *Journal of Communication Disorders*, https://pubmed.ncbi.nlm.nih.gov/
20970811/ (archived at https://perma.cc/JR3X-3VHA)

6 Evans, L (2016) *Ban the Box in Employment: A Grassroots History*,
https://prisonerswithchildren.org/wp-content/uploads/2019/10/
BTB-Employment-History-Report-2016.pdf (archived at https://perma.cc/
J2MN-968J)

7 Recruit (2020) Ban the Box: Removing the criminal record tick box from job
application forms, http://recruit.unlock.org.uk/fair-chance-recruitment/ban-the-
box/ (archived at https://perma.cc/2A7W-VJBE)

8 Smith, T (2020) *Neurodiversity: Eliminating Kryptonite and Enabling
Superheroes*, Ep 26: Shelley Winner – a Winner's Story, from prison to tech giant
[podcast] 29 Nov, https://anchor.fm/neurodiversity/episodes/Ep-26-Shelley-
Winner---A-Winners-Story--from-prison-to-tech-giant-en3vs6 (archived at
https://perma.cc/HS6R-3EJV)

06

Policies and procedures

What's the legal stuff all about?

Introduction

For the purpose of this book, we focus more on UK law as an example of the processes in place in one country. However, we would always advise you to take advice and guidance from your legal counsel or external advisers in this area. The law is evolving all the time and therefore it is best to look for the most up-to-date information.

It's important to remember that we are dealing with human beings, and our advice is to take a human-first approach. If we could all just take a step back and consider how we can help and support our fellow human beings, it would make for a better work environment and ultimately a far more inclusive world.

This chapter contains some case studies coming from different sectors that describe what some companies are doing and how this has been going for them and the gains they have seen.

We think it really helps to see examples of the processes people are putting in place, especially coming from different sectors.

The chapter also contains some of the guidance stuff that needs to be considered too, and if legislation changes, of course, this will require review.

CASE STUDY
Autotrader – National Autistic Society's (NAS) first autism-friendly UK
company

We spoke with Christos Tsaprounis of Autotrader about the work they did to become autism friendly. Sometimes we can get wound up in legal aspects of supporting our workforce with reasonable adjustments and our internal policies and practices, and actually we forget what's really important: keeping our policies simple and accessible to those that use them. This means that our employees can benefit from the support and direction they offer, rather than seeing them as the 'police' and fearing the information they provide, making them hyper-sensitive and risk-averse to their content, which helps nobody.

We're going to be brave and call it out! HR needs to take responsibility for this and if they also fear making mistakes they need the support from those professionals that can help.

Autotrader, with the support of the National Autistic Society, have done some fantastic work, including making their policies and practices clearer for 'everybody'!

Here we discuss Christos's work around making his organization 'autism friendly', but don't be fooled into thinking this is in spite of other neurodevelopmental challenges; in fact they have championed assistive technology for those who are dyslexic and ultimately they are taking an individual approach to ensure 'ALL' their employees are given the platform they need to succeed.

Something that a lot of people can hopefully relate to and appreciate is that everything that they have done has required a lot of care. One of the things that people are always finding difficult with things like this is where do you start? Do I need to be an expert in order to actually do this?

So the story started with a colleague reaching out to Christos personally; they had an autistic colleague in their team, and they just wanted to find out more about autism in order to be able to support them.

They didn't want to just put that ownership on the individual to educate them. It was a very responsible approach. They worked very closely with this individual and they really genuinely cared about them, but they thought that they needed to educate themselves, through some learning and other resources, not just depend upon that person for information and guidance.

Christos recalls, 'I had no idea how to do that and I knew very little about autism. Hopefully I know a bit more now.'

So he asked himself, who is the expert on this? That's how he came across the National Autistic Society (NAS). He then just picked up the phone and called them and explained the situation and asked them, as one of the leading charities in the UK, what support would they suggest? They said that actually they ran a specific workshop of about a half day on managing autistic people.

'I felt that sounded like a really good way to start and that it would increase awareness for managers. That manager, myself and a few more managers participated in the workshop. Then the National Autistic Society said they had this new initiative on making organizations autism friendly. They felt because of meeting us, and seeing our managers, we might be a good fit, and we'd be one of the first ones to do it.'

So they agreed on NAS doing a full audit of their offices, both in Manchester and London, to look at the physical environment in which their colleagues work. The second part of that was to look at all the policies, or the people policies and all the people-related procedures, and make sure they were autism friendly. Then the third and equally important part of it was raising education and awareness for their colleagues.

So in the first two parts NAS made about 60 recommendations for things that they needed to change, both in their physical environment and their policies. Then there was a series of workshops, some specific workshops for the people team, that were more around recruitment, and then workshops for managers.

The guidance that they offered was what impressed Christos the most. The second thing that impressed him, and what he's so proud of, is the involvement of his colleagues who lead this work. They were the network leads of their disability and neurodiversity network, their environment team, technology team and their people team. They really embraced the recommendations and they made sure that all the recommendations were completed in order for the workplace to become autism friendly. So it became such a collaborative effort!

'All the credit needs to go to all these people that actually made this happen. It was really just a collaborative project between the two organizations, and those people are just brilliant.'

The role of their champions, their network leads, is to lead the disability neurodiversity network, and help their people understand it's part of their day job to continuously improve the employee experience. The same goes for the environment team as well, which is responsible for the physical environment and also the technology that their colleagues use. So the people team, the environment team, and the network leads worked and collaborated with NAS to make this happen.

Some of these people are neurodiverse themselves, and bringing their lived experience into this was very important for Christos, because they were involved in the solution, utilizing their own lived experience.

'At Autotrader we have a "value" which is "community minded"; they really live that value. It wasn't necessarily something that was very personal to them, because they're not autistic. But they are very caring towards their colleagues, and they wanted to make these changes in order to improve the experience of their colleagues. All that combined is what made this really successful. So autistic colleagues didn't feel this was being done to them, they were involved as well.'

There were a lot of improvements made in the building. What was really surprising to them was that you didn't actually have to make major adjustments in the building; they did change some of their meeting rooms and created four different pods that would allow the opportunity for people to work by themselves in that busy open-plan environment. A lot of the feedback from colleagues was that they don't need to be in them all day – sometimes they just need to have the opportunity to go and do that for an hour or a couple of hours, while they're concentrating on a particular piece of work.

A lot of work was also done on the signage, coming into the building all the way from the lift and the staircase into the offices, making sure that everything is clearly signposted. 'When it comes to our policies and procedures, when we reviewed them, or when the NAS reviewed them all, their advice that they gave was fantastic, because they made their policies and procedures a lot more clear.'

The beauty of it all is that by making them more clear, they're more clear for everyone. So a lot of the changes were inspired by and were targeting autistic colleagues, but actually they ended up being good for everybody in the workplace. A lot of people enjoy the fact that they have those quiet rooms, and everyone that's reading their policies feels that they're a bit more clear now than they were before.

Their staff networks have been very influential and heavily involved in them becoming Disability Confident leaders.[1] A lot of the Disability Confidence scheme is around recruitment, which has made their recruitment process more inclusive. Their team members are becoming real-life role models, sharing their experience with blogs, at internal conferences, and really talking about their experience.

A very interesting one was very recently, one of their graduates, who had been on the graduate programme the year before. When they were going through the application process, they didn't let Autotrader know that they were dyslexic because they were really worried about how it would impact their application and the decision that would be made on them. Then, when they joined Autotrader, they realized that they should have let them know, because it wouldn't have impacted their application in a negative way. So they decided to write a blog and make that blog available on their social media and careers website. This year, all their careers fairs for graduates are virtual. And so the blog was shared and as a result of that, a graduate who applied this year read it and shared the fact that they were dyslexic, and asked for the adjustment that they needed in order to do their best at the assessment centres.

By creating those stories, by showcasing people, they are breaking down the stigma and making sure applicants feel reassured that if they share that information, it will be used in the right way to support their application process and to offer any adjustments they may require.

Autotrader also introduced the hidden disability sunflower scheme. It's about wearing a sunflower lanyard or a sunflower bean to share with your colleagues that you have a hidden disability and potentially might need some support. But it's also about raising awareness and education about the different hidden disabilities so people become more understanding and increase their knowledge and awareness. It's also for the individuals themselves to be able to share – it's not something that they have to hide.

The network has been very active and during Covid-19, they have provided a safe space for colleagues to come together and support one another. They can chat about what's going on in their lives, how they're dealing with any given situation. It's been so important for them to have that support network, that safe space where they can talk to their colleagues about things and support each other.

Christos gives this clear advice to others. 'I think from my point of view, and speaking out as an HR professional, and a D&I professional, I think, engage with the experts. I also think that you need to have a genuine interest, and a desire to increase your personal awareness, keep on learning, and remember you don't have to be an expert.

'Create meaningful partnerships with those experts, so that they can support your people. Make sure that you involve your neurodiverse colleagues. You might feel that you might not have many neurodiverse colleagues, but statistically speaking, you probably have quite a few.

'If you're not aware of any, I would do something as simple as an open call to the business, and see if people will come forward. Explain to people what you're trying to do, and the fact that you want to start doing some work in order to make the working environment more inclusive to neurodiverse people, and see if someone comes forward, and be very open and clear about why you would want to involve people.

'Finally, just do something. An awareness session is easy to organize, it will spark that interest, it will give you more confidence by increasing your knowledge and awareness.

'Just never stop. It's never ending; you should never see this as a project that we've done, this project is finished, now, let's move on to the next one. Because it's something that should always be a part of your overall people strategy.'

The business case for investing in diversity and inclusion in the workplace has been well documented and we have given some examples across the book. But Christos makes a great point that the one thing he thinks, in general, for businesses, one key factor of it, is that it's the right thing to do.

For this reason we wish every commercial business could have a Christos! He goes on to say, 'Sometimes, we keep forgetting businesses are for people and looking after your people; making a positive contribution to the communities that you're operating in is the right thing to do. I think we shouldn't always look at the impact on the bottom line. If you're a responsible business, you should be doing the right thing by your people, not necessarily looking at the correlation to profit.

'I think that should really be the ultimate reason why you do something. The tangible result that we've seen though personal experience, is if one of your employees can be themselves, be who they really are, they will put all that energy into their work, because they don't have to spend any energy hiding things from their employer and from their colleagues.

'If they are supported, that security they have will also make them more productive, more creative, they will enjoy their job more. So that practical support, that we haven't really touched upon, when they go through a workplace assessment, so that you can identify what the needs of the individual are. So you can provide them with support, which could be technology, it could be changing what they do, or how they do it or how they perform their job. It could be education, and awareness for themselves and their colleagues and all the things that are usually outcomes of workplace assessment. These things will eventually make the individual happier and more productive at work.

'It's really that simple.'

Some of the feedback Christos now receives from the teams at Autotrader, is how much happier, how much more productive and engaged they are when they can be themselves and have support, both from their colleagues and any other tools that they need.

When it comes to neurodiversity, there's so much technology that is already built into what we currently use. Microsoft as an example – there's a lot of technology that's already built into the products that we all use every day. There are other products that are more specialized, that you can subscribe to. But again, it is available to individuals.

Christos reminds us that we've got 'Access to Work' in the UK, and we're so fortunate to have it, that individuals can actually benefit from getting support for what they need. Unfortunately a lot of people don't realize what is available out there. So he thinks it's so important!

Ultimately, this all should be centred around the individual.

We think that should be the guiding principle that should really drive all these different initiatives and all these different projects. Because focusing on individual needs means everybody and that's what we are hoping to achieve through the inclusion of neurodiversity at work.

Putting in the policies and procedures

Putting the policies and procedures in place can feel a little nerve-wracking because there is a legal imperative to do so. Amazingly, in the UK the Equality Act is more than 10 years old but is really only being embedded in many workplaces relatively recently. An increase of cases relating to neuro-diversity has highlighted the role of the employer.

Yvonne Saxon is Head of HR, Diversity and Inclusion Services at Vista Employer Services Ltd in the UK. She describes some of the challenges for employers and how they can avoid getting into trouble.

'HR professionals often find themselves immediately navigating legal and medical processes when an employee or job candidate presents with neurodivergent needs. This is done with the primary aim of establishing if the person is disabled and, if so, what reasonable adjustments need to be made to meet the requirements of the Equality Act 2010. [2]

'Taking this legally focused approach isn't surprising when you consider the responsibility HR and Employee Relations functions have to prevent employers falling foul of the legislation and facing the potentially significant financial and reputational damage of a successful disability discrimination case in a tribunal.

'So, I, like most other HR professionals, have in my career, quickly headed for reports to get a medical opinion on whether an individual is disabled or not. However, the law is never that straightforward and the onus is actually on the employer to decide if the individual satisfies the disability test. The case of *Gallup vs Newport City Council* in 2013 firmly established that an employer cannot solely rely on a medical adviser's opinion to come to that decision.[3]

'The employer must gather specific and practical information to assess whether the individual meets the legal definition of disability, ie they have a physical or mental impairment which has a substantial and long-term adverse effect on his or her abilities to carry out normal day-to-day activities. Normal day-to-day activities can include the normal activities associated with their job.'

In her current role, she says, 'Nowadays, when advising corporate HR and ER teams on issues of neurodiversity and disability, I encourage them to broaden their approach and explore the issues with the individual. This results in a better understanding of the individual's needs, how the organization can enable them to perform well, establish whether the individual would meet the legal test of disability and also the reasonableness of any adjustments required.'

Yvonne also describes some straightforward questions to ask, which we have reiterated in other areas of this book.

Ask the individual:

- Find out what they feel they need.
- What do they find helpful?
- What do they find difficult or what makes their work harder?
- What might a job candidate worry about that they don't know about the set-up or environment of the selection process?
- What has worked for them previously?
- Would it be helpful for them to involve a family member or friend in these discussions?

Consider the job role and the work environment:

- What aspects of the role may be more challenging for them than others?
- What could be done to overcome these challenges?
- Would Access to Work fund any equipment or adaptations needed?
- What might they need in terms of work routine, structure or flexibility?

Don't forget training and development:

- Are there any difficulties with where and how training activity takes place?
- What format of learning materials work best for them?
- What might someone delivering training or development need to know about them?

Make sure to consider social interaction:

- What might they need their manager or colleagues to be aware of?
- If online meetings are necessary in the role, how might this hinder or help them?

Yvonne, from experience, has found this a useful approach which is do-able by us all.

'By taking this very practical approach, I have found HR and ER professionals are much better equipped to consider and get the right support in place for the individual. A medical report can then provide more focused information or address specific areas of medical complexity. From a legal perspective, the resources of an organization will influence what is considered 'reasonable' in terms of making adjustments with it often being deemed reasonable for large organizations to provide more support than smaller ones.

'Sometimes an employee or candidate's performance issues may be due to neurodivergence but the employee does not know they have this, or it might be suspected but not diagnosed.'

She makes an important point that not everyone will have a medical diagnosis and neurodiversity profiling can be just as useful in many cases. 'Asking the same questions can still be helpful as they are still likely to know what they struggle with and what helps. Undertaking neurodiversity profiling in these cases could also be just as helpful as a medical report when it comes to determining what might be needed to assist them.'

The hardest thing in many cases is when you have put in place adjustments and nothing seems to be making any difference. At this point you need to consider whether you have allowed enough time to embed the training or if the person has had time to gain the skills. If sufficient time has been given then sometimes a difficult conversation has to be had. Is the job right for the person and is the person right for the job?

Yvonne says, 'There will be times when it just isn't possible to accommodate an individual, regardless of the size of the employer. In my experience, where this happens and everything above has been explored together with the employee or job candidate, they are much more likely to feel that they have been listened to, treated fairly and be understanding of the employer's position. Whilst they probably won't end up feeling positive about the situation itself, they are less likely to have suffered the additional stress of feeling unfairly treated and also less likely to make a claim to a tribunal.'

No one ever wants to go to an employment tribunal. This is awful for everyone. Yvonne makes an important point that by carrying out procedures thoroughly this can hopefully be avoided: 'Of course, should such a claim arise, then an employer can have greater confidence in demonstrating to a tribunal that all the facts have been sought and presenting good evidence of adjustments considered and why they weren't reasonable in the circumstances.'

What's the key legislation?

The key act for employers to be aware of in the UK is the **Equality Act 2010**. In other countries there are different standards in place. Since 1919, the International Labour Organization has maintained and developed a system of international labour standards including:

> Freedom from discrimination is a fundamental human right and is essential for workers to be able to choose their employment freely, develop their potential to the full and reap economic rewards on the basis of merit. Bringing equality to the workplace also has significant economic benefits. Employers who practice equality have access to a larger, more diverse and higher-quality workforce.[4]

What is the UK Equality Act 2010?

The Equality Act consolidates previous discrimination and harassment law in order to ensure uniformity in what employers and employees need to do to make the workplace a fair environment and to obey the law. The Act became law in October 2010.

WHAT LAWS DID IT COMBINE?

It is a combination of these previous acts:

- The Disability Discrimination Act 1995
- The Equal Pay Act 1970
- The Sex Discrimination Act 1975
- The Race Relations Act 1976

WHAT IS A DISABILITY IF WE ARE CONSIDERING THE SOCIAL MODEL?

The UN Convention has also been incorporated into European case law by the European Court of Justice's decision in the Ring v Dansk almennyttigt Boligselskab case (C-335/11 and C-337/11, 2013).[5] That judgement introduced a new definition of disability, which reads as follows:

> The concept of 'disability'… must be interpreted as including a condition caused by an illness medically diagnosed as curable or incurable where that illness entails a limitation which results in particular from physical, mental or psychological impairments which in interaction with various barriers may hinder the full and effective participation of the person concerned in

professional life on an equal basis with other workers, and the limitation is a long-term one.

WHY IS IT IMPORTANT FOR EMPLOYERS TO KNOW ABOUT THE LEGISLATION?
All employers of any size in the UK have to comply with the Equality Act. There is no minimum number of employees. Temporary staff are also included in the Act.

WHAT IS YOUR ROLE AS AN EMPLOYER?
Employers are under a duty to make *reasonable adjustments* for disabled workers, job applicants and potential job applicants.

In the UK, The Equality Act 2010 states that 'it is unlawful for employers to discriminate against disabled people in their selection and recruitment practices unless there is justification for such action.'

WHAT ARE THE MAIN FEATURES OF THE ACT?
Whether at work as an employee or in using a service, the message (or purpose) of the Equality Act is that everyone has the right to be treated fairly at work or when using services.[6]

It protects people from discrimination on the basis of certain characteristics. These are known as *protected characteristics* and they vary slightly according to whether a person is at work or using a service.

Since April 2011:

- As an employer you can take a protected characteristic into consideration when deciding who to recruit or promote.

- However, you can only do this when you have candidates who are 'as qualified as' each other for a particular vacancy. This does not mean they have to have exactly the same qualifications as each other.

- It means that your selection assessment on a range of criteria rates them as equally capable of doing the job.

All processes before, during and after employment need to be considered:

- recruitment;
- working arrangements;
- working hours;
- promotion, development and training;
- grievance and appraisal procedures.

There are nine protected characteristics:

- age;
- disability;
- gender reassignment;
- marriage and civil partnership;
- pregnancy and maternity;
- sex;
- sexual orientation;
- race;
- religion or belief.

WHERE DOES PROTECTION RELATING TO THE PROTECTED CHARACTERISTICS APPLY?

The law protects individuals against discrimination in these situations:

- at work;
- in education;
- as a consumer;
- when using public services;
- when buying or renting property;
- as a member or guest of a private club or association.

Lawful measures can include:

- Targeting job training at people of particular racial groups, or either sex, who have been under-represented in certain occupations or grades during the previous 12 months or encouraging them to apply for such work.
- Providing facilities to meet any specific educational, training or welfare needs identified for a specific racial group.

WHAT IS INCLUDED AS A DISABILITY?

You are disabled under the Equality Act 2010 if you have a physical or mental impairment that has a 'substantial' and 'long-term' negative effect on your ability to do normal, daily activities.

You will see from the following list there are a number of conditions associated with cognitive diversity:

- sensory impairments eg **sight or hearing**;
- impairments with fluctuating or recurring effects such as rheumatoid arthritis, epilepsy;
- progressive conditions eg motor neurone disease, dementia;
- organ-specific conditions eg asthma, heart disease;
- developmental conditions eg **dyslexia, dyspraxia (DCD), ASD**;
- mental health conditions eg depression, schizophrenia, eating disorders;
- produced by injury to the body or **brain**.

WHAT TYPES OF CONDITIONS ARE <u>EXCLUDED</u> IN THE ACT?

- alcoholism;
- drug and substance misuse;
- nicotine addiction;
- the condition known as seasonal allergic rhinitis (eg hay fever), except where it aggravates the effect of another condition;
- tendency to set fires and/or to steal;
- tendency to physical or sexual abuse of other persons;
- exhibitionism and voyeurism.

WHAT DOES 'SUBSTANTIAL' MEAN?

Substantial is more than minor or trivial eg:

- it takes much longer than it usually would to complete a daily task like getting dressed;
- the individual finds it difficult to get around or access certain spaces due to limited mobility;
- the way in which an action is carried out in comparison to how you might be expected to carry out the activity if you did not have the impairment;
- the overall cumulative effect if the effects of more than one activity are taken together.

Long-term means being present for 12 months or more.

WHAT IS DISCLOSURE?

The *Oxford English Dictionary* defines disclosure as the action of making new or secret information known. When talking about the Equality Act, disclosure is when someone with a disability makes their employer or other employees aware of their disability and how it affects them.

There is no legal or professional duty to disclose a neurodivergent condition to an employer. The challenge is often the difficulty of whether you do or you don't and this may be related to past negative experiences rather than avoidance. Shame and fear may be a part of this. A worker may not have disclosed that they have a neurodivergent condition, or they may not know themselves that they have a neurodivergent condition.

WHAT IF AN EMPLOYEE DOES NOT DISCLOSE?

You cannot make reasonable adjustments for a disabled worker if they do not disclose their disability to you, and you cannot reasonably be expected to know that they are a disabled person. As an employer, if you have reasonable grounds to believe that a person may have a neurodivergent condition, and fail to investigate that possibility, then a tribunal may find that the employer should have known about the condition. This is why anticipatory adjustments are so important so you don't disadvantage someone by lack of awareness about fair recruitment, induction and support processes.

WHAT IF AN EMPLOYEE DOES DISCLOSE?

The employer can make reasonable adjustments to allow them to carry on doing their work or to be on equal footing *during* their recruitment process and *throughout* their employment. The employer can apply to **Access to Work**[7] in the UK which is a government programme to help people with disabilities into work; it can help fund adjustments and also supply training for your workplace.

An employee may disclose their disability:

- in application form;
- at the interview stage;
- when they first start in their role;
- during their employment;
- when they receive a diagnosis.

WHAT IS POSITIVE ACTION?

'Positive action' means the steps that an employer can take to encourage people from groups with different needs or with a past track record of disadvantage or low participation to apply for jobs. Reverse or affirmative action is illegal in the UK.

Putting something in place

The Code of Practice (6.19) in the UK advises that, for the purposes of making reasonable adjustments 'the employer must, however, do all they can reasonably be expected to do to find out whether [a worker is disabled and subject to a substantial disadvantage]'.[8] What is reasonable will depend on the circumstances. This is an objective assessment. When making enquiries about disability, employers should also consider issues of dignity and privacy (where is the conversation taking place?). It is important to ensure that personal information is dealt with in confidence and to have a discussion with the person with whom this is shared.

Example: A worker with speech and language challenges (has difficulties articulating words and is slower to process information) and dyspraxia (which affects their recording skills) receives both verbal and written instructions. The employer's annual performance reports consistently record that the worker's verbal comprehension and output appears to be of a higher quality than their written work. It is noted that they appear to have challenges with spelling and the pronunciation of unfamiliar words. In this case, a tribunal may conclude that the employer should have known that the worker had a disability within the meaning of the Act.

What is direct discrimination?

Direct discrimination is where someone is treated less favourably than another person because of a protected characteristic.

Example: A worker with ADHD is singled out for capability proceedings after disappointing performance results for their team. All their co-workers have similar responsibilities but only the worker with ADHD has been placed on capability. The employer cannot justify this treatment when challenged. A tribunal is likely to find that this employer has directly discriminated against the worker because of their disability.

Example: A parent of a child with ADHD and autism requests flexible working because of their caring responsibilities. Their request is denied. A colleague is granted a similar request to work flexibly on some days of the week. An employment tribunal could find that the employer has directly discriminated against the worker because of her association with someone who is disabled. (One real example of this is the case of McLeod v Royal Bank of Scotland plc, 2016.) [9]

What is indirect discrimination?

This can occur when the employer has a condition, rule, policy or even a practice in your company that applies to everyone but particularly disadvantages people who share a protected characteristic. Some examples are as follows:

1. THE EMPLOYER APPLIES, OR WOULD APPLY, THE PROVISION, CRITERION OR PRACTICE TO ALL WORKERS WITHIN THE RELEVANT GROUP

Example: An employer required all applicants for a particular post to pass a psychometric test. An autistic applicant said that the test discriminated against people with autistic spectrum conditions. The employer's own equality and diversity monitoring data showed that only one self-declared autistic applicant had previously passed the test. The claim of discrimination succeeded at tribunal. This example was the Brookes v the Government Legal Service, 2017 case.[10]

2. AN INDIRECTLY DISCRIMINATORY POLICY MAY BE 'PROPORTIONATE' IF THERE ARE NO REASONABLE ALTERNATIVE MEANS FOR REALIZING THE LEGITIMATE AIM

The employer can defend claims of indirect discrimination by arguing that a provision, criterion or practice is a proportionate means of achieving a legitimate aim. A legitimate aim may include health and safety considerations.

Example: A dyslexic employee is required to transcribe fridge temperature readings in a coffee shop. The tribunal concluded that the practice did place a dyslexic worker at a disadvantage, but it also found that investigating the way temperatures were recorded for health and safety reasons was a proportionate means of achieving a legitimate aim. The claim succeeded on other grounds. (An example of this was the Kumulchew v Starbucks Coffee Company UK Ltd, 2017.)[11]

3. THE PROHIBITED CONDUCT CATEGORY OF 'DISCRIMINATION ARISING FROM A DISABILITY' IS ADDITIONAL TO DIRECT DISCRIMINATION AND INDIRECT DISCRIMINATION

This category of discrimination occurs if:

a An employer treats a worker unfavourably because of something arising in consequence of that worker's disability.

b The employer cannot show that the treatment is a proportionate means of achieving a legitimate aim. These provisions have subtle but important differences from the previous two categories of direct discrimination and indirect discrimination.

For discrimination arising from disability (Section 15 under the Act), the question is whether the disabled person has been treated unfavourably because of something arising in consequence of their disability. An example is dismissing them, when this act was not a proportionate means of achieving a legitimate aim. (As in the case Wells v the Governing Body of Great Yarmouth High School, 2017.)[12]

Example: A worker was dismissed for sickness absence caused by depression and anxiety. The tribunal concluded that the worker's anxiety and depression were linked to their autism.

What is discrimination by association?

This is a situation where an individual is discriminated against through their association with another person, eg their colleagues may subject an individual to harassment because they are married to someone who is gay or of a particular religious affiliation.

What is harassment?

Harassment is 'Unwanted conduct related to a relevant protected characteristic, which has the purpose or effect of violating an individual's dignity or creating an intimidating, hostile, degrading, humiliating or offensive environment for that individual.'

Under the Act, an employer engages in unwanted conduct related to a neurodivergent condition, and the conduct has the purpose or effect of:

a violating a worker's dignity;

b creating an intimidating, hostile, degrading, humiliating or offensive environment for that worker.

'Unwanted conduct' covers a wide range of behaviours. The Equality and Human Rights Commission's Code (EHRC) of Practice[13] describes it as 'unwanted conduct... [can include] spoken or written words or abuse, imagery, graffiti, physical gestures, facial expressions, mimicry, jokes, pranks, acts affecting a person's surroundings or other physical behaviour.'

Harassment has a precise meaning under the Equality Act. It occurs in relation to specified 'relevant protected characteristics' which include disability (Harassment Section 26).

Example: A manager incorrectly assumes, based on flawed stereotypes, that a neurodivergent worker is unable to complete certain tasks. They repeat this view to other workers and make patronizing comments regarding the neurodivergent worker's capabilities. This behaviour is likely to constitute harassment.

Example: A worker has medication prescribed following a diagnosis of ADHD. A manager becomes aware of this, and refers to that worker being 'off their meds'. The taking of medication is related to their protected characteristic. The manager's behaviour is likely to constitute harassment.

Victimization

Victimization is described when a worker has been victimized if their employer subjects them to a 'detriment' because they have performed a 'protected act'. 'Detriment' has a broad meaning and could be the denial of promotion, opportunities to train, or being subject to disciplinary or capability proceedings.

The protected acts are defined in Section 27 as:

a bringing proceedings under the Equality Act;

b giving evidence or information in connection with proceedings under the Equality Act;

c doing any other thing for the purposes of or in connection with the Equality Act;

d making an allegation that an individual or employer has contravened the Equality Act.

Example: A dyslexic worker initiates early conciliation with an arbitration organization on the grounds that their employer has not made reasonable adjustments. After the issue is resolved, the employer changes the worker's place of work. This forces the person to have to undertake a longer commute. When they complain, a manager comments that 'well you caused us trouble'.

Example: A union representative supports a neurodivergent colleague who brings a tribunal case against their employer. Some time later, the representative fails to obtain a promotion that they thought they were qualified to obtain. They request copies of the interview notes. An entry in the notes says 'concerns about loyalty to the company (tribunal)'. The representative has been victimized because of their activities on behalf of someone with a protected characteristic.

Human Rights Act 1998

A second key law to consider is the Human Rights Act 1998.[14] Human rights are the basic rights and freedoms that belong to every person in the world, from birth until death. In the UK, our human rights are protected by the Human Rights Act 1998. Article 14 of the Act requires that all of the rights and freedoms set out in the Act must be protected and applied without discrimination:

> Discrimination occurs when you are treated less favourably than another person in a similar situation and this treatment cannot be objectively and reasonably justified. Discrimination can also occur if you are disadvantaged by being treated the same as another person when your circumstances are different (for example if you are disabled or pregnant).
>
> It is important to understand that the Human Rights Act does not protect you from discrimination in all areas of your life – there are other laws that offer more general protection, such as the Equality Act 2010… Article 14 is based on the core principle that all of us, no matter who we are, enjoy the same human rights and should have equal access to them (from the Equality Human Rights Commission).

Health and Safety at Work etc Act 1974

This is the third key Act in the UK:

> If you are an employer, you're required by law to protect your employees, and others, from harm. Under the Management of Health and Safety at Work Regulations 1999, the minimum you must do is: identify what could cause injury or illness in your business (hazards); decide how likely it is that someone could be harmed and how seriously (the risk); take action to eliminate the hazard, or if this isn't possible, control the risk.[15]
>
> Employers should already be managing any significant workplace risks, including putting control measures in place to eliminate or reduce the risks. If an employer becomes aware of an employee who has a disability, they should

review the risk assessment to make sure it covers risks that might be present for that employee (from the Health and Safety Executive).[16]

Performance appraisals

Ideally we should be anticipating challenges or support needs rather than having to consider the performance of the person. It may be worth considering the type of reviews that are taking place and seeing if there are some themes that would allow a more proactive stance. Are there more challenging appraisals with some line managers than with others? Is there a need to provide training or help to understand communication differences?

It can be useful to stand back and consider the following before the review takes place so that a complete picture of the situation is gained.

The 4 Ws: What, When, Where or Who has changed?

- Was the person performing well before and this is new?
- When did this happen?
- Has the work setting changed so that the person is working with less supervision or working remotely and doesn't have the skills or tools to do their work sufficiently?
- Has the job itself changed but this has not been clarified with the employer?
- Is there a difference or clash in communication styles or expectations that have not been clarified?
- Has something changed in the person's personal life meaning there are additional mental health challenges in place impacting on performance?
- Has there been a period of illness for themselves or someone close to them?
- Is there new line management?

Have adjustments been put in place?

Has there been adequate time to embed the learning and has coaching or support been provided? Has a regular review taken place on progress or if new barriers have emerged?

Giving someone some software without training can be unhelpful and put added stress on that person. There is good evidence that someone with DCD (dyspraxia) for example may need longer to learn a new skill and require additional opportunities for practice. It's important to allow adequate time and sufficient training for someone to use new tools as part of their everyday practices. Sometimes, with the best will, we provide a list of strategies for someone and new tools that can be overwhelming and end up being more confusing for that person. Regular short reviews can help to check progress.

Considerations for preparing panels or performance reviews

- Where the review process takes place is important. Lots of noise outside an office with colleagues around can cause anxiety.
- Information beforehand can be very helpful. Not knowing what will happen or not having time to prepare can make it harder for someone to process information and respond easily to questions. The person can also arrange to have someone with them to help with communication if needed.
- How long will the meeting last? What will happen during the meeting? What will happen after the meeting and when will this happen?
- Have all the panel members had neurodiversity awareness/unconscious bias training and feel confident knowing how to make adjustments during the panel session?
- Is there clarity over the processes and has this been conveyed to the person, ie when, where and with whom? Consider the best way to transmit this to the person, eg verbally/email, and ensure that you have checked their understanding of the process.

Adjustments for the meeting

- How will you put in place any adjustments that may be required during the session? Is there sufficient time to put these in place? For example, questions in a written format beforehand; limiting use of multipart questions; providing additional time to respond; the avoidance of use of acronyms; slowing down speech and checking understanding; being prepared to reframe questions if required.

- It's also important to allow the person sufficient time to provide their view of what has happened. Some people will need longer to process information, and may need someone with them to explain it and/or seek clarification.

Support in place

- What support is there before and after the session to check understanding and provide a debrief for the person so they are clear what the next steps are?
- Larger organizations may have a union member to support the person but in smaller companies there may be no one specifically in place with an HR role.

Has the line manager had training or support?

Sometimes there can be a real lack of understanding of why the person is not performing as well. Increased pressure by a line manager without appropriate guidance can add to someone feeling anxious and can become a vicious cycle.

One person Amanda was working with was so worried about what their line manager was going to say to them that they were physically sick before coming to work. Their anxiety caused them to question their work and check it over and over again, slowing down their productivity and resulting in them making more errors.

What can you do in general to limit your risks of tribunals and having to do performance reviews?

It can sometimes be too easy to misconstrue the signs of a neurodivergent condition as a sign of poor performance. If there is no adequate awareness in the organization it can also be seen as easier to deal with poor performance than it is to try and remedy the workplace for the individual. This is not often due to malice but more often to ignorance.

Someone who is late providing a report may not have the tools to help them such as the software to proof a document and so takes much longer to complete the task. If this happens repeatedly it can be seen as laziness or someone not bothering. In some cases this may be masked by the person and they end up working longer and longer hours (unknown to others) to ensure their work is up to standard.

It is essential that line managers who are dealing with performance or conduct matters are aware of how neurodivergent conditions can present and of the supportive processes that exist if it becomes apparent that they are working with someone who simply thinks differently to others.

Increase awareness about neurodiversity in order to challenge stereotypes. One example is that it is often cited that people in IT are all autistic or… people who are autistic are usually good at IT. Other stereotypes we have heard include people saying that someone who is on the autism spectrum can't empathize.

Awareness-raising sessions can be helpful to provide line managers with the skills and confidence to have more sensitive conversations and refute these stereotypes. It can also reduce the risk of 'banter' where someone makes a comment that is seemingly funny but in reality is not and can be deeply hurtful.

Don't make assumptions and think that all people with a diagnosis of X need Y type of support every time. An example of this is thinking that people with dyslexia will need specific support of a certain type such as having to have everything on buff-coloured paper. Not everyone with dyslexia finds that useful as they may not have visual difficulties and may have specific challenges with writing but not reading (and could have other challenges with anxiety or attention difficulties as well).

Assumptions about someone with autism are they may be viewed as rude, inappropriate or aloof by another person. While neurodivergent conditions shouldn't be used as a licence to excuse clearly inappropriate behaviour, it is important to gain information on the context in which a specific behaviour was seen, especially if this was a one-off occurrence. It is essential to stand back and see why someone may have responded in a certain way. We don't always know all parts of a person's life and there may be a number of factors why someone is sad, angry or irritable.

Keep an open mind and open dialogue – someone behaving in a certain way may not always be related to their neurodivergent traits. For example, someone not looking directly at you or not turning on their camera in a web meeting could be seen as a 'behaviour' associated with autism. However, it could also be because their camera is facing the other way, or their IT system is not working, or they are embarrassed about where they are working or they can focus better listening to someone than seeing them.

How confident are you of your knowledge relating to neurodiversity and the actions you would take?

What would you/should you do in these three scenarios?

Scenario 1

You know one of your employees has dyslexia as someone else has told you. The employee has not disclosed this to you. They are making lots of errors in their work. You would like to help them and provide some reasonable adjustments, but you are not sure how to go about it. What would you do?

1 Just tell them that you think they are incompetent and unless they improve, they will lose their job.

2 Talk to them sensitively and privately about your observations regarding their work, being specific, and suggest they could have an Access to Work assessment, or you could review how they are doing with some suggestions for improvements.[17]

3 Tell them their colleague told you they have dyslexia, and you think they need to have some help.

4 Give them the address for the British Dyslexia Association and tell them they should contact them.[18]

The answer is 2. Keeping a conversation going and finding support is key.

Scenario 2

You have an employee leaving your employment to move to another area of the country and they have ADHD and autism. They have asked for a reference. You have written a positive reference about what they contributed to the business and have included information about their disabilities and how the individual has overcome lots of the challenges in their work. Is this OK?

1 This is a really positive idea and will raise awareness of autism and ADHD in the workplace.

2 You should not disclose on behalf of the individual about their disability without their consent to do so.

3 You could send them an additional letter separately and let them know how your organization helped them and what adjustments were made.

4 You don't have to give someone with a disability a reference.

Which would you choose? 2 is the correct answer.

Scenario 3

You are a line manager and undertaking annual performance appraisals on all your staff. You have arranged for the meeting to take place in your office on the second floor of your building. The building is old, but it is where your business is based. One of your staff has disclosed she has dyslexia. Do you need to consider any adaptations?

1 If you are the line manager it is up to you where you have your meetings. They should come to you.

2 The individual with dyslexia could ask for notes to be written down for them, or they could use a tape recorder.

3 You only need to make adjustments if someone has a physical condition which is impacting on accessibility, eg someone with cerebral palsy.

4 You could have the meeting instead in the busy café around the corner.

Much of the focus for many employers has been around disability as requiring physical considerations in buildings. Adjustments relating to communication are less often considered. 2 is the correct option.

KEY POINTS
Policies and procedures

- Understand local legislation and what you should do as a legal duty.

- Start at the top and get support from your board in order to think about neurodiversity as integral in your equality, diversity and inclusion plans.

- Engage leaders from across your organization and with other similar organizations to share ideas and best practice – this shows others inside and out that you are a neurodiverse organization.

- Encourage team members to share experiences and ensure all voices are heard and listened to including asking for staff feedback post hiring.

- Check your blind spots, such as biases that may exist.
- Be consistent in your efforts and put EDI in your DNA.
- Audit, measure and track your progress so you can see where change needs to be made.

Notes

1 Department of Work and Pensions (2014; last updated 2020) Disability Confident employer scheme and guidance, https://www.gov.uk/government/collections/disability-confident-campaign (archived at https://perma.cc/2M2J-6AFM)

2 Equality Act (2010) https://www.legislation.gov.uk/ukpga/2010/15/contents (archived at https://perma.cc/5ZGD-6XJW)

3 Gallop v Newport City Council (2013) EWCA Civ 1583, https://www.employmentcasesupdate.co.uk/site.aspx?i=ed19473#:~:text=Appeal%20against%20the%20rejection%20by,claimant's%20claim%20of%20disability%20discrimination.&text=The%20claimant%20claimed%20unfair%20dismissal,discrimination%20(which%20was%20dismissed) (archived at https://perma.cc/42VV-QHK4)

4 International Labour Organization (2021) International Labour Standards on Equality of opportunity and treatment, https://www.ilo.org/global/standards/subjects-covered-by-international-labour-standards/equality-of-opportunity-and-treatment/lang--en/index.htm (archived at https://perma.cc/K4QT-KP2G)

5 Ring v Dansk almennyttigt Boligselskab case (C-335/11 and C-337/11) (2012), http://curia.europa.eu/juris/document/document.jsf?text=&docid=131499&pageIndex=0&doclang=en&mode=lst&dir=&occ=first&part=1&cid=400074 (archived at https://perma.cc/Q2RX-LG2D)

6 Equality and Human Rights Commission (2011) Equality Act 2010, Statutory Code of Practice, https://www.equalityhumanrights.com/sites/default/files/employercode.pdf (archived at https://perma.cc/GPQ5-QV83)

7 Access to Work Scheme, https://www.gov.uk/access-to-work (archived at https://perma.cc/4XRH-KTHS)

8 Equality and Human Rights Commission (2011) Equality Act 2010, Statutory Code of Practice, https://www.equalityhumanrights.com/sites/default/files/employercode.pdf (archived at https://perma.cc/GPQ5-QV83)

9 Ms K McLeod v The Royal Bank of Scotland plc (2016) https://www.gov.uk/employment-tribunal-decisions/ms-k-mcleod-v-royal-bank-of-scotland-plc-4110836-2015 (archived at https://perma.cc/4TSK-4EMX)

10 Brookes v the Government Legal Service (2017) https://www.gov.uk/ employment-appeal-tribunal-decisions/the-government-legal-service-v-ms-t-brookes-ukeat-0302-16-rn (archived at https://perma.cc/7BSK-FAU3)

11 Kumulchew v Starbucks Coffee Company UK Ltd (2017) https://www.gov.uk/ employment-tribunal-decisions/miss-m-kumulchew-v-starbucks-coffee-company-uk-ltd-and-others-2301217-2017 (archived at https://perma.cc/2V3J-NNRX)

12 Mr I Wells v The Governing Body of Great Yarmouth High School (2017) https://www.gov.uk/employment-tribunal-decisions/mr-i-wells-v-the-governing-body-of-great-yarmouth-high-school-3401100-2015 (archived at https://perma.cc/3CBM-Y4PH)

13 Equality and Human Rights Commission (2011) Equality Act Codes of Practice https://www.equalityhumanrights.com/en/advice-and-guidance/equality-act-codes-practice (archived at https://perma.cc/2MHT-RVGP)

14 Human Rights Act (1998) https://www.lcgislation.gov.uk/ukpga/1998/42/contents (archived at https://perma.cc/FZ2B-L3LN)

15 Health and Safety Act (1974) https://www.legislation.gov.uk/ukpga/1974/37/contents (archived at https://perma.cc/TJ97-GNJS)

16 Health and Safety Executive, https://www.hse.gov.uk/ (archived at https://perma.cc/EQH3-HQ2M)

17 Access to Work Scheme, https://www.gov.uk/access-to-work (archived at https://perma.cc/4XRH-KTHS)

18 British Dyslexia Association, www.bdadyslexia.org.uk (archived at https://perma.cc/L5HZ-WB77)

07

How can employers attract neurodiverse talent in recruitment?

Introduction

Do you remember what it was like going for your first interview or even going online to look for jobs? This requires a new set of skills in understanding what is the best route for success. For some of us word of mouth can be really powerful but knowing that may work can be something that we don't all know.

Who prepares you for getting your first job? Is it the role of school, college or university to prepare you and provide the training and skills to be confident to do so? How confident are you in a changing world of remote hiring and the need to demonstrate your transferable skills?

How many jobs have you started, but found that the job is nothing like the description? I don't think many of us have seen a job description that matched the job. The culture and values of an organization may be something that is not written down anywhere. Most places use acronyms and phrases that can seem to a new starter like a new language. A lack of confidence at the start of the job may mean that you don't ask someone what the terms mean and then months later you still don't know but you are reluctant to ask.

Understanding the 'social rules' in a workplace can be complex for some people but can be so important for team engagement. You're still not sure what people do for birthdays, or what the rules are around making tea or coffee for others. It's not just the complexity of the role or the words used that can create anxiety, but also what appears to some to be small inconsequential day-to-day things. However, in a team, if you don't make the tea, or bring in cakes on your birthday, you can be misjudged as unfriendly.

Onboarding processes that provide an understanding not only of the job itself but the values and behaviours of an organization can make a real difference. It is also an opportunity to discuss skills gaps or training needs. In the UK, there is a scheme called Access to Work, run by the Department of Work and Pensions at the present time, which allows for assistance, coaching and tools to be put in place to help with adjustments to the work setting. It has also developed support for people who are working in a blended way, both at home and in an office. It is so important to put in support in a timely manner. It can make a real difference to someone being able to do their job; not having support in place can lead to performing under par and line managers and peers losing confidence in you.

Bidirectional communication strategy

For some people working with others and understanding 'banter' and getting their interactions can be confusing and frustrating. Starting a new job can be learning how to work as part of a team with everyone communicating in different ways. Damian Milton, an autistic scholar in the UK, describes the concept of 'double empathy' and the reality that communication is not one-way and there is not one right way to do it. He talks about empathy being a bidirectional phenomenon[1] and notes that both autistic and non-autistic individuals may have difficulty understanding and feeling for one another because of their differing outlooks and experiences with the world. This perspective is a really important one for the workplace, as in the past support for people who were autistic was about 'normalizing' and teaching someone to communicate in a 'more neurotypical' way such as guiding someone to look at someone's ear if they found looking directly at the person difficult.

There is a growing realization (which in many ways is no surprise) that there is a responsibility of both parties to ensure that communication is two-way. Awareness of this is important when working in teams otherwise there can be misconceptions if someone doesn't 'look you in the eye'; this could be construed as being unfriendly or even worse. Autistic author John Elder

Robison in his book *Look Me in the Eye* talks about how his discomfort in making direct eye contact was often interpreted as a sign that he was 'no good', a criminal, or a sociopath.[2]

The reality of the situation is that there is still a huge amount of bias through the recruitment process. In a *Harvard Business Review* study, they found that humans categorize others in milliseconds and we make lasting judgements about an individual's character in just 30 minutes, the average length of an interview minus introductions and any questions.[3]

So if we are categorizing others so quickly and making lasting judgements about their character, based on the small amount of information we take and observe in that time, you can bet some pretty poor and very biased decisions are being made.

The fact that the candidate being interviewed may lack eye contact, have a perceived weaker handshake, have English that isn't their first language, or have cultural nuances that change our understanding or perception of what's being said, are all easy (discriminatory) ways for us to reject suitable and talented applicants. Sadly this often happens without us even giving it a second thought. Bias can start with our misinterpretation of a spelling error on an application form. We can think that the person doesn't care about the job enough to check it but in reality they may not have noticed the error even after checking it (but still have the skills for the job).

If we are not explicit around what we are looking for we risk missing out on diversifying our talent pool. The less we share information about the specific job as part of our recruitment and selection process, the less we can hope to get back in return from the candidates.

Importantly, when we consider the 'candidate experience' we often focus on the bright and shiny things. How can we make the process exciting and what cool tech or images and videos can we produce? The reality is that if you want to attract neurodiverse talent and give them an incredible candidate experience, you just have to give everyone equal access to applying for the role, describing accurately what it is and what is expected, and choosing methods to be assessed in a way that allows each person to best show their skills.

Seems simple, right?

Well it is. However, you'll find that the majority of those who are cognitively diverse often don't experience it, or even worse can't get past the first discriminatory gatekeeper.

One of the simplest things you can start doing today!

Repeat as often as you can throughout the process:

> We encourage neurologically diverse applicants from all backgrounds, so is there anything we can do to make this process better for you and to allow you to show your best self?

You could then go on to say:

> We recognize that some people require extra time to complete tests, or require alternative methods of presentation and can benefit from having the interview questions or a guide to the type of questions pre-interview. We are open to any suggestions or requests you may have and are always looking for creative ways to assess talent.

This will not only encourage more applicants who think and act differently, it will also give you great insight into how you can improve your recruitment and assessment process so that it is accessible for all.

This goes beyond any legal obligation for 'reasonable adjustments' and really shows the external market that you care about an individual's needs. It will also help you identify early on what needs an employee may have and therefore what support you can give them to be successful in the job.

We'll discuss in the rest of this section all the other ways in which we can consider how to attract neurologically diverse talent to your organization. It's not rocket science, but it will take a conscious decision to rethink 100 years of interview and assessment methodology.

Depending on the size of your organization and the jobs you are hiring for you can use a specialist sector recruitment company. Alternatively, if you want to proactively seek a neurodiverse workforce you can use specialist neurodiverse/disability organizations who support you and the person to find the best job for them and for you and often bridge the interview and onboarding stages. Examples of this are Evenbreak and Exceptional Individuals in the UK. Alternatively, there are firms that employ staff from neuro-minorities and will outsource them into work settings for contract work. For example, Specialisterne and ComputerAid in the United States employ people on the autism spectrum who also have excellent IT skills.

General recruitment guidelines

How you represent your company regarding your values, what your company does or doesn't do, can make a real difference in whether somebody wants to apply for a job with you. Amanda sometimes plays the game of looking on company sites to see if anything pops up when you search for dyslexia, disability, Access to Work or neurodiversity (it usually doesn't!).

Create a neurodiversity policy or make neurodiversity a distinct part of your current inclusion policy

You could include a statement such as:

> Diversity of thought is an important part of our organizational makeup. We will look to offer adjustments across our recruitment, selection, assessment, workplace and work practices to help those who apply for our jobs and work within our organizations to have a better experience and to be able to bring their real whole selves to work. We don't just see this as a legal obligation to provide reasonable adjustments, but an opportunity to offer the best experience possible for all involved.

Look inside before you venture out

We'll talk later in the book about creating champions safely, but it's important before trying to run off and hire lots of new neurodiverse people that you consider your current work environment and employees. It may well be that you are already a highly neurodiverse organization, but you are just not aware!

There are likely to be mums and dads of children who have dyslexia, ADHD or dyspraxia, for example, as well as employees who know or think they are but have not been diagnosed. It is through these employees that you can start to understand what it's like to work in the environment and some of the challenges they may face, as well as identifying poor work or recruitment, selection and assessment practices you may have that are not inclusive or accessible. They can provide you with vital information as they already know your organization.

Be cautious in how you approach this as it may be that your current employees do not yet feel ready or in a safe enough space to share this information with you, so you may want to consider bringing in some external support to help, either in the form of an evangelist who can generate some interest in the subject and/or a consultant, charity or advisory/support group like Amanda and her team who can help assess where you are currently at and what steps can be taken to improve. Sometimes some awareness-raising allows different people to start talking to each other in the room and can generate a support group that can blossom into really celebrating the diversity that's in your workforce.

Warning! One person's experience doesn't make them an expert in a specific condition or the expert in advising adjustments for others. We will be reiterating this and will hear from others saying the same thing.

The words you use mean different things to different people

JOB ADVERTS

What is the job? Do you need everything on the long list of skills? Do you assume that everyone needs a degree for a specific job because that's how it has always been? How can you best understand a candidate's values, skills and their motivation for the job?

Amanda was working with one firm where they did 'reverse job matching' to look at the skills they really needed. They looked at existing people doing the job and then measured skills, attitudes and qualifications and asked the line managers to 'blind' mark their skills using a defined matrix. They also looked at other factors that may have been important for the person in the job such as whether performance was better in those with a short commute. What they realized was that qualifications were not a key factor for the specific call centre job. They also interestingly found out that having too much empathy in an outbound call centre work wasn't very good. This may be because that person worries too much about the customer at the end of the phone and takes their clients home with them at the end of the day, worrying if they have upset them in some way or not.

There is good research evidence of gender bias in the words we use for job descriptions and how this can impact on whether someone applies for the job. We often associate some words as more male, such as leader, competitive and dominant, and some as more feminine, like support, understand and interpersonal. It has been shown that when job advertisements were constructed to include more masculine than feminine wording, participants perceived more men within these occupations and, more importantly, women found these jobs less appealing. Results confirmed that perceptions of belongingness (not skills) affected the level of job appeal. When some cognitively diverse people apply for jobs and see a long list of skills, the assumption is often that they need all of them to apply and so they don't, when neurotypical (and often more confident) people will have a go even if they don't have the full set of skills cited.

PRACTICAL TIPS

- Consider and avoid words specifically that are gender associated such as strong, driven or competitive.

- Avoid superlatives such as best, leader, world class, industry leading.

- Avoid slang words that may mean something different to some people such as rock star, guru.

- Avoid terms that may have a double meaning such as fast paced, flexible, dynamic, opportunities for growth.

- Consider the font you use in an advert and try and avoid pictures obscuring the words. If there are pictures ensure they have an 'alt tag' so someone using a screen reader can know if the picture has some additional meaning.

- Check the content for readability level, especially if the role is likely to attract someone who doesn't have a high level of literacy. This benefits everyone. You can imagine if you are hunting for jobs, if you can read the advert easily and quickly you will be attracted to it.

- Be specific and consider your true requirements and limit the number you ask for. Try to avoid a whole list of other 'nice to haves' and focus on what is really required.

SHOWING YOU CARE

- Demonstrate your commitment to equality and diversity and state this on your site and on job adverts and application forms.

- Think about the time, place and structure of the job. Obviously if you are in the retail, customer-facing sector then you may need to have someone in the job for certain hours. But one thing we have seen during Covid-19 is the flip to working from home for many people in many jobs in a way we could not have imagined.

WHAT ALTERNATIVES COULD YOU CONSIDER?

- Could the person work from home (all or some of the time)?

- A compressed working week, working four longer days instead of five.

- Flexible start and finish times to allow them to miss rush hour traffic and be able to use public transport when there are fewer people around.

- Term-time working in order to balance family and work commitments.

- Or could they be offered project-related working?

This is a useful discussion to consider in general. We need to recognize that we are all different and some people will be most creative early in the morning (or even in the middle of the night); others work really well not doing regular hours but being given project-related work (allocated packets of work and a deadline and they decide when in the day they work and then deliver it). This latter approach can also be mixed with some fixed time points in the week for meetings/reviews.

For other people, having regular hours is essential to them in a regular work setting. They may find that hot desking is a stressful nightmare. Not having your own space and tools around you can cause real concern. Amanda was told by one person that he left his job because of it. He was so worried each day where he was going to end up, who he would be working next to or even if he had a desk at all. Having to hunt each day for desk space had such an impact on his wellbeing and led to increased anxiety.

Further considerations

- **Ensure your website is accessible** and compliant with local/country guidelines, eg the words used, layout, whether it is text-to-speech enabled. You can use 'plug ins' such as Recite Me, or Browsealoud. These allow pages to be spoken; you can change the colour of the page and text and change the font style to suit the person.

- **Think about the accessibility of the actual application process** – how does someone complete a form? Does it 'time out' if you have not put in the information quickly enough? Some people may be less organized and not know what they require beforehand to be ready, such as personal details, passport number, national insurance number for example.

- **State that you offer an alternative application process** (if you do) such as by phone or on a video call.

- **Alternatives to a CV?** Could you allow other forms of information to demonstrate skills? Some companies use video CVs but there are pros and cons in doing so and the choice of representing yourself is ultimately most important. It also very much needs to align to skills needed for the job, as the person will require IT skills, communication and organization skills. If the job requires good verbal communication skills then this can be demonstrated but if the person is not 'customer facing' the need for a video CV may put off someone who has great technical skills but has a speech and language difficulty such as a stammer or a tic. This immediately puts them at a disadvantage despite having the required skills for the job.

- Does a two-page CV always really tell you about the person or does it benefit those most who have someone to teach them how to write a good CV, check the wording and proof it? This goes back to really considering how you want to find out about the skills of the person and this is dependent on an accurate job description. Someone working in engineering, IT or science may be brilliant at their job but just not be a good copywriter!

- You could accept a **portfolio of work** to demonstrate someone's skills, or if they need to have a particular skill could you provide a test for this?

- In the UK companies can sign up to be a **Disability Confident** employer – this is a programme run by the government (Department of Work and Pensions) that all sizes of business can sign up to. There are three levels of commitment requiring different levels of engagement. Showing the symbol on your website demonstrates to an applicant you are likely to provide an interview automatically if they disclose a disability.

- **How does someone 'disclose' or share information with you if they have support needs?** What words do you use on the application form? In the UK you can only ask about health or disability if there are necessary requirements of the job that cannot be met with reasonable adjustments; you're finding out if someone needs help to take part in a selection test or interview or you are using 'positive action' to recruit a disabled person.

- **Be explicit in saying how someone can get support.** We need to always remember that no one has to tell you they require additional support. Try to avoid a tick box with a long list of conditions. This could leave you open to accusations that you support some people with some conditions and not others. Sometimes the easiest approach is saying, 'Do you need some additional workplace adjustments and wish to discuss this further?'

- **In-work support.** In the UK there is a government scheme to get specific help with workplace adjustments, called Access to Work. This can help at all stages and even at the interview stage. It can also provide mentoring and coaching support as well as specific equipment (chairs, keyboards etc) as well as software.
- **Content of the adverts** – check for any inadvertent bias. Have someone else look over your job descriptions and person specifications to consider any unnecessary health and disability-related barriers.

There are a variety of online tools that can help in this area both paid for and free to use. https://textio.com/ (archived at https://perma.cc/T37K-J7GY) is one of the most well-known paid services.

Here are two free options:

http://gender-decoder.katmatfield.com/ (archived at https://perma.cc/KVB6-JDV3)

https://www.totaljobs.com/insidejob/gender-bias-decoder/   (archived   at https://perma.cc/62RR-RZ8E)

The good news is that tools are being created and implemented into recruitment and HR technology all the time, so be sure to check with your provider what is on offer.

Information about your company

Let applicants know about the culture and values of your organization. **Paint a typical day/month** and explain what will be expected in the first few months. Some people, if they are leaving education and entering the world of work for the first time, may be less familiar about expectations and the culture of working practices in an organization and this may need to be explicitly stated. Doing work placements in one place may be very different from another.

Although the practical hints and tips for what you can do to attract a neurodiverse workforce are incredibly useful, sometimes there comes an opportunity to do something big and bold, that is bigger than us, our organization or the people who work there. In this story from Jenny we get to hear about just that type of magic moment.

CASE STUDY
Umbrellas – symbols of hope

In early 2019 Jenny McLaughlin, a project manager at Heathrow Airport, sat on a train going into London for a work event, contemplating how her son Richie, who had been diagnosed with ADHD a year earlier, would fit in to the world she saw around her. She really wanted to be able to make a statement to the world that we need to recognize the strength and challenges of each of us who think differently and she thought, what better way to do that than host the ADHD Foundation's Umbrella Project at Heathrow.

The Umbrella Project has grown year on year to become the largest neurodiversity art project in the world. Its aim is to raise awareness of neurodiversity. The 'umbrella' symbol stems from the use of neurodiversity as an umbrella term for ADHD, dyslexia, dyspraxia, ASD etc. From humble beginnings in Liverpool in 2017, the Umbrella Project has become an art movement that celebrates the ability and talent of every human being including every neurominority individual, empowering and enabling the next generation of children and young people through the canopy of umbrellas.

The installation at Heathrow was at the time and remains the largest and most ambitious installation to date. It required weights and countermeasures to support the 300 umbrellas to ensure the artwork did not affect the integrity of the airport structures. The complexity of installing the canopy within an open space at arrivals at Terminal 5 required collaboration between multiple parties including MACE, Baker Hicks, Pascal and Watson and Heathrow's Operational teams.

Heathrow pre-Covid-19 had over 80 million passengers a year coming through its airport, which is a staggering amount to consider. It now has a number of initiatives including sunflower lanyards that allow passengers needing tailored help and support to discreetly identify themselves, complemented by investments in colleague training and equipment and signage to improve the airport's accessibility. It's a continual journey that they look to improve year on year through open dialogue with the airport users.

Jenny has dyslexia and ADHD and after the Umbrella Project she chose to accept the Lead role for the Disability Network at Heathrow. The installation created conversations within all areas of team Heathrow, which includes airline handlers, and pushed neurodiversity up the agenda. This has led to a cross-functional strategy to truly deliver and embed systematic inclusion in all areas of the business.

The initiative also went on to be recognized in neurodiversity awareness awards as the joint best inclusion project of 2020. It was specifically commended for its incredible educational effort in bringing about greater understanding of neurodiversity, allowing people to stop for a moment and take in the visual splendour of the umbrellas.

The ADHD Foundation (www.adhdfoundation.org.uk (archived at https://perma.cc/ T9QV-DGT8)), a key neurodiversity charity in the UK, which leads on this initiative, is now extending to other areas across the UK (and internationally) and has also developed the neurodiversity awareness mark for companies to gain if they show they are embracing neurodiversity. This entails them getting staff to complete an online training course relating to neurodiversity in the workplace. The umbrella sign is then a means to show their customers and employees that they take neurodiversity awareness seriously within their organization.

KEY POINTS
How can employers attract neurodiverse talent?

- Create a neurodiversity policy so that people have a map and processes to follow. Review this on a regular basis.
- Look inside your business and check on the talents there.
- Look at the words you use in the job adverts.
- Ensure line managers have training so they are confident to have conversations.
- Demonstrate you care and you are interested in attracting a neurodiverse range of skills and talents.
- Ensure your website is accessible and your application forms are too.

Notes

1 Milton, D (2012) On the ontological status of autism: the 'double empathy problem', *Disability & Society*, https://kar.kent.ac.uk/62639/ (archived at https://perma.cc/M6AX-GLNE)
2 Elder Robison, J (2007) *Look Me in the Eye: My life with Asperger's*, Crown, New York
3 Elsbach, K D (2003) How to pitch a brilliant idea, *Harvard Business Review*, https://escholarship.org/uc/item/1w82h22c (archived at https://perma.cc/ PL2Y-TVGT)

Further reading

Milton, D (2017) *A Mismatch of Salience*, Pavilion, https://www.pavpub.com/ a-mismatch-of-salience/ (archived at https://perma.cc/P7W7-ETDG)

08

Apprenticeships, internships, work placements and hiring schemes

Introduction

The value of work-based learning and training is something that cannot be disputed. The opportunity to see what a workplace is like, speak to people working in the organization and work alongside them and learn real-life skills can be a game changer for many neurodivergent people.

Training and gaining experience can take place in different ways either as work placement which may be undertaken while in training or through organizations whose task is to find employment for someone brokering this placement, or through supported internships, or lastly gaining by an apprenticeship.

An apprenticeship is different, as this is work-based training while an internship is work-based learning. An intern gets the chance to work in a trade or at a company for a limited period of time, for example a summer. They may be offered full-time employment after internship completion. Supported internships are designed to enable people with additional support or learning challenges to achieve sustainable, paid employment by equipping them with the skills they need for work through learning in the workplace. In the UK there are some specifically funded schemes in some areas for 16–24-year-olds who have already had support during their education.

The aim of these programmes is that they support the young person to move into paid employment at the end of the programme. Students complete a personalized study programme which includes the chance to study for relevant substantial qualifications. The internships normally last for a year and include unpaid work placements of at least six months. Young people on supported internships are expected to require a higher level of support than a trainee or apprentice, and to be offered workplace support in the form of a job coach, as well as support for their non-workplace learning. Usually there are no specific entry or completion requirements for supported internships, and each learning provider will work with their interns and the organization to develop a personalized programme that meets their needs and provides progression.[1]

Gaining a precious place on any of the above schemes is still dependent on the organization understanding the needs of the individual in the context of the work being asked to be done and being motivated to put in place the additional support that may be required. It requires the organization working sometimes with outside agencies to help and guide them. This collaboration can be very helpful to achieve success. Funding for some schemes has been an incentive to take on placements and some companies have seen this as part of their corporate social responsibility.

In this chapter you will hear some case studies of how organizations have set up schemes and gained from the experience and their reflections about this. Remember to think about ways to widen participation otherwise we tend to attract white, middle-class men to all these programmes (of course there is nothing wrong with white, middle-class men but it would be more inclusive to ensure equal chances for all to gain success). We provide some tips for recruiting at the end of the chapter.

While a number of organizations have established successful specific placements for neurodivergent people, these have been primarily focused on those who are autistic. While it is great there has been increased interest in supporting people with autism into work, the narrow view does potentially have some challenges as we also need to remember that most people with a diagnosis of autism will be different from each other and have varying co-occurring conditions. Some people may have dyslexia traits as well and others ADHD and/or dyspraxia traits; others could be in a wheelchair or an ex-Olympic athlete; and some may be visually impaired or diabetic. Each person will require different support depending on their suite of skills, challenges and the work being undertaken.

Gaining a placement on a scheme may come from working with a specialist provider brokering this and supporting the person during their time with the organization, or alternatively some organizations have developed their own in-house provision. One example of the latter is the Microsoft programme cited here.

CASE STUDY
Microsoft becoming autism-inclusive

Michael Vermeesch is Digital Inclusion Lead for Microsoft and he describes how becoming autism-inclusive has made a profound difference to the business and their culture.

'We launched our first pilot project to hire autistic people in 2015. When Mary Ellen Smith, our Corporate VP for Operations, spoke about it at the United Nations we received around 800 CVs. Now a CV may not be the best way to assess talent, but that response told us something – that there are a lot of brilliant people disabled by society. We learnt that our traditional hiring processes could be a major barrier to entry for many talented candidates – so we set out to change them. In the years since, we have continued to refine and develop our recruitment and onboarding so that we reach more people on the autism spectrum and enable them to demonstrate their abilities in a comfortable and supporting environment.

'Today, each qualified candidate attends a week-long hiring academy with a variety of Microsoft teams and hiring managers. We partner new autistic talent with job coaches and mentors who help candidates understand our structures and processes. We've profiled candidates and used those profiles to remove barriers during recruitment and beyond.

'As one single measure of success (and there are many) there are Microsoft engineers hired through the Autism Hiring Program who have written code used by millions of customers every day. Becoming autism-inclusive has made a profound difference to the business and our culture. Our leaders and managers are better at their jobs because the new strategies they have learned – to share written recaps of meetings, to set clear expectations, to give more regular feedback – can benefit everyone.

'That increasingly inclusive feel has encouraged more of our employees not hired through the Autism Hiring Program to self-identify and feel comfortable in coming forward in being themselves. And that has shown us that the issue is often not "how do we hire people with autism?" – but recognizing that they are already here.'

Another company, CAI in the United States, provides workforce training and employment for neurodivergent adults through partnerships with disability agencies, universities, support groups and forward-thinking businesses. Their programme is called Autism2Work (A2W). CAI describes one person's experience and what they did that resulted in success.

CASE STUDY

CAI: Workforce training and employment for neurodivergent adults

For nearly two years after graduating from college, Nick Muench filled out applications and submitted resumes to as many as 10 job postings a week. Even with a degree in chemistry, a minor in computer science and a clear aptitude for problem-solving and programming, the job search was slow and difficult. 'Searching for a job on Google can produce thousands of links,' says Nick, 'but it's hard to tell what is a real opportunity and what is spam.'

He found chemistry an especially difficult field to break into without real-world experience, so he focused on computer science, which he could continue to teach himself in his free time. In two years, he secured a handful of job interviews but sadly no job offers.

Nick says his employment challenges were related to his Asperger's syndrome, a neurodivergent disorder diagnosis that he received in grade school. It means Nick has strong verbal language skills and intellectual ability but struggles with social interactions. 'What quote-unquote "normal" people would think is not at all a task,' Nick explains, 'feels like a task to me. Formal interviews are difficult because you are supposed to follow a set of rules, which everyone seems to know. But the rules are opaque to me. I have to guess when to make eye contact and when to speak up, which is a lot of stuff to figure out if you have trouble picking up social cues.'

Nick had excelled in high school and college, especially in settings where people were invested in the subject matter they had come to study. But the job search was oriented so clearly on first impressions, which was exactly where Nick struggled. 'Interactions are always easier for me when they are less formal,' he says. 'First impressions are the hardest part. As soon as you know people, the syndrome becomes a lot less relevant.'

Nick learned about CAI's Autism2Work (A2W) practice offering technical job openings in his area. After completing the initial competency call and attending a local 'Meet & Greet' session, he was invited to the next A2W Job Readiness Training (JRT). The JRT is a 60-hour workforce development training and competency assessment designed to prepare candidates to be successful in the work environment. 'It felt more like a structured audition than a training,' says Nick. 'They wanted to give us a sense of what the work would be like – we learned about quality assurance, testing, and agile – and they got a better sense of our skills. For me, it was much better than a formal interview.'

Throughout the JRT, Nick showcased his strong problem-solving skills, attention to detail, and ability to integrate into a team environment. After the JRT, CAI immediately offered Nick a full-time position as a Quality Assurance Analyst working with a large pharmaceutical company. The A2W team was expanding there, and Nick became one of 17 A2W team members working in the CAI offices in Allentown, Pennsylvania.

On day two of the new job, Nick volunteered to put his programming experience to good use. With the help of his A2W Team Lead, he began creating reports that would monitor the testing of the custom applications the company was building on top of its SAP platform. This work leveraged two of Nick's strengths: the ability to see the big picture and the ability to break it down into individual steps. 'I got to learn SQL, which I didn't have much experience in,' says Nick, 'but, to me, programming is programming. Once you figure out how to think through a problem logically, you can easily translate it from one language to another.'

Over the next few weeks, Nick quickly learned the SQL programming language and the firm's application lifecycle management (ALM) software. 'Figuring out how to link the data is an interesting problem,' he says. 'Tests, test scripts and design steps are not stored together for technical reasons. So you have to pull the test scripts together and integrate that with all the information about requirements, bugs, and fixes related to the testing.'

And the results are clear. The company relies heavily on the reports Nick generates. Decision-makers use them for daily monitoring of user acceptance testing and execution and deferred defects progress as part of the SAP upgrade. 'Nick learned the ALM software in less than a month and now sends reports to global business managers twice a day without fail,' says CAI Director of Solution Delivery Madhu Chinnambeti. 'He is a true professional and has quickly become an expert in report building!'

Today, Nick is expanding his role, working to automate report generation so he can batch the scripts and run the reports at one time. Though his role has evolved into a distinct one, he is an integral part of the A2W team. 'It's nice knowing the A2W support is there,' he says. 'My bosses and managers are aware of both my strengths and my challenges. And it's a relief to have a job that offers fulfilling and challenging work.'

So what have we learned?

We have met so many talented people who have not had the same opportunity as Nick and as a result they are increasingly anxious and despondent about gaining a job. This leads to lost confidence and this can become the real barrier to enhancement. One person Amanda knows who finally gained a great job couldn't believe his success and thought it must be fluke or that he had been lucky rather than because he had the skills to do the job. A good work placement and guidance can be life-changing.

Nick's case is one example where the employer has taken a little time to understand the skills and perspective someone has, and how their talents can be best used. This very positive tale is one of success for Nick and for the company but it reminds us that a neurodiverse workforce delivers gains for all.

What to consider if setting up a neurodiversity placement or internship scheme

Start off creating a plan (see Figure 8.1)

- What is the programme and who is it aimed at? Is this in one department or across a business?

- How long is the supported internship programme for?

- Do you need partners to work with internally and externally? What expertise have you in-house or will you need professional expertise to help you, eg occupational psychology, workplace assessment or strategy coaching, specialist support organization?

- How much time, on average, will interns or placements spend in the workplace and where will that be? Is this remote working or at a fixed place of work, or a mix of the two, and what is the actual structure of a working week? Is this flexible and may it change over time?

- How will the interns/placements be selected? What criteria will you use? Are you going to be specific that this is people with autism for example, and if so will you require them to be diagnosed? (Do consider why you are choosing to do this and not considering a more neurodiverse grouping.)

- How will you decide the support needs for each intern?

- What will be your onboarding process and induction, especially if this is done remotely?

- How will you agree on forms of communication for different tasks?

- What learning or training will the people be expected to do while they are there and will there be coaching support for this?

FIGURE 8.1   Flow diagram for internship schemes

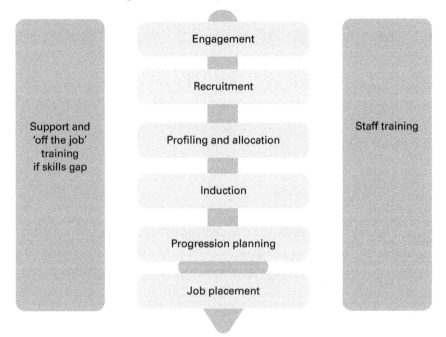

- How will your staff view the placement? What information and training will be given to them so they can provide appropriate support?
- What forms of ongoing support might interns need during their time with you and how will you meet those needs?
- What process is there for reviewing the progress of the intern?
- What processes will you put in place to consider what has worked well for future interns? It is useful this is captured during the placement and not at the end, as recall may be less accurate.

Considering your selection process

Engagement and recruitment

How do you want to recruit people if you want to attract neurodivergent talent? A two-page CV may not be the answer. The quality of the content can be influenced by the support that person has got to write it. A supportive parent or partner may be a copywriter or be in the industry the placement is in. How can you elicit the skills and motivation and interests in a way that isn't purely determined by whether someone can spell and format? Some people also have gaps in their CV that can be difficult to explain. After the tragic times of Covid-19 we will see many people with 'spotty' CVs and start /stop placements. We may also see some who have had to take a break relating to challenges with their mental health. We need to ensure we don't make assumptions.

Think about the skills you actually want

For example, if this is an entry-level job, formal qualifications may exclude bright and capable candidates who have had poor experiences of education or lack of opportunity to show what they can do. What you really want is someone enthusiastic, who has new ideas and is creative. If this is the case, you could ask for this to be described to you in different ways, eg a portfolio with examples, a video or audio presentation, or a series of photos.

One organization described how one person who had a severe stammer was so anxious they could not get through an interview. He was brilliant at DIY, and had helped his father build a brick BBQ and mend a wall. His attention to detail was fantastic. He created a film of himself mending another wall and sent this to one company who were looking for apprentices. They were so impressed they took him on because they could see his potential.

The important point is that in offering alternative ways of showcasing skills you open up the doors to more people who could have been missed altogether.

Create a checklist

- Essential qualifications required for the position that anyone needs to have to participate in the programme, eg someone may need to code in a specific computer language.
- Are you providing alternative ways for applications such as on the phone/ via portfolio? State a named contact if someone needs assistance and how to go about contacting them.

- A 'clean' description of what the internship/placement will entail, how long, and expected outcomes for the person, eg is there potential for a job at the end of it?

- Detailed information relating to the interview process, eg online, offline, interview panel, expectations, length of interview, when they will hear outcomes.

- Information easily available on how someone can gain help if they need adjustments for the interview.

- Information about the session, for example if it is going to be virtual – then what system will be used and could they do a test run before the day to check the software all works. (When you are already nervous about the interview having to download new software can be one step too many!)

Painting a day in the life of...

What's a day in the life of an intern like? This could be painted by someone who has already completed the internship. You could ask what they would have liked to have known at the start of their internship. Think about providing a peer mentor who they can call beforehand to check on any specific details, eg dress code, lunches, transport. You may also want to think about any cultural aspects to the organization that need to be understood or specific terms or acronyms that are used that would be helpful to know about.

Onboarding – making the first day a good one

From the point that the intern or placement has been told they have the place, this is the start of onboarding. There is a balance between giving too much information and not enough but clarity on what will happen during the first couple of weeks can make a real difference to reducing anxiety. Providing information on expectations from the line manager and the organization itself helps.

The person may lack confidence to ask and sometimes what seem small things to others may be important to that person. In some places a pre-visit to have a walk around to check out transport, toilets, café, see how people are dressed and just get a lay of the land can make a difference to a good first day. In times of virtual working this could be done virtually too! A low-pressure first induction day with some of the ground rules can help ensure confidence remains for day two. There will be some things that need to get sorted such as reading company documentation and if this is an organization using lots of acronyms then including a glossary of terms (make sure this is in an accessible format), any security elements such as use of passwords, email, internet, use of specific types of software tools. Obviously, this may depend on the type of work and work setting. What is always key is that the person knows where to go for help and how to do so.

In the placement

How will workplace adjustments be put in place for each intern in a timely manner? Will they have a work coach to support the person (in addition to the line manager)?

Introducing the person to the team and how everyone works together and communicates is helpful especially if this is remote working. We forget how much we pick up about people if we are in the same place as them. We see micro-gestures and movements that provide information. When you first start in a new place you may be reticent to ask for help. You usually look for clues when it seems OK to do so. Is your line manager looking so busy that it's hard to approach them or is it the right time because they are chatting to others? The challenge if you are working from home is that you don't have any clues to go on and so rules of engagement and communication need to be more explicit for both synchronous and asynchronous communication.

Synchronous communication is communication that happens in 'real time' – two or more parties are exchanging information in the same moment with one another. Synchronous communication can be in-person or virtual, scheduled or impromptu. People use different actions for different tasks and will have their own style. Agreeing this will reduce the potential for misunderstandings.

Some examples of synchronous communication methods:

- In-person meeting.
- Phone call.
- Video conferences (eg via tools like Zoom, Teams, GoToMeeting).
- Synchronous learning environments such as online programmes that use class time for group discussion.

- Asking a peer across the desk a quick question (the value of this is often forgotten when you are working remotely). A quick clarification can reduce mistakes being made resulting in a lot of effort but doing the wrong thing!

- 'Water cooler' conversations – again the value of this to gaining an understanding of workplace politics and what are the common ways for social interaction will be lost completely when working remotely. This is the micro-chatter and some of the gossip.

Asynchronous communication is any type of communication that includes a lag between when the party imparting the information sends the message, and when the party receiving the message interprets it. Asynchronous communication is generally not in person, and it's usually unscheduled (although there are exceptions, such as using an email marketing tool to schedule sending an email at a certain time).

Examples of asynchronous communication methods:

- Email.
- Letters or other direct mail.
- Project management tools.
- Company wikis and workspaces.
- Text messaging via mobile devices.
- Direct messaging (via tools like WhatsApp, Twitter or Facebook).
- Video messaging.

It is important that we distinguish in the organization how and when each approach is used (or not). Synchronous communication demands live interaction and is useful for someone building rapport, for example getting to know the person on the work placement and exploring their support needs. However, it is important to determine when and how that will happen and if it suits both parties. Critical and sensitive feedback is always better given in real time but may be assisted with notes afterwards to clarify any key points and next actions. The first induction meeting has to be live either in person or online.

KEY POINTS
Apprenticeships, internships, work placements and hiring schemes

- Some detailed planning can lead to successful life-changing work placements.

- Consider how you open the door to ensure you are providing opportunities for all and have inclusive practices in place that are person centred.

- Ensure your staff have adequate training and feel confident in having an open and ongoing conversation about providing support and the 'manager' also knows where to go if they need help.

- Check communication preferences and understanding of expectations.

- Review progress and ask apprentices and work placements for feedback.

Note

1   Department for Education (2014, revised in 2017) Supported internships https://assets.publishing.service.gov.uk/government/uploads/system/uploads/attachment_data/file/620920/Supported_Internship_Guidance_updated_with_EFA_funding_advice_May_2017_2.pdf (archived at https://perma.cc/8J58-82GU)

09

Interviews and assessments

Introduction

Interviews and assessments can be entrenched in archaic processes that were designed via outdated research and evidence and often can be kept the same for many years with little invigoration and specialization. Hiring managers often also lack the proper guidance and support, especially when it comes to neurodiversity and how to ensure we get the best from every individual who walks through the door to attend an interview.

Before a candidate even sits in the seat to begin the interview, they have often already faced so many hurdles designed to eliminate them from the process. They are lucky if the application process has offered anything more than a blanket tick box statement of: 'Do you have a disability?... Do you require a reasonable adjustment?...'. We still assume that most people know how to write a succinct two-page CV which describes their skills and how they apply them in the context of the job being applied for.

As we heard from Christos Tsaprounis at Autotrader UK in Chapter 6, candidates coming through the process who may be dyslexic or ADHD or... can be suspicious of oversharing at this early stage as they will be fearful the information could be used to discriminate against them, even when an organization has put every effort in place to ensure that is not the case.

Candidates are given very little opportunity for personalization or adaptations for the process, or to have tools at hand to help them have a great interview and a fair assessment process. As we digitize the process more and more, we can be at risk of potentially perpetuating outdated and discriminatory processes.

When a candidate does finally sit down, they could benefit from not having their interview in a fish bowl room with a chaotic workplace swirling about them. Small things can make a difference. Anxiety can make our mouths feel like the inside of a cardboard box. A glass of water to wet lips can be wonderful as it can not only allow a pause for thought but can allow you a means of cooling down too. We sometimes forget how it can make us feel and act when an interview room is too hot.

In the modern world of remote interviewing, a person could be sitting in their small bedroom in a shared house, or a one-room space which is a bedroom, workspace, and dining room/kitchen. To add to this could be an internet connection that belongs to the '90s. Either way we need to consider when designing interview processes other challenges that may be facing a person that are above and beyond the interview itself.

Alongside this is the interview team. The candidate may be faced with an interviewer or interview panel that lacks experience or support. What may be even worse is an overconfident panel who believe they have the ability to weed out the weak from the strong, and even in the 21st century still believe a firm handshake and/or good eye contact makes the difference to a successful interview!

If organizations do one thing it should be to simplify the essential criteria they use to assess and select their talent – what really matters in the role and how can a candidate demonstrate this skill/knowledge?

CASE STUDY
The interview from the perspective of a manager who identifies as on the autism spectrum

Hunter Hanson is a business analyst at one of the leading tech innovation companies in the world. He also shares highly engaging video diaries on the YouTube channel 'The Life Autistic'.

Hi, I'm Hunter. I'm here for the interview.

I've been 'here' a lot. On both sides of the table. Not at once.

I've been an interviewer and an interviewee many dozens of times. It's not remarkable. But as a mildly successful autistic professional, that combination of experience affords some unique and helpful perspective into what is often an intimidating and nerve-wracking process – even for neurotypicals!

As a one-time hiring manager and practised interviewer, here's my neurodivergent take on the process. From the interviewing standpoint as a hiring manager, I'm ultimately answering one burning question: 'Who is this person?'

That's right. Who. Are. You?

You'd expect that question to be 'Can they do the job?' That's fair.

But sometimes I know all my interviewees can do the job. Sometimes I'm looking for the right fit on my team. Or the right person to grow. Or a near-term successor. Or a challenger.

But I can't answer any of those without answering 'Who is this person?'

For a literal, autistic person, it can be jarring and surprising to hear and address questions that aren't really getting to 'the real question'. Since I'm giving you this heads-up, at least it won't be a surprise.

You have a key advantage: you know you better than I know you.

For those 'Tell me about a time' questions, I'm trying to answer for myself who you are by how you've reflected on your experiences, how you respond to situations, and what you learn from mistakes.

For the 'How would you' questions, you may not have had the experience, but I'll need to know you – enough to know I can lean on and support you in the work you'll do. Or if it's about a specific task, fact, or how something works – you are a sum of your knowledge. If you don't know how or what, are you the type who learns how and what?

That's what I'm after as an interviewer.

But I still interview for things here and there as well. It helps to stay fresh, test the waters, make some moves. Apparently I do well with this. Not despite my autism, sometimes because of it.

If you're interviewing for a job, a role, or a whatever, here's the one thing you NEED to get across: **You.**

Yeah, I know. I hate hearing 'be yourself' too. It feels like anti-advice. But when people see more of 'me' in an interview, then I want them to know who they're hiring, who they feel they're really getting. Who wants to be wanted for something they're not?

On a practical level, I have appreciated some of my traits. When I share stories for the 'tell me about a time' questions, my precision, memory, and enthusiasm can come through unbridled. When I prepare, I'm very good at sussing out many and too many possible scenarios to where I'm almost over analytically prepared – not surprisingly. I've masked through enough small talk to spin the conversational wheel and buy time before articulating an answer.

Either way on either side, it's a daunting experience. It doesn't have to be one that consistently leads to defeat.

Hunter raises some important points here and when we consider the individual in an interview, we ask a lot of them. Sometimes it can be confusing and other times it can just be overwhelming! We need to consider the evidence and unfortunately, as we are about to find out, the evidence in this area is a little old and potentially outdated, but sadly it's all we have to hang onto. It does, however, paint a picture of a process that is still even more outdated than the outdated evidence.

Who is the perfect candidate?

So surely the holy grail we are all after is the perfect candidate. The one who'll save our company from the evil empire, drive sales through the roof and be an ambassador for all things ambassadorial!

The perfect candidate!

Must have dark hair, brown eyes, handsome, good handshake, a conversationalist, Intelligent with a capital I, speaks the Queen's English and rises at 5 am every day to run a marathon before putting on their smile for the day ahead!

Really?

No such thing. Well, there might be, but we certainly wouldn't want a room or team full of them![1]

Dare we say it's just like there is no one perfect life partner. We could indeed find many people to share our lives with. We are sure Disney will have something to say about this with their Prince Charmings and pretty princesses! But in real life perfection is indeed a distraction from the reality of what we need and what will work. There is no perfect person, just as there is no average person.

It's the little idiosyncrasies and quirks that make us human and we should celebrate these differences whilst focusing on what we really need a person to deliver versus a false perception of what we need. One that has been drummed into us by the media, consumerism and false negatives.

This is the type of misinformation that insists boys fight with Action Men and think blue is cool and girls play mummy with dolls and love pink. And that love has to be gender specific, between a man and woman. It unfortunately feeds into everything we do and the way we think, including the way we interview and assess our candidates.

For example, a role that requires somebody to deliver exceptional customer service, doesn't necessarily require the candidate to be a great verbal communicator with the ability to 'talk the hind legs off a donkey' or to hold great eye contact with a smile like a Cheshire cat who's just stolen the cheese. They just need to demonstrate that they can offer exceptional customer service, which may manifest in many styles and variations of experience.

When Theo spoke with Anne Cockayne, a researcher in autism employment, she shared a story of a restaurant business she had encountered as part of her research. One of their restaurants needed somebody to stand front of house and welcome families in. Clearly, they required somebody personable, a social butterfly, great with eye contact and a good handshake.

So the last person you'd expect to select is somebody who may struggle with direct eye contact, may be introverted, may not like bright lights and noisy environments! Someone who is autistic would surely be a completely unsuitable selection; they are not going to be fantastic at customer service. There are loads of wild assumptions we can make about them because the media has done such a great job of telling us Autistic = severely mentally disabled.

In fact, that's exactly the opposite of what happened. An employee already working at the restaurant (who is autistic) wanted to take on the role. They worked in the kitchen, but had a special interest in animal balloon making and the manager saw an opportunity to utilize this talent as part of the role. Hence the individual stood at the front entrance to the restaurant welcoming guests with animal balloons, much to the delight of children and adults alike – brilliant customer service!

This employee was able to focus on something they loved doing as part of their role and the guests received a very personal and welcoming invite into the restaurant. Any Mum or Dad will know how important it is to keep the children happy when eating out. We think most will admit, first and foremost, that they want the kids to be happy. And we're sure a few romantic young couples going to the restaurant would also appreciate a heart-shaped balloon.

So what is important?

It is important when assessing the skills we require for a role that we don't get caught up in things that don't matter.

Customer service role = ability to deliver great customer service.

The key is to be hyper-focused on the few skills required to do the job and assess against them. You need to give the candidate every opportunity to SHOW how they would do the job.

Past performance can predict future behaviour, but too often those who have a range of neurodiverse skills have not been given the platform to work to their significant strengths and therefore carry a lot of anxiety and lack confidence in their abilities and what they have achieved. Even when they have been very successful, they may struggle to demonstrate it in a way most organizations will assess for it.

You'll also find that some people will have trouble remembering facts, figures and percentages, especially when they are anxious and have to respond in the here and now with no time to process the questions and plan a response. This may be despite having successful and positive experiences in past jobs. This hesitancy can give the interviewers the perception the candidate has poor memories or in fact didn't really deliver what they are sharing. In a heightened situation like an interview this can then impact on their confidence and as the interview goes on they start to make more errors or forget or confuse some details. Their confidence falls through the floor.

One person Amanda knows well prepares for days before an interview. He finds out more about the organization he is going to be interviewed with than the organization does. He has notes and more notes. The problem comes in the interview that he now has so much information he is worried about remembering it all, or thinking about what is the best response to the questions asked. Any question requires him to sift mentally through all this data and he gets himself increasingly panicked and then he doesn't get the job. This then results in a spiral of increased anxiety, sleeplessness and self-medication (with alcohol and sleeping tablets). This person is hugely talented but in an interview process his talents would be missed completely.

This example is not isolated and can actually impact anybody under the stressful false situation that is an interview. There is plenty of evidence to show us the poor state of the way we interview and assess, but for some reason we are struggling to recreate the crooked wheel.

While researching for the book, Theo spotted an article written by Mathea Kangas and John Vlastelica of Recruiting Toolbox: 'Validity of

Interviewing and Selection Methods'.[2] Now you may not immediately know who Recruiting Toolbox are, but you may know who John Vlastelica, their founder, is. He is one of the most engaging and knowledgeable influencers who takes to the stage at major recruitment and HR conferences on the subject of recruitment training.

Recruiting Toolbox has built custom interview training for startups and world-class brands, for thousands of hiring managers across 20+ countries. The article highlights the archaic nature of some of the processes, and does outline some hope and the fact that there are alternative options available to us to help bolster our interview and assessment processes. It also points out the need for an evidence-based approach, and that there is a science to interview and assessment.

We have not included the 'Validity Coefficients', which was part of the article, as we're in danger of sending the reader down rabbit holes. For the purpose of this book we want to give laser focus to the impact on those who are neurodiverse and how the current interview and assessment process might impact them.

In their article, Kangas and Vlastelica describe some important issues relating to the validity of interviewing and selection methods that need to be considered to reduce bias. We share a large extract from the article here to open up the debate.

CASE STUDY
Interviewing and selection methods

We want the best person for the job to get the job. Sounds easy, right? But you know that it's not that simple. We all have biases and assumptions about who will be best. The best person for the job might be someone without a fancy pedigree, or someone from a historically underrepresented group. They might not match the hiring team's idea of a perfect candidate (which is one reason why the ideal target candidate profile is a myth that needs to end). So, what's a hiring team that just wants to make the best decision (but is, like all teams, made up of biased humans) to do? In order to make the most informed hiring decisions to select the best talent, we turn to the help of science.

WHY ISN'T INTUITION ENOUGH?

Why does science come into this? Well, we tend to think we're good at knowing intuitively who the best candidate is. Turns out, we're often not great at predicting on-the-job success. We can be blind to our own biases, and that leads to suboptimal hiring decisions. And that can lead to discrimination (and missing out on good hires), lower-performing new hires, and even – potentially – lawsuits... all bad things.'

When hiring decisions are made primarily based on intuition and personal judgement, that leaves room for a whole party of biases and cognitive distortions. Scott Highhouse, an industrial-organizational psychologist, reviewed many studies on the effectiveness of hiring decisions, and found that people tend to overestimate their own ability to make good, intuitive decisions. He called this the 'myth of expertise'[3] – the belief that experienced professionals can make subjective hiring decisions that are more effective than those guided by impersonal selection methods. Actually, results from many studies show that more intuitive selection methods, like unstructured interviews, are less effective at informing good hiring decisions than more structured, rigorous methods, like work ability tests. It turns out that we make better hiring decisions when we trust the results of validated, research-supported assessment methods.

WHAT ARE 'VALID' SELECTION METHODS?

So, that prompts a question: what does 'validated' even mean? How does a validated selection method provide more useful decision-making evidence than just an unstructured interview? For our answer, we've got to go back to statistics class – just briefly, I promise!

To be considered good to use, a selection method needs to be both *reliable* and *valid*.

- *Reliability* refers to whether a selection method is consistent – for instance, if five people are interviewing a candidate using the same questions, would they rate the candidate similarly? If so, that's a reliable interview. Think of a dartboard – to be a reliable dart thrower, you want to hit the same spot every time.

- *Validity* refers to whether a selection method actually tells us anything about what we really care about: future job performance. Going back to that dartboard, what we really care about is hitting the bullseye. That's our target – just like a candidate's future job performance is the target in the hiring process.

Both reliability and validity are important – if you were a *reliable* dart thrower, hitting the same spot every time, but that spot was off to the side of the board, you're still not going to win many games! And, if you think about it, you can't have validity – hitting the target every time – without being consistent. So, leaving our imaginary dartboard and heading back to the world of recruiting, this all means that a validated selection method is one that researchers have shown to consistently provide useful information about a candidate's ability to perform in the job they've applied for.

Pretend you're in a team-based dart-throwing contest that you really want to win – if you can either partner with an unknown player who says they have a great instinct for throwing darts, or a world-champion player who consistently hits the bullseye every time, which person would you want on your team? Obviously, you'd choose the world-renowned player known to deliver results! (Okay, now we're putting the dartboard metaphor away, I promise.) The same thing is true in hiring – if you want to consistently hire world-class talent, you need to use selection methods that have been found to provide reliable, useful information about candidates' ability to do the job.

So what information and encouragement can we glean from this article in the context of neurodiversity?

Firstly, what is the sample that systems have been validated against? If you only trawl in the pond of goldfish you will never scoop up a sea bass! This can be a fundamental problem with some of the standardized tools as there is inherent bias. The words used in an interview or assessment process and how questions are asked can change the response, the meaning and interpretation. There is extensive research showing that women are less likely to 'brag' about their skills than men in an interview.[4] There may also be cultural biases where modesty in some societies is regarded as an appropriate behaviour and being part of the 'greater good'. We know far less about the behaviours of different neurodivergent candidates, some of whom may be more concerned about being honest about saying what they cannot do rather than selling what they can, especially if disclosure is being encouraged.

This is unsurprisingly complicated! We not only have to take the scientific evidence into consideration on the best approach to interview and assess a candidate. We also have to consider the impact that approach has on the individual in any given situation.

What's the environment like, and the conditions of the interview setting? Are there things like bright lighting, or is there a lack of good internet connection that could impede communication? Have accommodations/adjustments been considered to make sure that the interview and assessment are accessible to all beforehand?

It's not enough to say that one assessment over another will work for everybody if other conditions are not considered and catered for, and the stark reality is that often they are not.

We put all the candidates through the same proven assessment process; however, some are dolphins, some are rats, whilst others are birds! We may process candidates in a certain way so we can use the same marking grid but this will only be marking characteristics and traits in that setting and in reality have nothing to do with the job.

Appropriate training and development is essential for anyone conducting interviews to consider whether the interview and selection method has validity for the job. We recognize gender bias in terms of questions asked and the candidate response, and we need to consider this even more widely.

Too often we see organizations implement competency-style interviewing, but without good structure, poor interview questions can lack clarity and meaning, and don't have follow-up questions to allow more in-depth exploration. They can be too vague and ambiguous.

How many times have we seen this or sadly been involved in an interview like this?

- Interview only lasted 30 minutes (normally an hour).
- Interview questions seemed to have no relevance to the job.
- Candidates gave brief answers, because they could not fully understand the questions and didn't ask for clarification because of lack of confidence in doing so.
- Candidate's skills and experience on paper didn't translate to the interview.
- Candidate had a bad experience and didn't get an opportunity to share their full skills.
- Both the interviewer and the candidate feel dejected, impacting their confidence and interest in being involved in interviews in the future.

One predictor of job performance is probably a work sample test. From a neurodiversity perspective, it makes sense. As we discussed earlier in the chapter, the best way to know how well a dart-thrower can throw darts is to watch them throw darts; the best way to know how well a software engineer can write code is to ask them to complete a sample project. This works in jobs where you already have the skills but it can be harder to do if you are new to a job or apprenticeship and need to learn the skills along the way.

Structured interviews can be better at predicting job performance than unstructured interviews. Personality assessments can also provide useful information, but they aren't nearly as powerful as other tools and often have the problem of being developed on a neurotypical population. There is a challenge also that taking grades and years of education as a metric for skills can exclude those whose education may have been a bit bumpy. In reality, combining multiple selection methods can help provide a comprehensive picture of candidates' ability to perform well in the position you're hiring for.

There is some evidence of the challenges of using some assessments that have not been validated on a wider population, including those who are neurodivergent.[5]

Hiring diverse talent

If using psychometric assessments is the norm for neurotypical people, is this the right thing if you actually want to attract a neurodiverse talent pool? Is there a better approach? If we rely too much on one approach it will kick out a selection of people who may have actually been able to do the job.

The reality is that there is little research looking at what predicts job performance in truly neurodiverse populations. Too often we have relied on the 'culture fit', or a specific grade achieved at school, college or university, or intuition to make hiring decisions.

Work samples are a better way of assessing someone's capability to do a specific job than any of the other forms of assessment. It has what is called 'face validity'.

It therefore begs the question of why more organizations are not finding better ways to include this as part of the process. A key challenge is when there are a lot of applicants and a need to effectively manage this. We then often resort to a standard process that may keep excluding a specific demographic.

One of the challenges we face as a neurodiverse community is that we are not all created equally. For example, some people with ASD can often outperform their peers when it comes to completing some technology tests, but they may struggle with group-based exercises presented in an unfamiliar setting. How can we make sure we offer variation and allow our assessors to comfortably gain the information they need to make fair decisions, but also equally allow an individual to showcase their skills in a way that suits them?

This is where often we fall down. Jen (who is ASD) scores 9/10 on the test, but scores 5/10 on the group exercise. Kelly scores 7/10 on the test and 7/10 on the group exercise. Who gets the job? We need to move from 'culture fit' to 'culture add'.

> **Culture add** is a term that is now starting to be widely used to describe people who not only value a company's standards, workplace culture, values and purpose, but also bring an aspect of diversity that positively contributes to an organization.[6]
>
> Whereas **culture fit** has received some negativity towards its use, seeing if people fit into the current set of boxes, which can end up creating 'like for like' hires and ultimately an organization and teams that can suffer from groupthink and a very one-dimensional environment.

So Kelly gets the job, and all of a sudden we have five Kellys who are all really good all-rounders and perfect for the team. They all get on together from day one and agree with each other's ideas. But are we missing that individual who can crack the code and look at what can be done and achieved from a different perspective? The team may continue to perform well enough, so we would never question their performance, but just imagine if we had added a Jen to the mix.

Who would you rather have in your team – the person who will fill the gaps in your knowledge and expertise and offer new solutions, or the person who would make the same decisions as you and reinforce your viewpoint?

John Vlastelica from Recruiting Toolbox goes some way to combat this. 'In our interview training, we teach recruiters or decision facilitators to ask the hiring manager and her interviewing team these related questions: "What will this person ADD to our team? How will they complement the capabilities and insights we already have on our team, to make us better, to help us better reflect the diversity of our customers?"'

Sure, it feels nice to have somebody agree with your perspective, but without these perspectives being challenged and put through the wash, we are in danger of not progressing at the speed the world now demands of us.

It is also often harder as a manager to lead a more diverse team; however, the ultimate rewards are much greater. It's like an athlete who has worked hard on every part of their training and finely tuned each muscle in their body. It takes more work, but the outputs are greater. You can't have a football team with only attackers and no defenders.

We therefore need managers and organizations who are willing to challenge the status quo, and until we really look at our interview and assessment processes, very little will change. This needs to start right at the beginning with the application process and the job descriptions themselves.

Work sampling or even work visits can provide opportunities for a more neurodiverse workforce to see and try out the type of setting they may end up in and what works best for them. This is especially useful when we consider entry-level roles where a traditional interview fails, either in a structured or unstructured format. It creates a real-world situation where you can see how the person gets on in the role.

To go back to the animal balloon maker, the best way to see the impact they make would be to test it out in real life, allowing them to show their skills and how it positively impacted on the customer, creating an amazing customer experience. This is often easier when this person is already an employee, because you can put them on a trial fairly quickly and retain their other position if it doesn't work out. However, it becomes a greater challenge if you're assessing skills during an interview process and the applicants don't currently work for you. If you are then unable to offer work samples or placements or direct work-related experience, it becomes necessary to utilize a variety of assessment touchpoints.

Employers will need to find a balance between the need for variety and giving individuals every opportunity to showcase their skills without over-burdening the process and creating too many barriers to entry.

Sometimes we end up going the other way, making it so lengthy and complex that only the most robust survive the process. This can end up being a five-stage process with three tests, a psychometric test/assessment, and then a 'meet the team', followed by a one-to-one with a manager… before an offer is even considered!

So choose wisely. Try to consider offering a variety of options to attract all talent rather than throwing the lot in and not really being able to pool the results and draw robust conclusions. Try gaining feedback during and after the process and from those in your workforce. If you're open and honest in what you're trying to achieve, you will attract a range of neurodiverse candidates and others will be more likely to provide the feedback that can help you further enhance the process so that it can be improved for all.

Remember to also ask what adjustments people may need so they feel able to show and communicate their talents.

Assessments and skill tests

When considering organizing assessments, start by thinking whether you are actually testing a skill that is essential and relevant to the job and does not put the person with a disability at a disadvantage because of specific challenges they have. This is important from a legal perspective as an employer.

For example, would you expect someone with dyslexia to write something in 20 minutes in their actual job with no access to a grammar or spell-checker? Would they not have time to review their response before sending it to you? What would be the typical processes in the job itself? Have you provided reasonable time for the assessment or are you actually testing speed over accuracy? Some people may also need to have the context of why this is needed and how the information will be used, and then can do a great job.

Have you told the candidate what assessments will take place so they know what adjustments to ask for? Have you provided sufficient information? Do you know how to make adjustments to any assessment process?

Keep thinking about what you are testing for and this goes back to checking the accuracy of the job description.

Examples of adjustments could be (but need to be determined for each person):

- placing someone in a different room away from noise from others;
- a verbal rather than written assessment or vice versa;
- alternative format of assessment such as avoiding the use of 'Situational Judgement Tests' in some situations;
- use of IT accessibility tools such as text-to-speech or speech-to-text software instead of expecting handwritten responses;
- ability to change font, colour of on-screen work;
- presentation of information on paper of a certain colour;
- hardware such as a larger screen;
- rest breaks between tasks;
- one-to-one and not group interviews.

Check your internal dialogue too!

Be honest with yourself. How do you feel when someone is asking for more time, or a separate room, access to a grammar or spellchecker? What is going on in your head? Are you reluctant or think it's a bit of a pain to organize?

Very rarely do we mean 'take your time' when we say it; it's one of those strange things we have just become accustomed to saying. Very much like with reasonable adjustments, often we don't really think they are reasonable. The additional time needs to be built into the process and easy for the person to access. If someone really does need more time, help or additional support, we can fail them by making it difficult to request and access. Think about if it was your relative or a close friend who was asking for an adjustment and you knew they could do the job so well!

The future of assessments

The way we assess candidates has the potential to change significantly in the coming years. With advances in digital technology, gamification and use of artificial intelligence and all other kinds of weird, scary and wonderful tools, this really could be the time where we drop the old and bring in the shiny and new.

But we do need to be cognizant of the fact that if we keep designing the new, fashioned from the old, we are in danger of just digitizing a system and process that is already problematic and discriminatory for many.

We interviewed Bas van de Haterd on what the current assessment landscape looks like and what we can consider for the future. Bas is an independent expert on modern (pre) selection tooling. He helps organizations select and calibrate the best selection tools.

Bas had this to say: 'In the past years we've seen a great number of new assessment technologies emerge that can be easily applied on a massive scale. Because of enormous amounts of data and ever-increasing computational power many years of academic research can now be validated and refined. For example, the academic research on linguistic analyses started after the Vietnam War, but only because of the data provided by social media and the technology of machine learning was a viable and working product able to be created. And of course this is when the fine-tuning and improvements begin and it's still very early days for this technology.

'Although questionnaires are usually considered the most reliable and scientifically valid method, they have two main flaws. First of all they can be easily manipulated. The other flaw has to do with reference. For example, HR people who ask questions about using data to support decision making, will most likely describe themselves as very analytical. Accounting department employees might consider this so common that they would actually rate themselves less analytical, as they compare themselves to their very analytical peers.

'Currently, game-based assessments are the most mature of all new technologies, with the greatest scientific validation. Yet they are still in their adolescence.'

Another challenge is how the tools have been constructed and the populations they have been tested on. From a neurodiverse perspective, just like with any single form of assessment there are some who like gamified assessments and those that don't. Often they are impacted, like many assessments, by how they are framed and presented and the opportunity to experience them beforehand. Clarity of how the data and information will be interpreted and what will be assessed is often lacking.

We dream of a day when a candidate will be able to select between a multitude of assessments that all provide the information and validation required as part of the process but in a way that suits the candidate rather than the budget or expertise of the company conducting the interviews. Maybe we will see Virtual Reality Scenarios which allow us to test competencies and actually train people in the tasks as well.

However, with every new form of assessment we need to consider if it is a fit for everyone and it is unlikely to be so. The trend towards gamification of psychometric tests doesn't necessarily make things easier either for everyone. Between the need to both read and interpret the questions, and understand the expectations of the task, alongside managing anxiety in completing the 'game', and have the digital skills to do so, some candidates can perform poorly in these tests but this doesn't necessarily translate directly to the workplace. The virtual test demands may be greater than reality.

The key will be focusing on the key skills and empowering the individual to show them in an environment that they feel comfortable in. The future could be anything from building and designing Lego buildings, or creating a working world in Minecraft, to answering technical questions or showing how you can solve real-world problems.

It's no secret that GCHQ have been known for their interest in those who think differently for some time, and they take a fun approach to creating challenges that are open to many, to not-so-secretly find the few who could make the cut as the next 007 agent![7]

The Dutch military are also looking at actual game behaviour in games like Minecraft and League of Legends to predict potential fit for military jobs. There are also experiments with this technology within the social services. In the future your gaming data could be the key to your next role!

But don't worry all you 'non-gamers', you could just give up a hair follicle as your CV instead. Bas goes on to say: 'On the other end of the spectrum are DNA assessments and brain scans. Both have been in development for some years and, in the case of DNA, there is even a supplier offering an assessment based on an individual's DNA. This is all very new and we know so little about what specific DNA markers actually mean and how our brains technically work that no company would even think about using this technology now or in the near future. That does not mean the technology isn't there and the scientific progress isn't happening. Before we actually start using this in business I would hope clear rules are established regarding privacy, data security, and disposal of the samples.'[8]

Amanda thinks the new and exciting recruitment tools will require advancements in machine learning and artificial intelligence to ensure they don't exclude specific groups of people. During Covid-19 we have seen those with learning challenges and who are living in poverty doubly disadvantaged.

New forms of digital assessment will of course disadvantage those who lack digital skills, or if they have to record their responses this will be problematic for those with indistinct speech patterns. If you need to use a keyboard for entry or if it is a reaction time test this may be challenging for someone with poor motor skills such as those with dyspraxia, for example.

The system may be assessing some of the skills or attributes required for a job but some talents that could compensate may be being missed altogether such as empathy, persistence, kindness. We also know that some people with dyspraxia are able to learn and automate skills with adequate practice and training. The challenge is often when this is a novel or unfamiliar skill.

In addition, speech-to-text software can still not recognize some accents and would have difficulties filtering in or out words someone was saying with a stammer or stutter. Humans can also interpret the semantics, nuance and context of what has been spoken and this is yet to be achieved online. Hesitancy or pauses could also be misinterpreted or scored wrongly.

The reality is that AI is based on the data you have and we need to ensure the samples are not biased in the first place and represent a truly neurodiverse population. The real question is are we wanting to recruit the average person? If this is the case then neurodivergent people will of course always miss out!

Bas finally goes on to say: 'Currently the most important and most validated modern forms of assessments are game-based assessments. By this

I mean games, developed in academia, that measure how you play them and are able to derive both cognitive qualities as well as psychometric traits. This can be anything from reaction speed, anticipation, being able to switch tasks quickly, to risk taking and persistence. Depending on the job at hand these traits can either matter or not. The major problem in matching currently isn't measuring the abilities of a person anymore, but matching them to the skills needed to perform in a job as for most jobs we have educated guesses at best.'

What's the reality?

The reality is that there are often multiple ways to excel in a job. We need to be able to have better processes for 'mapping' the different ways onc can excel in a job as this would greatly help to recruit neurodiverse candidates. A one-size dichotomous approach to hiring often excludes those with certain traits that might not even matter that much, or alternatively can be made up with other traits they actually excel in.

Another aspect of digital assessments that would help neurodiverse candidates is tools that can accurately showcase the degree of talent and ability someone has.

The first reason has to do with relativity. Remember *Good Will Hunting*? When Robin Williams and Stellan Skarsgård, the professor that won the Field's medal, were in the bar and Stellan said, 'There are maybe three or four people in the world that can actually see the difference between us, that know you are so much smarter than I am? That's because if some people are so much smarter in a specific area than you are, you can't tell the difference between someone who is four times as good at maths and somcone who is six times as good. Both are so far out of your capacity that you don't see the difference.'

When we consider the strengths and skills of those who are neurodiverse and the fact they may demonstrate very spiky profiles, if we are measuring all candidates on a scale of 1–10 on five cognitive skills but one candidate has the potential to go off the chart on two of those skills areas, the comparison has not been a fair one and the generalist will keep winning the day.

A second important point made is about inaccuracy in our estimation of our abilities. This may be over- or underestimated and can vary by gender, culture and experience.

Digital assessment technology may reduce bias in some ways but may introduce it in others. Digital poverty is a real thing and not all jobs require digital skills. Inclusion has to be considered at the time of design and not as an afterthought. Ultimately organizations need to be more open minded to looking at candidates' strengths rather than their defined weaknesses.

When we consider the performance of a Formula One racing car, we don't say, 'Wow it uses a lot of petrol; is very expensive to repair; it doesn't even have a roof or a SATNav/multimedia system.' We say, 'Wow, that's super-lightweight, with incredible driver safety, and incredibly fast, perfectly built for what we need it to do.'

Context is everything, and if we build assessment the right way, laser focused on the key cognitive skills we require, then we give ourselves the best opportunity to build high-performing diverse teams with complementary skills and experiences.

How 'game based' assessments are widening the talent pool[9]

Air traffic controllers

Air traffic control agencies in Europe have been using pre-screening assessments for several years now. One of the most important traits of an air traffic controller is, unsurprisingly, resilience to stressful situations. The main difference between a good and a great air traffic controller is being able to keep track of all the planes during high levels of stress, without becoming distracted. These traits have successfully been tested with game-based assessments, with no correlation to levels of education.[10]

In the past this was of course tested during the selection process, but the dropout rate during training was fairly high. After implementing pre-selection testing based on only the cognitive traits that are relevant for the job, the dropout rates in training significantly decreased.

Another key benefit to this approach is that air traffic control agencies have been able to open up their selection, not just to university or college graduates, but everybody with a high school diploma. As it turns out, you don't need a university degree to be an air traffic controller, but just need to be able to learn a detailed manual. A high school diploma is still a prerequisite, as some learning of theory is involved and this skills marker has proven successful at a high conversion rate. This has opened up the job for many more people, who may not have gone onto further education, but do have the qualities to be good at the job.[11]

Finally, Adam Grant, an award-winning occupational psychologist, in his latest book *Think Again* talks about the need to rethink the way we do things.[12] He also describes many of us as 'cognitively lazy' in the way we often favour continuing to do what we feel comfortable doing. One thing that struck a chord in his words was that in order for us to rethink the world we live in and how we recruit in the future we need to admit our failures and then truly reimagine our tools to truly recruit neurodiverse talent in the 21st century.

KEY POINTS
Interviews and assessments

- Ensure there is detailed information beforehand for the candidate about the setting and the interview process including time, place and length.

- If using activities/tests/group interactions describe what these will be.

- Ensure that if they ask for adjustments you know what you can offer.

- Train the interview panel in how to consider what their biases may be and to reduce unconscious bias.

- Consider tools you use and if they are selecting out talents rather than recruiting a neurodiverse team.

Notes

1 Vlastelica, J (2020) Why it's Time to End the 'Ideal Candidate Profile' [Blog] LinkedIn Talent Blog, 15 July, https://business.linkedin.com/talent-solutions/blog/recruiting-strategy/2020/time-to-end-ideal-target-candidate-profile (archived at https://perma.cc/2M3Q-8SDP)

2 Kangas, M (2020) Validity of interviewing and selection methods [Blog] *Recruiting Toolbox*, https://recruitingtoolbox.com/validity-of-interviewing-and-selection-methods/ (archived at https://perma.cc/U6M4-VDLB)

3 Highhouse, S (2008) Stubborn reliance on intuition and subjectivity in employee selection, *Industrial and Organizational Psychology*, https://onlinelibrary.wiley.com/doi/abs/10.1111/j.1754-9434.2008.00058.x (archived at https://perma.cc/R9QK-RM4B)

4 Smith, J and Huntoon, M (2013) Women's bragging rights overcoming modesty norms to facilitate women's self-promotion, *Psychology of Women*

Quarterly, https://scholarworks.montana.edu/xmlui/bitstream/handle/1/9028/ SmithJ_PWQ_dec14POSTPRINT_A1b.pdf;sequence=1 (archived at https://perma.cc/8KUX-TUUE)

5 Miciak, J *et al* (2015) The effect of achievement test selection on identification of learning disabilities within a patterns of strengths and weaknesses framework, *School Psychology Quarterly*, https://pubmed.ncbi.nlm.nih.gov/ 25243467/ (archived at https://perma.cc/AJN8-3ZQH)

6 LinkedIn, Talent Solutions (nd) How to assess for culture add, https://business. linkedin.com/talent-solutions/resources/interviewing-talent/how-to-assess- skills/culture-add (archived at https://perma.cc/WBN3-NXBL)

7 GCHQ (nd) Puzzles, https://www.gchq.gov.uk/section/news/puzzles (archived at https://perma.cc/8JGF-4HTJ)

8 Plomin, R (2019) *Blueprint: How DNA makes us who we are*, Penguin, London

9 Assessment Day (nd) Gamified assessments, https://www.assessmentday.co.uk/ gamified-assessments.htm (archived at https://perma.cc/7X49-KGES)

10 Smy, P *et al* (2020) Training air traffic controllers through digital mobile applications versus traditional methods, Proceedings of the 14th International Conference on Game Based Learning, https://rke.abertay.ac.uk/ws/portalfiles/ portal/30891640/Donald_TrainingAirTrafficControllers_Published_2020_2_.pdf (archived at https://perma.cc/K7A6-FLAL)

11 NATS Air Traffic Controller (2021) NATS Air traffic controller aptitude tests preparation, https://www.jobtestprep.co.uk/nats-air-traffic-controller (archived at https://perma.cc/4RC6-W9P4)

12 Grant, A (2021) *Think Again: The power of knowing what you don't know*, WH Allen, London

10

Making workplace adjustments

Introduction

In order to make adjustments we need to think about why we need to do so and consider the context, such as the specific job or tasks needing to be undertaken. We also need to consider the differences between equity and equality.

Why do we want to know about the difference between equality and equity? It is important to consider what we want. Is it doing the same thing for everyone or supporting each person according to need?

What is equality?

Equality is about ensuring that every individual has an equal opportunity to make the most of their lives and talents. It is also the belief that no one should have poorer life chances because of the way they were born, where they come from, what they believe, or whether they have a disability. Equality recognizes that historically certain groups of people with protected characteristics such as race, disability, sex and sexual orientation have experienced discrimination.[1]

What is equity?

Equity is about giving people what they need, in order to make things fair.[2]

In this chapter we will explore workplace adjustments, with some good examples of what type of adjustments can be made. The reality is that every single person may have slightly different needs, and this may be dependent on the work setting they are in, but broadly, often adjustments can benefit the many, not just the few.

For example, designing something for someone with only one arm may seem like it's not something you'll be asked for very often. But let's consider the wider impact of an adjustment for somebody with one arm to a piece of technology or to an events space or workspace. It could also benefit a parent who's holding their baby in one arm – why should they be excluded from attending events and using tech? It can also benefit the many people who only have limited use of an arm, due to a stroke or cerebral palsy for example, or due to a short- to medium-term injury like a fracture or a tennis elbow.

If when considering requests that seem in the extreme we could broaden our thinking to how it can have a wider positive impact, then the adaptations stop becoming a challenge and become an opportunity for innovation and inclusion!

We'll also share with you examples of adjustments, so if nothing else you can prepare yourselves for the type of adjustments that you could put in place. Theo was approached at a Manchester TRU UnConference (recruitment conference) in the UK and was asked by a head of recruitment of a leading UK tech company: 'A candidate has asked if their Mum can join the telephone interview for support as they have disclosed they are autistic. What's your advice on how I should approach it?'

Which was brilliant! Brilliant because this head of recruitment was thrown by the request as it was unusual, but wanted to do the right thing and approach it in the right way. So the advice that was given to him was that this is a perfectly reasonable request:

- the candidate is autistic, has disclosed this and is seeking support;
- this could be their first interview;
- interviews are not normal situations, so there is often heightened anxiety involved;
- their mum may help them interpret some of the questions and inform the interviewer to rephrase them, but most of all she is there as a support mechanism to help get the most out of the situation.

Ultimately what do we want from any interview process? An opportunity for a candidate to demonstrate their skills and abilities so that the interviewer can assess whether they fit the needs of the organization and the job. That's recruitment 101!

The feedback after the interview from the head of recruitment was that the telephone interview went well and they were glad they approached it with an open mind.

Some adjustments may seem unusual or scary, but we need to try and think of it from the candidate's perspective rather than just from our own. It's often too easy to see requests or adjustments as a pain in the process. So we will also give you some further information in this chapter on who actually determines if it is 'reasonable' and whose responsibility it is for making the adjustments. Of course we'll also give you some hints and tips on how to get started.

What are workplace adjustments?

Awareness of putting in workplace adjustments (often described as 'reasonable adjustments') is variable and may be seen by some as a privilege and not a necessity or a right. For some, an adjustment is the means to working or not. Someone who is visually impaired who doesn't have accessibility tools such as a screen reader cannot access information online for example. A person with coordination challenges can't take notes in a meeting if their handwriting is illegible to them and others. Neither person may be lacking the competency to do a job but will need adjustments in order to do it. Delay can have an impact. Many people needing workplace adjustments can face long waits for these to be put in place, and this can significantly damage their own and corporate productivity. It can also impact on the person's confidence.

Disclosing a disability is an individual decision, and there is no obligation on anybody to do so. Not everyone has obvious (to others) challenges and these may also vary from setting to setting. Legislation in the UK is in place under the Equality Act 2010 to assist and protect a person with a disability in employment or seeking work, but in many cases the protection and assistance that legislation offers is dependent on the individual disclosing their disability.[3]

There are many reasons why disclosing a disability to a potential employer is a positive action that will empower, protect and assist the person in the workplace. However, for some, past experiences of doing so may not have gone so well and resulted in negative comments or changes in attitudes by others.

A '**reasonable adjustment**' is a change to remove or reduce the effect of an employee's disability so they can do their job. In the UK this is embedded in the Equality Act 2010, where legislation exists to help and protect those who choose to disclose. Under the Act an employer has a legal duty to make 'reasonable adjustments' for both job applicants and current employees who disclose a disability.

Reasonable adjustments may relate to working arrangements or any physical aspect of the workplace. In the Equality Act they are described as 'provisions, criteria and practices', 'physical features' and 'provision of auxiliary aids'.

Examples of adjustments are:

- **A change in working patterns** – for example delegating some duties to another employee or allowing that person to be absent during working hours to attend treatment or rehabilitation. Another example of this may be providing flexible start and finish times for someone who is very anxious travelling at peak times on public transport.

- **Having extra equipment to enable the employee to carry out duties,** such as the use of specialist computer software. An example of this is providing someone with handwriting difficulties with speech-to-text software or an audio recorder to record their ideas or take down information in a meeting.

- **Physical changes to the working area** in order for a person to access and carry out their work easily and safely, such as providing a ramp or increased space to work. Another example could be providing a person with dyspraxia or cerebral palsy with a specific chair or a desk that can have the height altered so they can sit or stand in a stable position.

- **Adaptation to processes may need to be undertaken.** An example of this could be a candidate with spelling difficulties (this could be related to dyslexia) applying for a job and the potential employer requiring them to do a written task as a part of the interview process. This person could have an adjustment made to use a spellchecker and also be given more time to complete the task.

In the workplace one great change that has benefited most of us has to be the introduction of the computer. Okay, technically this is not an adjustment but more of a complete technological transformation but it provides huge opportunities for adjustment to an individual's needs. Through the pandemic of Covid-19, technologies have been used in different ways because of immediate needs (for example flipped workplaces and virtual meetings) and then translated on a mass scale. We can only wonder how many people have benefited from having access to a computer to complete their work, but on the other hand there are challenges for those without this. We have seen the changing work setting and how this has improved working practices for many by allowing them to work from home and construct the environment that works for them. Access to assistive technology in different formats, such as text-to-speech software (hearing what is written), speech-to-text software (recording your thoughts and ideas) and organizational tools, has had a huge impact for many people. It's amazing to think of the time when we didn't communicate via text or email or even have video conferencing in the way that has become mainstream for many of us in work.

We don't want to trivialize in any way what 'reasonable adjustments' are and what they mean to someone in gaining and sustaining a job. Clearly for some it is the difference between them being able to access the building or not, or completing a task, or participating in a conversation with others. That's why it is so important in the way we design our systems, processes and environments with inclusivity in mind.

We can see just how quickly change can be implemented when we want to. Imagine the technological advances to come that we've never dreamed of and how they will transform where we work, how we work and why we work.

Who determines it is reasonable?

This is a big question. Various factors influence whether a particular adjustment is considered reasonable. The test of what is reasonable is ultimately an objective one and not simply a matter of what you may personally think is reasonable.

When deciding whether an adjustment is reasonable you can consider:

- how effective the change will be in avoiding the disadvantage a disabled worker would otherwise experience;
- the practicality of implementing it;
- the cost;

- your organization's resources and size; for example, if you are a small organization the change to a building or implementation of some adjustments may not be possible;
- the availability of financial support.

> Remember always that the overall aim should be, as far as possible, to remove or reduce any disadvantage faced by a disabled worker.

Whose responsibility is it to make the adjustments?

It is the responsibility of the employers. However, in the UK, there is a government scheme called Access to Work that can help with extra costs which would not be reasonable for an employer or prospective employer to pay. The level of support can be dependent on the size of the organization. Support is based on the needs of each individual. The grant may include in some cases help to cover the costs of travel to and from work or practical support in the workplace. It can include interpreters, equipment or software, a support worker and even include disability awareness training for colleagues. A person may be able to get advice and support from Access to Work if they are:[4]

- in a paid job;
- unemployed and about to start a job;
- unemployed and about to start a Work Trial;
- self-employed;
- AND if their disability or health condition stops them from being able to do parts of their job.

Getting started

Start with the view that support tools don't have to be complex or expensive and often a positive can-do attitude is a big part of successful implementation. An adjustment could be extra time given for a test or exam, so that the person can read at their usual pace, which may be slower than the average reader. It could be about adjustments to the ways you and colleagues agree to communicate or about times and places where you work.

For example, Theo finds being provided with the questions to a competency-based interview beforehand allows him to have greater focus on expressing the answers so that his brain can have time to consider the questions. It's a small adjustment that could have a huge impact on the success of the candidate in showing the talent they have.

Another adjustment in an interview setting could be allowing a person to be given the opportunity to follow up their interview with a short written statement to cover any points that may have lacked clarity. This can ensure the candidate has a fair opportunity to show their skills and capabilities. Reflection after the event can be really useful for some people but is not often allowed.

The above are two examples used at NICE (National Institute for Health and Care Excellence), a UK organization, that are focused around the individual at the point of need.[5] Having an open approach to providing support and making this easily available can mean a huge amount to someone wanting to apply to an organization.

Words are important

Be mindful when it comes to your words. A string of some that don't mean much to you, may stick with someone else for a lifetime.[6]

RACHEL WOLCHIN

The words you use and how you demonstrate as an organization that you provide support are very important. It's all good and well offering a statement at the beginning of the process saying 'We are happy to offer reasonable adjustments' versus making sure that at each stage you explain how your organization is one that is open to adapting this part of the process to meet individual needs.

It's amazing how quickly candidates and employees respond to the latter approach of a positive message. Do remember that most requests are reasonable and not costly and can help both the candidate and the hiring managers have a better overall experience.

Adjustments are not about specific conditions and sometimes this is where mistakes are made. There can be a fixed view that dyslexic people need X and dyspraxic people need Y, and while there may be some common ground to consider as a starting point for a conversation, each person will be different and dependent on the tasks being asked of them. Importantly, adjustments will need to be reviewed if changes to tasks happen or the work setting changes (see Figure 10.1).

FIGURE 10.1   Aspects to consider for best outcomes

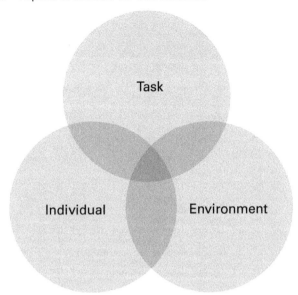

SOURCE Kirby, 2021, www.doitprofiler.com

Taking a person-centred approach

What do we mean by 'person-centred'?

'Person-centred' is an outlook or philosophy that (as you might have guessed) puts the person at the centre of all plans, discussions and interventions. This is in contrast to a traditional model where the focus is on a disease or health condition.

A biopsychosocial approach

A person-centred approach is often seen as a **biopsychosocial** one, taking into account all aspects of a person – their body (bio-), mind (psycho-) and their environment (social) and the ways these interact – and considering how best to support the learner (see Figure 10.2).

The biopsychosocial model states that 'health' and 'wellbeing' depend not only on the biology of illness but on **the whole person** (body and mind) **and their social environment** (family, friends, socioeconomic background, etc). To ensure good health, you need to look at the whole person and their

FIGURE 10.2   Biopsychosocial model

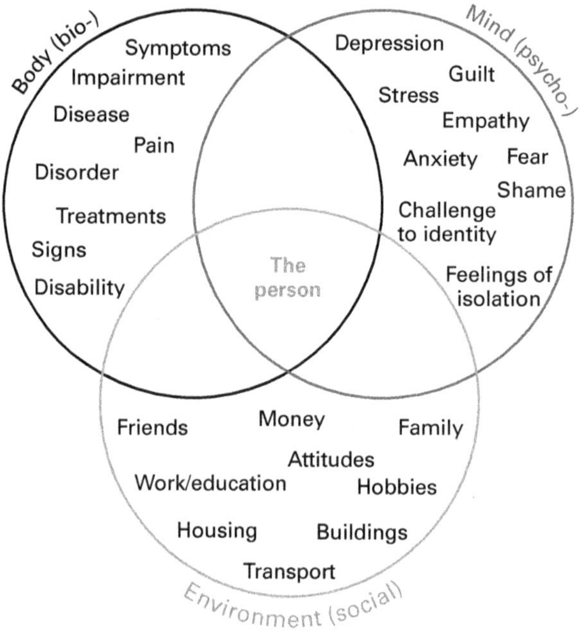

Body (bio-)

Symptoms
Impairment
Disease
Pain
Disorder
Treatments
Signs
Disability

The person

Depression
Guilt
Stress
Empathy
Anxiety   Fear
Shame
Challenge to identity
Feelings of isolation

Mind (psycho-)

Friends   Money   Family
Attitudes
Work/education   Hobbies
Housing   Buildings
Transport

Environment (social)

SOURCE Kirby, 2021, www.doitprofiler.com

environment. It aligns to the World Health Organization's International Classification of Functioning of Disability and Health approach (ICF).[7]

For example, one person's cognitive profile might cause them to struggle with maths. They may therefore think themselves 'stupid' and have low mood, which affects their work and social life. To improve the wellbeing of this person, their underlying poor maths skills and maths anxiety need to be considered. Simply treating the anxiety alone would not necessarily be effective.

Some adjustments to get started

This chapter provides guidance that is not related to one condition or another but is about individual people and finding solutions and strategies that can allow them to participate and appropriately support each person. It would be lengthy to list every adjustment that can possibly be given because the environment and job that someone is doing can determine the specific adjustment. For example, a dental nurse and a bus driver do different tasks every day, but we want to just show you some more common approaches as a starting point. However, the best adjustments are those that are considered in the context of the individual, the tasks they are doing and the environment they are working in, and are also reviewed on a regular basis.

Think about different aspects of support and where and when they may need to be provided. The ideal process is to make anticipatory adjustments so that there are inclusive processes already in place. This means the need for specific adjustments is lessened and someone doesn't have to disclose a challenge unless they feel comfortable doing so.

Starting in a new work setting

A good induction meeting provides the opportunity to check if there are any specific adjustments that need to be put into place. Remember you don't have to be an expert in everyone's medical conditions (you are not a doctor – unless you are one!):

- Ask the person if they have any specific challenges or support needs that need to be addressed.
- Discuss if they wish to tell anyone else and how they wish this to be done.
- Discuss what has helped in other settings or workplaces.
- Describe the potential work setting as much as possible. Unpack the job description, and be as explicit as possible. You may want to use timeframes such as in the first month it is expected you will do X, especially if there is on-job training.
- If there are 'rules' in the workplace then describe these, such as dress code (including 'dress down' days and what this means to your organization). Provide specific expectations such as what people do at break/lunchtimes.
- If there is a 'language of the workplace' provide specific terms, phrases or acronyms that are used in the organization (a glossary of terms could be put on the intranet for everyone to access).
- Ensure the person knows who to speak to if there are specific challenges.
- Set up regular and short review meetings so if challenges are arising, they can be quickly addressed.

Generic principles

A long list of strategies can seem unwieldy, but these are being provided to help as a starter for ideas, as small changes that are specific to the person can have a big impact. Every organization and work setting is different and so this is not an exhaustive list of adjustments.

It is sometimes useful to take a 'whole day' approach to making adjustments so that all aspects are considered. This could extend to a whole week if the person works from home some days, or has meetings out of the office or in a specific work setting on others, as different strategies may need to be considered across the week.

Arriving at work

- Information for all employees about travel options to and from work may be impossible to provide but any help to know where to come or what public transport is around may be helpful for all new employees. Some larger organizations set up carpools to share car journeys together and information relating to this is useful too.

- Some people may be very concerned about where they may park each day, which can result in increased anxiety, and it may be reasonable to provide a parking space for some people. There have been employment tribunal cases in the UK where this has not been provided despite a person having a specific health need. It is always worth remembering that if a policy is put in place and staff don't know about it, then this cannot be used as an excuse for failing to make the adjustment (if it is deemed as reasonable).

The work environment

This includes the type of job being undertaken, the skills required, and the task complexity. This may change the support required. A list of common approaches relating to conditions can be a starting point, but it is a crude way of supporting each person because of the above variables. We need to move away from the 'dyslexics need X' approach to understanding each person.

Different environment means different adjustments

Different environmental settings mean different adjustments may need to be considered. It is very different working in an open plan office setting or working at home or being on the move. Static settings mean the environment can be controlled whereas dynamic changing settings require greater adaptation.

For example, three people may all be dyslexic but may need different strategies. One person delivers parcels and needs to record actions on a tablet or phone or by hand, another is a fire officer and needs to read signs and documentation on the go and at speed, and a third person works in an office from the same desk using a computer with spellcheckers and grammar checkers available to them all the time.

The following strategies are not exhaustive but provide some ideas of the challenges some people may have and some suggestions to help.

Office working

If working in an office environment, consider the following:

- **Hot desking.** Some people need to have a consistent space to work in so that the layout of their work area and their possessions are always in the same place. One person told Amanda how having a desk drawer with key items such as their pens and paper (and including an emergency bar of chocolate) was important to them. Being in the same place also may reduce anxiety for some people due to working next to the same person rather than having to engage with different people every day.

- **Movements of others around you.** Busy traffic can be very distracting for some people, ie if you are placed near the toilet or by the 'water cooler'. Sitting away from the 'flow of traffic' can help some people, such as being placed at the end of a row of desks or facing away from other people, or working in a booth or with the use of desk dividers.

- **Smells.** Some people have heightened responses to specific senses. This can be related for example to food smells, or someone's perfume or aftershave. Amanda really hates the smell of boiled eggs, so someone eating egg sandwiches next to her would be a really unpleasant experience for her. Discussing this in general with teams can help people become more aware.

- **Sounds.** Noises in an office such as voices or background music playing can make it much harder to focus on work or to be able to listen to someone else. It may be helpful to be able to move to a quiet area for one-to-ones, wear noise-cancelling headphones, or work from home on specific tasks where possible.

Home working

One thing that has happened in response to the Covid-19 pandemic has been the flip to home working for many people across the globe. This can provide advantages for some people, especially those for whom external noise is distracting and the need for movement can aid productivity. However, for some, virtual meetings and online communication can result in misunderstanding.

Long emails for some may mean a way of getting their ideas out and the crucial information may be at the end of the email. However, the person receiving it may not recognize what was a key action in the email unless it has clearly been highlighted.

Virtual meetings set up a whole new level of interpretation. Turning off cameras in a meeting may be wrongly seen as someone disengaging from the meeting but for some it may be a means of being able to focus their thoughts and not be distracted by a bank of faces (including their own). A discussion about preferences helps everyone to see that there are choices and there are not misinterpretations.

For some people, also having information about expectations of specific meetings prior to the event where possible can be of help, along with an agenda and timings. If you are working from home and you know this is a camera-on meeting it also means you can be conscious of how you and your surroundings look.

Universal design principles

Universal design principles can reduce the need to make specific adjustments as they are available if you want to ask or if you don't. Every organization has their own jargon and acronyms. Provide an in-house glossary of terms on your intranet as this can help everyone.

Thinking about accessibility in all that you do

This is useful for anyone you want to engage with. Below are some examples for considering usability and readability of websites or written materials:

- Check the readability of the main content before you release information, for example:

- use the readability features built into MS Office (see the Help section);
- use an online site, eg www.readable.io/text (archived at https://perma.cc/JA69-F5WS);[8]
- simplify the text content where possible, eg using www.rewordify.com;[9]
- avoid italics, all-caps and fully justified text;
- use plain, jargon-free English and avoid unnecessary and undefined abbreviations;
- preferably use sentences shorter than 25 words.

- Font/background contrast colours when designing content:
  - use colour with care and try to provide several options;
  - high contrast, eg black and bright yellow, are favoured for visually impaired people but are a poor choice for people with dyslexia;
  - an off-white (eg pastel-coloured) background with dark text is best for someone with dyslexia.

- Keyboard, mouse and touch-screen use:
  - any and all of these may be difficult for people with low computer literacy, motor and/or coordination difficulties, etc;
  - where possible, ensure you can move around the website using both mouse and keyboard – note there are standard guidelines online, so that everyone uses the same key combinations for similar tasks.

- Colour and information:
  - ensure colour is not the only way of conveying information, especially on graphs and charts – up to 8 per cent of men have some form of colour blindness, with red-green colour blindness being most common;
  - check colour combinations using a colour-blind simulator, eg www.color-blindness.com/coblis-color-blindness-simulator (archived at https://perma.cc/B3VH-S2NF).[10]

- Font type and size:
  - ideally, incorporate an accessibility toolbar that allows the user to change fonts;
  - otherwise, use a clear, easy-to-read, sans-serif font, eg Arial, Verdana, Calibri;
  - use a 'normal' font size as standard (12 pt or larger);

- – check that you can increase the font size by up to 200 per cent in the browser without losing information.
- Screen readers:
  - – make sure your text can all be accessed easily by screen readers/ text-to-speech software – this is important for dyslexic and visually impaired users;
  - – do not use images to present text boxes or quotes, as these will not be read;
  - – ensure all images and videos have appropriate 'alt text' and descriptions;
  - – when considering your alt text tags:
    - – always try to use the shortest amount of text possible to convey the appropriate level of information for the context;
    - – think about whether or not the image needs alt-text; most of the time you do, but don't force your users to listen to unnecessary descriptions;
    - – avoid using punctuation – !!! announces as 'exclamation point exclamation point exclamation point';
    - – avoid using abbreviations unless they are known to the person accessing the information;
    - – avoid using articles like the, an, a, 'one of', etc.
- Links:
  - – avoid using 'click here' for links;
  - – all links should make contextual sense when viewed on their own.
- Accessibility plug-ins:
  - – plug-ins such as ReciteMe and Browse Aloud allow the user to change font, colour, text size and to translate. This allows the user to make their own personal choices to suit their needs.[11]
- Use people who practise what they preach:
  - – before you take on someone to 'redesign' your site to make it more accessible, check that their website follows the simple guidelines listed above.

Keep thinking about the readability of the materials you provide, especially if the content is being used widely internally or is customer-facing.

You can check readability level of content using a readability index which allows you to know the average reading age required for the content. This can be done automatically in Microsoft Word, for example. Think also about offering alternative formats so it can be read aloud as well. Images can aid understanding but ensure they have 'alt tags' with a description of the content so a screen reader can tell someone what the image is.

Getting it right from the start

Getting support in place in a timely manner can make a real difference to someone feeling engaged in a new job and being productive. Confidence, once lost, takes longer to regain.

SOME TIPS

Regular short meetings to check in with a new employee can mean that feedback is provided promptly, and any small adaptations can be put in place. It can be harder for some people to recognize if they are doing OK if they have no previous benchmark. The person may be reticent to ask for guidance as they may have had poor past experiences or lack confidence in doing so.

Do be explicit about what is expected. Consider the type of tasks that need to be undertaken and also the environment where they are taking place. Does information need to be given in a quieter setting to limit background noise? Is flexible working more appropriate for some tasks and on some days? Are you expecting the employee to come to specific meetings on a regular basis? Discuss if changes are required too so the person can adapt to these.

Demonstrate where possible new or less familiar tasks and provide the steps required to achieve them if necessary. Allow sufficient time for someone to embed a new skill. Remember that none of us learned to drive in five minutes and some of us needed more lessons and more practice. If it is a complex task with multiple steps, consider if appropriate video or photographic information can support training. Provide instructions for the person (in the agreed format) and highlight specifically something that is important, eg if changing the order of actions has health and safety implications such as a carer using a bath hoist.

Supporting someone with organizational challenges

Starting at a new job means understanding the pace of work and what others' expectations are. For some people, executive functioning skills (which include planning, organization and time management) may be problematic. If you are someone that can prioritize and self-organize it can be hard to see why it is so difficult for others. Some people use the analogy that being someone with ADHD can feel like having all the files (ie the knowledge and skills) without being given the filing cabinet!

SOME TIPS

Having some support in organizing workflow can make a big difference at the start of a new job or piece of work. Often what seem small adjustments have a huge impact, such as checking if the person understands the work diary systems. In the UK there is coaching support available in some jobs and if this is put in place early it can have a profound impact on that person doing their job successfully.

Other strategies include putting task lists in place with reminders and alarms as prompts for work deadlines. Some people find the use of colour coding for folders for different projects can be helpful to organize paperwork. Most of us have optimum times in the day to focus on more complex tasks. Recognizing how to pace and complete low-interest/high-boredom tasks across a day can increase productivity.

Supporting someone with social, language and communication challenges

Start by making an agreed time and place that is quiet without people and noise distractions to discuss key information.

SOME TIPS

- Sit alongside the person rather than opposite where possible.
- Look at the person and not your phone!
- Don't be distracted by doing other things at the same time.
- Start by asking the person about the support they require. Use **I** and **We** rather than **You** to reduce feelings of anxiety and allow the person to feel supported, eg 'How can "we" work together to provide support?'

Show you are actively listening:

- Slow your speech down to the pace of the person.
- Provide sufficient time for response.
- If someone seems not to understand your question or request, try asking it in another way – don't just repeat the question again. If they didn't understand the first time, repetition of the same thing several times will not help a great deal.
- Allow the person enough time to process the information and think of a response and don't jump in too soon.
- If you don't understand what the person has said to you then ask in a non-judgemental way for it to be repeated.
- Reframe what the person says to you to show you are hearing what has been said.
- Avoid jargon, abbreviations, metaphors: 'We run a tight ship here', 'Don't be lippy'.
- Avoid using double statements: 'You weren't coming to the gym, were you...?'

Discuss steps and actions so a work plan can be created. Check their preferred communication style for information flow. Different people have different communication styles. Some people need to have a chat between tasks they are doing, and others find 'small talk' really difficult. Some people are at ease meeting new people and know intuitively when to start, extend or end a conversation. This may not be easy for some people who need a bit longer to process what is being said or are not readily picking up the cues that it is time to stop talking. Try to allow the person time after the meeting so they can consider and process what has been said.

Recognizing your own style of communication also helps you to be more patient if someone interrupts you. Strategies such as writing down what you want to say while the other person is talking seem so simple but can allow the person to maintain focus on what is being said while not worrying about remembering their points they want to say.

Discuss the different types of communication settings as strategies may vary for each, eg face to face; online and via email; group meetings; and one to ones.

Explain the 'rules' of each setting, what is expected and be explicit, including ones that are less obvious such as team meetings, social activities and meeting with line managers.

- **Phone calls.** These can be challenging if you need to remember information, follow oral instructions, and especially if someone is speaking too fast or not clearly, or there is background noise. Some people, for example in a call centre, may have to manage dual tasking such as listening, seeking out information online and writing down information accurately.

- **Face-to-face meetings.** Think about the setting and the other person's pace of conversation.

Supporting someone with numeracy challenges

Seeing a list of numbers or an Excel sheet can for some people result in real feelings of anxiety. Dyscalculia or number difficulties may be something that someone has not discussed with others. Small changes can make a big difference.

SOME TIPS

- If there is maths content to interpret try to make the message or task clear.

- Provide, where possible, additional visual representations of numbers to reinforce concepts such as use of bar graphs or pie charts.

- Show how to set up speed dialling if remembering specific sequences of numbers is harder for the person.

- Consider providing a method of using alternative passwords and codes not requiring numbers if this is harder for someone to recall.

- Show how to set up templated expense forms.

- Encourage the use of timers and set alarms to know *when* a task needs to be completed if time concepts are harder for some.

- If the person is needing specific formulae, then create a table with common conversion formulae in the workspace available.

Supporting some people with coordination challenges

Some people with dyspraxia and other coordination challenges may find writing down information or doing specific tasks needing good fine motor skills, balance or movement harder to do or may take a little longer to learn to be confident and competent.

- Try to demonstrate new skills sitting beside the person, not opposite them.

- When teaching a new skill, SHOW what is expected rather than assume skills. Allow the person to practise skills slowly to start with for accuracy before speeding up.

- Encourage the person to say their strategies aloud as this can help to reinforce the steps in a task.

- Handwriting is often more challenging for some people with dyspraxia/developmental coordination disorder. Encourage practice of typing skills if this is slow or there are inaccuracies. Consider templated reports and forms to minimize the need for handwriting.

- Where possible, use of speech-to-text software can be very helpful but may need to be practised.

- Video a series of tasks or provide photos to help with remembering a sequence of movements – especially important if there are health and safety implications.

- You may also need to consider a workplace assessment for modifications to seating, desk height and computer screens.

Supporting people with literacy-related challenges

Some people with dyslexia or literacy challenges may have difficulties with reading, spelling or writing. This may mean writing reports, reading documents or taking notes down can all be harder.

SOME TIPS

- Provide a template for reports or forms if a standard approach is to be taken.

- Consider the use of software that allows for text to be read aloud.

- Dictation software (speech-to-text software) can help if writing is difficult.

- Grammar checking software can spot errors and offer correct responses.

- Spellcheckers are in most word processing programs but setting up autocorrect for specific work-related terms being used all the time can be helpful.

- There are some specialist spelling programs for helping in some sectors such as for medicine to help with medical terms.

IT support strategies

There is a growing range of apps and software that can make a real difference to people's everyday functioning, many of which are now being built into software programs as standard:

- To-do list reminders/scheduling apps can help with reminders and alarms for deadline setting and meetings (eg Todoist) or built into Outlook or Google Calendar.[12]

- Text-to-speech software (on Macs and PCs, Adobe).

- Speech-to-text software (eg Apple, Dragon Dictate, Siri, Alexa, Google dictate).

- 'Blockers' can be used to eliminate distractions from social media/smart phones when wanting to complete specific tasks. This stops someone from going on other sites for set time periods.

- White noise/ambient noise apps can be helpful to block out other noises (eg Focus@will) or the person may use music that they find helps them to focus. Some people love classical music and others rock; it will be personal to that individual.[13]

- Note-taking apps (can be as simple as 'Notes' on a phone).

- Microsoft has a lot of inbuilt accessibility features including Immersive Reader.

Spellchecker and proofing software e.g such as Ghotit and Grammarly can highlight errors and suggest where corrections can be made.[14,15]

Rewordify[16] and other programs built into software, such as Microsoft Office Immersive Reader,[17] have a range of accessibility features built in, such as tools that can simplify the words and sentences.

CASE STUDY
Helen Needham, Founder of Me.Decoded and Neurodiversity Lead, Capco

Helen Needham is a management consultant at Capco, a global management and technology consultancy. She powerfully describes how it felt gaining a diagnosis of autism in adulthood and what this has meant to her from a personal and work perspective. She also describes the impact that the commitment from her organization has on becoming neuroinclusive:

'At first I felt neither happy nor sad when I was diagnosed as autistic in my forties: it was a fact. My son had been diagnosed as autistic three years earlier and I had been struggling at work for years, questioning what was wrong with me. I was managing teams of four to six people and my feedback each year was that I needed to work on my people skills, but nothing I tried seemed to work. Most of my peers had been promoted past me, and I was battling with increasing anxiety. I was tired of struggling and feeling like an outsider. Something needed to change, but I wasn't sure what that change was.

'A few days after my diagnosis came a feeling of relief. There wasn't something wrong with me, my brain was wired differently. I was different and I needed a different way of working. I knew from my son the difference that the right understanding and strategies could make. I felt empowered and positive as I thought, "this is me, no excuses".

'Then came the report and the recommendations after my assessment. I felt deflated and conflicted about wanting to be open about being autistic. The report mentioned the need for employers to be mindful of their obligations to disabled people under the Equality Act, and that I might benefit from acknowledging that I had a weakness in the areas of interpersonal relationships and managing people at work. It also mentioned that a traditional career development path of promotion to a supervisory/managerial role was unlikely to reflect my skill sets and I would require an element of job redesign or role sharing to meet my occupational potential.

'Was this really how I wanted to be perceived? Did I really want to go into work and tell them that I was autistic and that I wasn't able to fully do my job? The answer was no. I didn't want to say that I couldn't meet the expectations of my role. Everything seemed to be focused on what I couldn't do. There was no way that I was ever going to share my report with anyone at work. I needed to find a different way. I wanted to focus on what I could do, and create a working environment that worked for me. This meant needing to open up and talk to the people I worked with.

'My first attempts of telling colleagues didn't go to plan. It took them a while to process my being so open about my diagnosis, but we slowly worked our way through it. It felt empowering to talk about the situations that I found difficult and explore how we could try to do things differently. This change didn't go unnoticed, and I was promoted six months later and the team that I managed grew from five to 30 people. Despite this success I had only told a handful of people as I was still nervous about talking to HR or senior management. I was concerned about how I would be perceived.

'I am a management consultant, which is a people-based business, and I had no idea how my organization would react to me being autistic. Would they be supportive, or would they be concerned? Would they really be supportive of an autistic consultant, who often struggles with people? I knew there were other neurodivergent people at work, who like me, had been struggling in silence. They needed a change as well. So, despite my concerns, I decided it was time to speak up.

'I met with the head of HR and the head of our UK practice to tell them about my diagnosis, and to discuss some of the challenges that I have faced as an autistic consultant as well as some of the strategies that I had adopted to work around them. I also highlighted some of the experiences that fellow employees had shared with me and put forward a business case for embracing neurodiversity inclusion within the workplace, starting with the establishment of an employee neurodiversity network. Before the meeting I felt sick with nerves. They might say no to a neurodiversity network, but they will never forget me telling them that I am autistic. Thankfully they were open and supportive, and our Neurodiversity Network was launched later that year.

'I was incredibly lucky to have a supportive workplace whose motto is "Be yourself at work", and with their support I have gone onto further successes including leading a team of 70 people. I am now a valued member of our leadership team, and last year I was highlighted as one of the top leaders in my peer group. Something that I am incredibly proud of, as this was based on nominations from fellow employees. Quite a turnaround from being viewed as the "difficult colleague" and thinking of myself as a non-people person.

'In the two years since we launched the neurodiversity network, we have hosted multiple events to promote awareness of neurodiversity and the experiences of neurodivergent individuals, neurodiversity inclusion is part of our induction and interviewing training, and my company has made a public commitment to develop a roadmap for inclusion. We have participated in numerous roundtables with other organizations to learn about the changes we can make in order to be more inclusive of the neurodivergent, and have found allies in the leadership team, HR, Recruitment and Operations who are open to bringing about these changes. The impact across the business has been more than I could have imagined when I first put forward the business case. Neurodiversity is now a part of the conversation at our organization, and employees now know that they have other people to talk to if they find themselves struggling. We have even had people choose to come and work for us because they have read about our Neurodiversity Network.

'At the beginning of 2020 the head of the UK practice signed up to a public commitment with the Valuable 500 to review our organizational practices and develop a roadmap for inclusion. I am now leading a small group of volunteers from our employee network, along with representatives from our different business functions to map out employee journeys at key employee touchpoints. This includes recruitment, onboarding and induction, daily tasks and performance management. Our objective is to identify potential barriers to inclusion and apply the principles of universal design to develop processes and a working environment which cater for a wide range of needs. We want to be able to reduce the bar for reasonable adjustments so that employees don't need to disclose in order to access support. My hope is that by creating an environment where support is readily available and the wider workforce is educated about neurodiversity inclusion, we can bring about a change where neurodivergent individuals are empowered and supported to fulfil their potential.

'I am proud to be part of a company that recognizes the value of supporting neurodivergent individuals and has been there for me as I strove to find a way of working that worked for me. A change that I hope more organizations will start to adopt, as I know first-hand what a difference it can make for organizations and individuals.'

KEY POINTS
Making workplace adjustments

- Be person-centred and ask the person about what they think their support needs are.
- Check the context.
- Ask for help externally if you are not certain how to support someone, eg arrange a workplace assessment.
- Adjustments need time to be embedded and need to be put in place in a timely manner.
- Some people need coaching support to plan and embed adjustments into their daily practices.
- Be prepared to review adjustments if the job changes in any way.

Notes

1 Equality and Human Rights Commission (2018) Understanding Equality, https://www.equalityhumanrights.com/en/secondary-education-resources/useful-information/understanding-equality (archived at https://perma.cc/96AY-HE98)

2 Social Change UK (2019) Equality and Equity, https://social-change.co.uk/blog/2019-03-29-equality-and-equity#:~:text=Equality%20vs.,people%20differently%20dependent%20on%20need (archived at https://perma.cc/3GSM-JEFH)

3 Equality Act (2010) https://www.legislation.gov.uk/ukpga/2010/15/contents (archived at https://perma.cc/5ZGD-6XJW)

4 GOV.UK (2021) Get support in work if you have a disability or health condition (Access to Work) https://www.gov.uk/access-to-work (archived at https://perma.cc/4XRI-KTHS)

5 NICE (National Institute for Health and Care Excellence) (2021) https://www.nice.org.uk/ (archived at https://perma.cc/P6LS-LXKX)

6 Wolchin, R (2014) Be mindful when it comes to your words. A string of some that don't mean much to you, may stick with someone else for a lifetime [Twitter] 1 January, https://twitter.com/rachelwolchin/status/418219133138792449?lang=en (archived at https://perma.cc/Z7ZG-2FSE)

7 World Health Organization (2001; last updated 2018) International Classification of Functioning Disability and Health, www.who.int/classifications/icf/en/ (archived at https://perma.cc/UDX6-KAMF)

8 Readable (2021) www.readable.io/text (archived at https://perma.cc/JA69-F5WS)

9 Rewordify (2021) https://rewordify.com/ (archived at https://perma.cc/T4EB-VR8Z)

10 Colblindor (2021) www.color-blindness.com/coblis-color-blindness-simulator (archived at https://perma.cc/B3VH-S2NF)

11 Recite Me (2021) www.reciteme.com (archived at https://perma.cc/PMN7-N9E8)

12 Todoist (2021) https://todoist.com/ (archived at https://perma.cc/QW2B-6965)

13 Focus@will (2021) https://www.focusatwill.com/ (archived at https://perma.cc/ZZK4-6JVF)

14 Ghotit (2021) https://www.ghotit.com/ (archived at https://perma.cc/27U6-QNSS)

15 Grammarly (2021) https://www.grammarly.com/ (archived at https://perma.cc/8X8B-84SP)

16 Rewordify (2021) https://rewordify.com/ (archived at https://perma.cc/T4EB-VR8Z)

17 Microsoft (2021) Learning Tools, https://www.microsoft.com/en-gb/education/products/learning-tools (archived at https://perma.cc/HLB2-Y3XB)

11

Induction and onboarding

Introduction

In this chapter we'll discuss the journey of a candidate as they become inducted and onboarded into the organization. We'll look at the details of the process and the structure and mechanisms by which you should approach it.

The first 90 days can often be key to an employee's long-term success. In fact, '28 per cent of employees quit in their first 90 days'.[1]

Of course that doesn't account for those who join an organization and don't leave in 90 days but feel trapped and potentially underperform due to lack of support and good induction and onboarding.

There is also the reality that prompt action helps everyone. Here in the UK, if a government-funded 'Access to Work' grant is applied for in their first six weeks, no cost will be applied to the employer. The grant enables the new employee to gain additional support. So it's not only about giving the candidate a great onboarding experience, it's about providing them with the tools they need to do the job, as early in the process as possible.

And remember that because being neurodiverse is understood to be a 'hidden' disability, an applicant may not have requested any reasonable adjustments throughout the recruitment, interview and assessment process; however, that doesn't mean they won't require any when they start their job. They can decide to share this information once in the job.

Appropriate and timely support will ensure good commitment from the new employee, and alleviate additional risk of costs for adjustments and legal challenges at a later date. But let us be clear, it is also the right thing to do! Organizations should be doing more to promote and highlight this fact rather than waiting for employees to request the help, as often they won't, for many reasons which we highlight throughout the book.

So as much as it's important to get the structure right, it's also once again imperative that we focus on the individual. It's important to have processes and policies in place, but some people get stressed out about what sometimes are perceived as the little things, like who makes the tea and when. Others find that a busy environment and winding corridors impact their performance and equilibrium. Some just find the idea of starting a new job too overwhelming to deal with all on day one and need a little time to embed in the organization and understand how the organization and team works.

The reality is that induction and onboarding really starts much earlier than you'd imagine; the process should begin the moment you make the offer to the candidate.

Imagine you've been searching for a holiday for weeks; you finally find the one you want, but it's the winter and the holiday isn't until the summer. Do you:

a Never think of the holiday again until you sit on the plane?

b Never stop thinking about it?

c Have a cheeky look now and then and look up places to see when you are there, and get more excited as each week passes?

d Try to contact the holiday company for further information to no avail and panic that you hadn't really booked it at all?

e Buy some new clothes and check your passport is still OK in readiness?

In reality there are many more options available for how we feel when we book something that requires a large investment. None of us books a holiday to go and have a bad time; we do it in the hope it will be amazing and all we dreamed of. But in reality, sometimes it's not what we'd hoped for. The more information we can obtain about the area, the hotel, the flight, places to eat, the more we can prepare for the holiday, the less chance we will be disappointed when we arrive.

It's all about managing expectations and being prepared for barriers to success.

Sometimes it might be around the accessibility of airports or hotels – do they have lifts, are they difficult to find your way around? Or are there restaurants nearby, how far is the beach? What's public transport like, can I rent a cheap car and is the area pedestrian safe? What language is spoken and do I have some phrases I can use to get started?

The more helpful information you can provide upfront, the greater opportunity they have to request alternative arrangements or to make slight adjustments that ensure a happy holiday.

Organizations need to be thinking in this way when offering someone a new role. It should be a part of your accessibility around the interview and assessment process as much as it should be part of the induction and onboarding. Providing the glossary of terms used in an organization is like providing a phrasebook for your holidays. You can start engaging with others around you.

A good holiday company will keep you well informed and update you of different options like car rental or upgrades, whilst also sharing with you places you can visit and what you can get up to in the local area.

The better experience we can give candidates from the point at which we make them an offer, the easier it will be to induct and onboard them and the greater chance we'll have of keeping them way beyond 90 days.

Imagine how incredible it would be if we could shift that 28 per cent by just an initial 8 per cent to 20 per cent. What would that mean to those employees who previously would have felt lost and alone in their new roles? What would that mean to business productivity, having a more engaged and productive employee? What would that mean to recruitment and retention? Not having to search for and onboard a new employee, with a whole new recruitment and interview process required and all the time and effort that takes.

Surely this is an easy win, as the employee has already put the company badge on their shirt; they don't want this to fail as much as the organization doesn't want them to fail.

Failing is a lose-lose situation. Retaining that employee is a win-win for all involved.

Induction

Induction is a process which may take place irrespective of whether or not there is an official probationary period. It is usually led by a supervisor and involves the collaboration of work colleagues.

We need to keep remembering that the person got the job on the skills they had. The induction process is about how to do the job in the specific setting and what forms of assistance are required to realize their capacity. It is not about whether or not the job can be done. The induction period may vary, depending on the complexity of the work environment or tasks involved. In some cases this can be short, but for some more time may be needed depending on the nature of the challenges the person has. This may need to be changed depending on whether it is a virtual or real induction.

A good induction process can even start before the person begins their job. Background information about the ethos and values of the organization can make a real difference to understanding what to expect. Talking to someone (even for a quick call) from the organization about working in there, along with some practical information relating to local transport links, where to get lunch or a coffee, and even guidance on dress code can mean the person can arrive not worrying about the 'small stuff' too. It's a bit like starting at a new school; you want to either try to blend in or deliberately stand out – having a choice is useful. For some people having a new work setting, new work colleagues, new tasks and new line managers and a new commute can be several too many 'news' all at once.

In the modern world part of the communications strategy and onboarding can be digitized and automated. It shouldn't replace the human touch, rather provide the manager with a platform to help remind them of actions they need to take as well as ensuring the employee gets everything they need before day one.

And yes, you can even make this a fun experience and as part of this onboarding create some Q&As, so that the team can learn some more about their new colleagues, and likewise the new employee can start to get to know their new teammates.

Putting in adjustments or reducing barriers early on in the process can result in the person doing the job they have been employed to do with confidence. Alternatively, a confusing induction process can mean mistakes are made or communication misinterpreted, which can result in the person becoming increasingly anxious and losing confidence and line managers becoming frustrated too. This is never a good start. We have also seen many cases where the person loses or leaves their job because of a bad start that is hard to come back from.

Your approach to induction will depend on whether or not your company or organization has a track record in employing a neurodiverse workforce or has flexible policies and procedures in relation to issues which may arise. This may also be dependent on the size of your organization. In some larger organizations there can be in-house workplace assessors that mean the person can have adjustments put in place quickly and reviewed regularly. Adaptations can be made even at a later date if tasks or workplace demands change. These trained persons may also provide relevant training to others relating to neurodiversity. They can consult with line managers to clarify any misconceptions and help with developing an agreed 'work passport' between the person and the line manager. This helps to document agreed adjustments and can then be amended or taken with the person if they move to another position in the company so you don't have to start from scratch.

Good liaison with HR or D&I (diversity and inclusion) managers can also address challenges that may arise at the earliest possible stage.

During the pandemic in 2020 we saw virtual hiring become the norm rather than the exception and this extended to many of us working from home. This has brought new challenges for induction. The new employee may not have been to the actual workplace at all or met face-to-face with their line managers or new colleagues. This may mean forming relationships and understanding the dynamics of the team is much harder to understand and may take longer to achieve. Explicit planning and teamworking activities may need to be put in place, including planning informal gatherings (but asking people their preferences) to increase understanding of the roles of all members of the team.

For some organizations, neurodiversity is a relatively new concept. Some organizations may have had some initiatives in place, eg work placements for graduates who identify as autistic, for example. But line managers may lack confidence in supporting someone who says they are dyspraxic or dyscalculic for example, as they genuinely may not have had experience or lack the knowledge about what to do (or may not have heard of dyscalculia altogether). Conversations may then be avoided or there may be misconceptions about the amount of support someone may need, and this can lead to nothing being put in place.

In one case we know of, a person was initially approaching the line manager for clarification of the quality of their work. They were in a new post and unfamiliar with the formatting of a report, which seemed to differ in layout from their last job. They were really keen to get it right from the start and wanted to have their work checked to ensure they were doing what was expected of them. They were also waiting for some proofing software to be installed on their computer as they were dyslexic. The line manager was under time pressure and kept putting off finding a time to comment. They came across to the new employee as irritated when they fed back how they were disappointed with the quality of the work. They highlighted all the errors the person had made despite them knowing the person was dyslexic. The new employee then became increasingly anxious about 'failing' and then took longer to complete their work. The individual ended up taking work home and ruminating a great deal over whether it was right or not. This impacted on their sleep as they were worried about what the line manager would say about anything they did. A breakdown in confidence happened as a consequence and the person was 'let go' in their probationary period.

A good induction programme could have perhaps saved this situation. It seems such a costly waste when the person has been through the interview selection stage to fall at this hurdle. It also has a big and often lasting impact on the person's confidence in future job placements as well as anxiety affecting work performance. All this can be avoided!

The management of the work environment, appropriate assistance, education and training, collaboration of management, work colleagues and the person involved require sensitive consideration and appropriate and timely actions. As the process continues, if barriers are identified and addressed effectively, it can be a confidence-building time.

Integration into the workplace

The nature of the relationship between new employees who are neurodivergent and their managers, supervisors and work colleagues will influence the extent to which integration and true inclusion can be achieved.

People can have different management styles which may be highly structured or more informal. Different approaches may suit different people. This is not a parent/child role but should be about having an adult-to-adult relationship. This also does mean that people who are neurodivergent need to have the confidence to self-advocate. This is important to feel safe and be able to discuss needs and to agree on what the work boundaries are so they remain well and don't become exhausted. It does mean that line managers need to have the time to support each person and get to know them a little.

Creating collaborative working is essential and bringing together different talents effectively to work as part of a team can increase productivity hugely. All workers need to recognize the differences in communication preferences and be sensitive to this. With home working and online meetings, we each need to understand individual preferences for synchronous (eg live meetings) or asynchronous (eg email) forms of communication.

Sometimes this will need to be teased apart with the whole team as it may not have been considered or discussed. Solutions can then be generated together. Some people may prefer information prior to a meeting to know what is going to be covered and have time to prepare and reflect. Other people like to turn their cameras off as they find it easier to listen and walk around at the same time. Working together we can also see if there are optimum times (where this is possible) for the team to work together and other times when people can work alone. Amanda is an early bird and works best at 5 am. She puts on her email signature that she doesn't expect other people to respond at that time! She is useless after 8 pm!

Clear guidance about roles and responsibilities is important. This may be especially true if job carving has taken place and other people have had changes made to their roles as well. It is important to be clear who the person should go to for assistance or clarification about their role. Organizations also often require neurodiversity awareness training, teaching problem-solving skills and an ongoing commitment and review cycle. Power dynamics when first starting in a new job can make it difficult to vocalize needs and in a time of global employability challenges it may be even harder to feel you deserve or should voice your needs as you may be concerned about keeping your job (the last in/first out principle).

Neurodiversity awareness training

Appropriate and targeted training is often key to improving communications, addressing misconceptions and building a positive environment before or during induction. The training should be available to all relevant personnel, tailored to reflect the individual roles and responsibilities in the company – managers, supervisors, HR and diversity and inclusion leads. This is something that should be scheduled on a regular basis. You may be thinking you don't have anyone neurodivergent working in your organization. It is likely you do but even if you don't there will be customers, your supply chain and many other people you will come into contact with and the knowledge will not go to waste.

Disclosure at induction may only occur if the person feels safe to do so. Some people may have plucked up the courage to tell the manager for the first time they have ADHD, and this may be a really important point in their life. Fear and shame may be the emotions being felt now or in the past. That first response by a manager may have a significant impact on that person and shouldn't be underestimated. A dismissive comment such as 'Everyone has a bit of ADHD!' or 'Everyone is somewhere on the spectrum!' can be harmful to that person's self-esteem.

Getting started

Think of the induction process as the first phase of onboarding. It should aim to identify the person's particular needs and provide appropriate accommodations and then set up the processes for ongoing support, as necessary. The initial induction process serves to build knowledge and awareness of the work environment and to provide initial on-the-job training. It may be necessary to review the way training is delivered in order to take account of the needs of the new employee. Remember to give sufficient time and to ensure that training materials and job instructions are available in the employee's preferred communication format. Some simple questions such as 'Are there any support needs you think you may have?' can lead to a supportive conversation and result in employee and line manager even co-producing practical solutions that can be put in place.

What can you do?

- Provide an induction pack about the organization.
- Think about the need for a longer induction process for some people.
- Provide a schedule of activities for the first week with regular short check-ins.
- Discuss specific support needs and arrange an assessment if necessary – check adjustments have been put in place and are working for the person.
- It is important to discuss sensitive handling of disclosure with the person so that there is an agreed plan of what is told to peers (if anything).
- Regular review meetings are important but even more so if the person is remote working as they may be reticent to ask for help.

What is the job and what are the rules?

Clarity is important. What does a typical workday in your organization look like? Can the person shadow someone in a similar role? Is flexible working allowed and how flexible is this? Be explicit.

If assistance is needed by the person can you explain the process and agree times that are convenient or a process to ask for help (eg email with a specific header)?

What on-job training is required? Some people (eg with dyspraxia (DCD)) may need additional time to learn a new skill if it requires coordination. They may also need more time to practise the skill to automate it. This could be a health and safety procedure for example.

The 'non-rules'

These are the rules of engagement in an organization that no one ever tells you about but cause challenges and conflict. Often the structure of the job is discussed but aspects of the day that can be more challenging are missed altogether. We often use the term 'soft skills' but sometimes these 'non-rules' or unspoken rules such as who makes the tea, how long to take for lunch (or not), whether you can eat lunch at your desk, what is 'dress down' day (such as if there is a no flip-flop rule), and how to address each other including the management team (in and out of work). All these can be things that cause a lot of angst if you get them wrong.

Finding your way around

- If you are a large organization, can you provide maps, walk-throughs with someone, a video?
- A peer mentor can be really useful as a go-to person to ask about the organization – this could be via email and doesn't necessarily have to be a person working directly with you. Peer mentors may be someone who does a similar job (in larger organizations) or someone who has worked in the organization for a while within a department or could be linked to a neurodiversity champion.
- Acronyms and language – provide a glossary of terms from the start.
- A detailed meeting going through the job description is important as well as discussing expectations for the first three months including discussing work settings. Will the person be required to come into a work base, travel or work from home?
- Ask about specific support or training needs. Recognizing skills gaps may need to be explored during the induction process if the person hasn't been

in a similar job before. It is important to understand the preferred communication style of the person and also that they understand other people's communication styles to prevent clashes or miscommunication. Use of online screening tools can assist in guiding you.

- Arrange a workplace assessment if required, so that adjustments can be put in place in a timely manner. The context of the work being completed is important and the assessor may need to speak with the line manager as well to gather sufficient information to suggest appropriate adjustments.

- Safe spaces to ask for help – it may be difficult for someone in a new post to feel they can ask for help. Having somewhere where not only the job but the impact of wellbeing can be discussed may reduce the risk of drop-out, leavism, presenteeism and absenteeism.

Getting support in place

Find out promptly what support needs there may be and set up a review to check they are in place or what further adjustments need to be made. Regular short check-ins can make a big difference in picking up small queries or challenges as they arise. Too often we wait until it's too late and the person has left or the line manager has lost confidence.

Life is not static

People change over time and jobs do too. Issues which were identified and addressed during induction may need to be revisited and appropriate actions taken. This doesn't need to be onerous but needs to be diarized so that it happens. This is especially true as we move to ways of working that are more 'flexible', with some of us spending all or some of the week working from home. This is open to different interpretations and may change depending on personal and professional demands.

Mentoring support

A mentoring system should be considered for new employees. This should be agreed between the new employee and the potential mentor and should have a specific timeframe. The system should operate during working hours and also include work-related social or training events. Neurodiversity champions can also be trained as mentors (but make sure that the champion does not get overloaded).

What does involvement mean?

Employers and managers need to be careful to integrate employees into whatever workplace arrangements prevail but not to expect everyone to want to join in with everything. Work dos, going to conferences or meetings can all be very daunting and stressful for some people. We can sometimes make assumptions about someone that may be false. Someone who doesn't tend to want to chat over the 'water cooler' or kettle could be seen as unfriendly or it could in reality be that some people need a break at lunchtime to recover from an intense meeting and manage their work time effectively (and their wellbeing).

Access to Work[2]

This is a government scheme in the UK that can assist organizations to make further adjustments, offer support if required and arrange an Access to Work or a workplace assessment to be undertaken; alternatively in larger organizations this can be undertaken 'in house'.

CASE STUDY
A tale of untapped potential at IBM[3]

Before Covid-19 brought travel to a halt, test specialist Dyllan Rafail would board a plane every Monday morning to fly to Boston, where he spent the week working onsite for global food retailer Ahold Delhaize. On Friday evening, he headed back home. A demanding schedule for anyone, but Rafail isn't your average employee – he's part of a small but growing cadre of neurodivergent IBMers.

The flight is just two hours, but Rafail's real journey began in third grade, when he was first diagnosed with autism. 'They found me spasming in class and thought I was having seizures,' he said. 'It turned out that I was having an anxiety reaction to the temperature in the classroom and to how crazy the other kids were being.'

Two IBMers on a mission

Rafail was hired as part of an initiative spearheaded in 2017 by IBM employees Paul Austin and Andrew Williams with the Specialisterne Foundation, which works with companies around the world to successfully bring neurodiverse candidates on board. It was one of several pilots launched across IBM globally to pave the way for a more inclusive workplace.

Austin, a New York-based senior manager in WebSphere development, has been on a mission to expand job opportunities for the neurodiverse since attending the first World Autism Awareness Day at the United Nations in 2015. He says:

> People from a number of companies spoke, but the one that really got to me was the company Ultra Testing – now they call themselves the Ultranauts. Their speaker said they ate IBM's lunch at testing by using an all-autistic staff.

Austin launched the 'Autism as a Skill' Business Resource Group (BRG), and within a few months 500 IBMers had joined. In 2018, the group became the ND@IBM BRG and now boasts over 1,400 members – neurodivergent employees and allies – in locations around the world:

> It's kind of similar to the LGBT+ movement – people are starting to come out more as autistic, and this group provides a resource both for those on the spectrum and for those who work with them. I have a nephew with Asperger's, but I think my real driving motivation is that I know what it's like to be on the outside. I've always felt on the outside, and I've always sympathized with people who are not quite understood. This is my chance to fight for people who don't get represented. Autism is a condition that crosses class boundaries, racial boundaries, gender boundaries.

Australia-based Williams found his way to the cause of neurodiversity in 2015 when a friend introduced him to the CEO of Specialisterne, founded in 2004 by Thorkil Sonne after Sonne's son was diagnosed with autism. Sonne chose to focus on the abilities often exhibited by the neurodiverse – attention to detail, high accuracy, innovative thinking, loyalty and honesty – rather than seeing it as a disability. At the time, Williams was the global technical offering leader for IBM testing services. He said, 'I knew IBMers who had autistic kids, and I saw their struggles. One of them turned to me once and said about his daughter, "I really don't know what her future is". So I had a personal reason to move forward with this as well as a business reason.'

Austin and Williams met at a design thinking workshop in New York and hit it off immediately. Austin said, 'Andrew was on the same mission that I'm on. And he came up with a way to build a business offering where we basically told potential clients, "We're going to test your stuff, and we're going to do it using a group of autistic people, and this is why it's going to be better for your company".'

Accelerating the hiring effort

In 2019, the grassroots initiative started by Austin and Williams caught the attention of IBM's Diverse Abilities Council, which decided to focus on two areas related to neurodiversity in hiring: making the workplace more accessible for neurodiverse employees, and developing hiring models to bring more neurodiverse employees into IBM.

'Nothing About Us Without Us' is the motto of IBM's #ActuallyAutistic Task Force. Formed in 2019, it's a support group for neurodivergent employees as well as a sounding board providing important advice and guidance, which is critical for the success of the ND@IBM programme.

Heading up that effort are Yves Veulliet, IBM's global disability and inclusion leader, and Diane Delaney, programme manager for IBM's global neurodiversity programme. 'So now we have a two-year plan to hire neurodivergent employees in various locations around the world, including Australia, Brazil, Canada, Mexico, the UK and the US,' said Delaney. One challenge is identifying locations that suit neurodivergent candidates. The design thinking model in place at many IBM locations tends to be noisy and ever-changing:

> Some autistic people may be comfortable with that, but more often they need a quieter workplace to be comfortable. An accommodation as simple as noise-cancelling headphones can make a huge difference for them, or making sure their desk isn't on a main hallway with a lot of traffic.

While the effort with Specialisterne is seeing great success – almost all of the neurodivergent employees hired early in the programme are thriving at IBM – a bigger challenge is creating an environment where the neurodiverse can successfully apply for opportunities across IBM.

Diane Delaney, Neurodiversity@IBM Global Programme Manager

> Some people have a preconceived notion that neurodivergent people aren't capable, but many are very high-functioning. A study by JP Morgan showed that 'after three to six months […], autistic workers were doing the work of people who took three years to ramp up – and were even 50 per cent more productive.' Once people hear the success stories and learn about the abilities that neurodiverse people have, then they're like, 'OK, how do we become a part of that?'

IBM developed a course with Uptimize called 'Neurodiversity 101' that employees can take. It's a 77-minute course on how to work with neurodiverse individuals. 'We would love for every hiring manager to take this training,' said Delaney.

Veulliet added, 'The goal is to have a neurodiverse hiring process fully integrated into the standard hiring process within the next few years. Nothing is ever perfect, but we want to make sure we're providing equal opportunity regardless of factors related to neurodiversity. IBM has a long tradition of welcoming people with diverse abilities, and we've developed a very structured process for onboarding people living with various types of disabilities, like vision or hearing loss. We need to make sure we reach that same standard of quality for neurodivergent candidates.'

KEY POINTS
Induction and onboarding

- Start as early as possible in planning your onboarding experiences. Imagine it was a close family friend starting in the organization – what would you tell them? The rules and the culture of the place.

- Imagine you are coming from another world speaking a different language and with different cultural norms and try to be explicit about a day in the life in the new workplace.

- Provide mentoring support within the organization to ask the questions you may not want to ask your line manager.

- Be explicit about your interpretation about the work day, eg talking about 'flexible working' and what that actually means for you and for the person.

- Put in place regular reviews to check for understanding.

Notes

1 Taylor, T (2017) Why do 28% of employees quit in their first 90 days? Poor onboarding practices? [Blog] *HR Dive*, 25 April, https://www.hrdive.com/news/why-do-28-of-employees-quit-in-their-first-90-days-poor-onboarding-practi/441139/ (archived at https://perma.cc/E74P-MCZ3)

2 GOV.UK (2021) Get support in work if you have a disability or health condition (Access to Work) https://www.gov.uk/access-to-work (archived at https://perma.cc/4XRH-KTHS)

3 IBM (2020) Neurodiversity: The Power of New Perspectives, https://www.ibm.com/thought-leadership/passion-projects/neurodiversity (archived at https://perma.cc/EH55-45YS)

12

Line management means having good conversations

Introduction

Having a good conversation with your line manager requires the other person to feel safe, valued and listened to. Sharing who we are, especially for those who have what is sometimes seen as a 'hidden disability', can mean we have to become visible and have a voice that is loud enough that it can be heard.

It perpetuates the notion that visibility is a central organizing tenet for understanding identity and accessing social recognition from our managers and peers. We have to feel confident enough to tell others who we are, and describe what we can and cannot do. For most neurodivergent people it needs to be worth it. Revealing our invisible identities successfully in the workplace can be the only option to access accommodations or adjustments. This can result in the need for complex decisions about when, where, and how much to disclose.

Is there increasing pressure on the neurodivergent person to be their 'authentic self' and for managers to have *that* conversation? In an inclusive society there would be no need to have to 'come out' at all, as each person's needs would be considered in an ongoing dialogue and reconsidered as times and/or the context changed.

When someone decides to withhold the conversation and not to disclose, there can even be a sense of misplaced anger by the manager, who might misinterpret that the person is being less than honest.

But not disclosing can be because of fear of oppression and being outed as a member of a marginalized or minority grouping, and this may relate to poor past experiences. We may also take the decision not to disclose because we think it may affect our line manager's perception of us and our ability. Our fear of the response may be a form of transference because of former challenges from school days. We know that people with neurodivergent traits are at a higher risk of having been bullied in school. Bullying is a sub-type of aggression that may be defined as a systematic abuse of power in which a person (ie the victim) is exposed, repeatedly and over time, to negative actions on the part of one or more other students. It can have serious consequences and has been shown to be related to later behavioural and emotional problems. We need to remind ourselves and be sensitive to not re-traumatizing someone by our actions.[1]

Up to three-quarters of school children with autism spectrum disorder have been noted to have been bullied. There is also research relating to those with specific language impairments[2] and with ADHD,[3] and also developmental coordination disorder (also known as dyspraxia).[4]

So where do we start in having a conversation and how do we get it right?

A good and positive place to start is with some research with input from the people at the coal face: the managers and their people. So we are sharing some of the results of three years of hard graft in order to get underneath the skin of what it is like to manage a person on the autism spectrum and some of the learnings gained so that we can help everyone to be better employees and managers.

Anne Cockayne is a researcher in autism employment and is particularly interested in what happens to people with an autism spectrum condition and their line managers.

Although we know quite a lot about autism as a condition, we hear lots of stories from autistic people about the various challenges and strengths that they have. Anne's research is focused on what it's like for organizations. She has looked at how managers can make a massive difference, both positively and negatively, to someone who's on the autism spectrum.

This is not about managers getting it wrong all the time or not caring; most managers want to do the right thing. They want to be able to help their employees, but often, either they're misguided, or they've misunderstood the situation or may be so cautious about doing the wrong thing they avoid doing anything at all. This can lead to conversations being delayed resulting in challenges growing even bigger.

Anne interviewed about 30 managers and HR people who granted her access to their organizations of all sizes. What struck her most was that her results weren't really organization size-specific; it was much more about the quality of the relationship between the manager and the person they were managing. With a team of five or six people, it's all about the person rather than the policies. Yet it's sometimes the company's policies that cause difficulty and tensions for managers, for example a reward policy that requires everyone to work according to a generic job description and doesn't allow for managers to give out tasks according to capabilities and preferences.

Anne believes that probably one of the biggest challenges for success is to ensure that all managers are given the right support, the right training and the right development, so that they can help their employees.

Does someone need a diagnosis to get support?

This is a question that is often asked. It is not an employer's right to know if someone has lung cancer so should it be the right of employers or managers to know whether you have ADHD or dyspraxia? They don't have to tell you their diagnosis but often are forced into a position of having to provide the necessary evidence.

What is the best way to support managers?

The way the law is set up at the moment, you can't easily access support through reasonable adjustments or any other changes unless you've got a clinical diagnosis, but it is not actually required. A challenge for some is that there are many autistic people or those who identify as neurodivergent who do not see themselves as disabled, whereas the law says autism is a disability. This extends to other conditions such as ADHD and dyspraxia too.

The law is sometimes hard to interpret in that respect, and can make it harder for managers. If they do see that a person is having some difficulty with the working environment, they are limited to what they can do until the person discloses it themselves. However, organizations do need to put anticipatory processes in place. We think that Universal Design principles such as putting in place accessible and inclusive processes, and awareness and training of staff, can help everyone including those who want to disclose and those who prefer not to do so.

Open dialogue with a prospective or current employee is the easiest way of providing support and gaining appropriate adjustments. The manager who fails to discuss potential need for adjustments with the employee can amount to a failure to make the actual reasonable adjustments. However, we do need to recognize that sometimes it is necessary to gain professional advice for the adjustments (not necessarily for a diagnosis) as the employee may not have the knowledge or experience to know what would be of greatest help.

Should it be HR's role to guide the manager?

Anne's research found that it was very rarely likely that someone in an HR role was seen to directly help, as they were often in larger organizations too distant or remote from the individual. In some organizations people are sent to the occupational nurse or doctor who may also have had little training relating to neurodiversity. So if anybody is going to hear someone talk about being diagnosed or going down the disclosure pathway, it's more likely to be the line manager, because that's the person they are closest to and can trust.

Once someone has disclosed that they require support or consider themselves as disabled, then the manager is in a great position to do something about considering and putting in place reasonable adjustments. Disclosure is the beginning of the dialogue and getting the next steps right is crucial for the person who may have not told anyone before or had bad past experiences. It is important to note that when we describe challenges in the workplace they may be interspersed with other challenges at home too and not be in neatly boxed silos relating just to neurodiversity. Remember we are all a bit messy!

It is important for the manager and the employee to discuss what is said to the wider team, if anything. Different people want different information shared and this is very personal and will vary. Not everybody also understands that autism for some people, for example, isn't seen as a disability in itself, but someone might be disabled by the setting they are in, or have support needs, but it is seen as a disability in the eyes of the law.

Managers have a real tightrope to walk between wanting to explain to others in a team why someone might find bright lights difficult, or why they might need to take a few more breaks, or why one person may feel upset by specific food or perfume smells too close to them, if they don't understand the reasons why themselves. But it's a confidential matter. So, the managers are right in the middle of trying to negotiate something that preserves the individual's rights and confidentiality, but at the same time helps other people understand what's going on.

Because it's that lack of understanding and lack of knowledge of what autism or other neurodivergent traits are, and how they show themselves in people in a working environment, that can cause some confusion and result in tension within the team.

Training is important

This is one of the real reasons why training in relation to neurodiversity is so important. If an organization takes it upon itself to make sure their frontline managers particularly are up to speed, then of course they can consider their work environment and for example can make sure the office is laid out in a sensible way, and discuss how in general accommodations can be made for all. This reduces the need for those 'special' conversations.

The challenge is when people within a team are at 'odds' with putting in the changes or adjustments. One person might say they can't work in dim light and someone else may want specific brighter lighting. This might not be about being awkward, they genuinely might need really bright light; maybe they've got eyesight issues. Every manager has to modify things to suit a number of different situations and has to consider each person's needs and also what is reasonable. This may also relate to the size of the organization as well as how many changes you can make.

The reality of the situation is that managing somebody who is apparently different from most of their employees may take extra time and effort. Tiny modifications can make a big difference to somebody's performance, but the time to implement them can add up. Delay in implementation is often a big issue for the person. But the law, or the company's reasonable adjustments policies, don't always say anything about the manager who has not been given any extra time and often has little support to deal with the challenges they may face and the changes they may need to implement. The minute you have a team where one person has quite a different set of requirements from the rest, it creates an extra workload and the manager needs some knowledge around what to do and how to do it.

Managers can vary hugely in their skills, knowledge and willingness to adapt and make adjustments. Some managers see the rationale for doing so and know that it's part of their job. Some don't. Anne's research found that most people were just curious; they wanted to know a lot more, and were open minded. Generally their experience with their employees was really positive. But there will always be some managers who just think, 'It's all a bit too much trouble, I don't really "get" what it's like to be autistic and I don't want hassle in my team, I want an easy life.'

That's the real challenge in managing, supporting and understanding diversity, especially when we are talking about neurological differences amongst minorities which can vary greatly from person to person.

It takes a really skilled manager to strike that balance between not exploiting an individual, not expecting somebody to do things over and above what they're paid to do or for which they have the skills, and also giving work that is interesting, productive and can benefit the team and the organization. Anne describes 'job crafting', which requires a really in-depth understanding of the overall skills and mix of your team.

A massive conclusion from Anne's research is that it is always important to consider the ecology the person is placed in. Success for a person relies on us considering not only their physical workplace, but also what good teamworking and communication looks like. An example of this could be somebody who sits on their own at lunchtime. This may be perceived by their peers as odd or unfriendly but this could be a complete misconception. Some people need time to themselves to decompress at lunchtimes and being on their own can help. Once managers (and all of us) have an understanding that we can all behave differently for a range of reasons that may not be obvious, and don't assume how someone is and this is not wrong or bad, we can focus on each person's strengths, of which there will be many.

So then we can start to consider how we each modify our style of inter-action, and how and what we ask every person to do. This is not just about modifying the environment, but focusing on and harnessing each person's individual strengths. Once we start to do this we will then start to have a more neurologically diverse and inclusive workforce that will be happier and more productive.

So with Anne's research in mind, what would it be like to see through the eyes of somebody else? The impact that light, sounds or communications have on that person. Not what it is to be autistic or ADHD or... but actually some of the experiences of those people who find their current working environment a challenge and what effect it is having on them physiologically and psychologically.

By putting ourselves in the shoes of others and specifically in the shoes of those we manage, we can better increase our understanding and become more accommodating.

When Theo went to the LinkedIn offices in London to meet with Clare Corrie, account director and dyslexic, he didn't count on what he was going to encounter. He had the pleasure of interviewing Clare for his podcast, but then was introduced to Clare's manager Christopher Barron who had this to say: 'Her verbal oral communication is outstanding! Her drive, tenacity and ambition contribute to her being a world-class sales professional. I think it stems from her dyslexia.'

What can we learn from this?

This is where we need to get to. A world where managers see neurodiversity and those from neuro-minorities as highly skilled individuals who can perform brilliantly well because of their neurological difference rather than in spite of that difference.

This brings us back to the importance of sharing our experiences and feelings to help eliminate stigma, but most importantly of creating an environment where we can all thrive.

Organizations should be giving their employees the opportunity to share their voice with others. Not just their work persona, but to choose what parts of their whole self they want to share. This should not be about enforced jollity (eg everyone being expected to attend Christmas parties where everyone has to join in even if they don't want to or find social settings uncomfortable).

A person's voice can be presented in different ways and can encompass a wide variety of thoughts, ideas, beliefs, aspirations… It should also not be confined to work, because what happens outside of our work significantly impacts on our approach, our wellbeing, our thinking, within work. To deny the experiences that come from outside limits the ability to maximize our internal strengths and ensure we are a progressive, productive and welcoming place of work, where we can all feel a sense of belonging. However, we need to remember that each person should have the right to choose what they reveal about themselves and it is a choice.

CASE STUDY
Talking with Leena and Sean from the BBC[5]

Leena and Sean work at the BBC and have been doing some incredible work over the years championing neurodiversity at work and beyond. You can access some of the content that they've been creating around neurodiversity and follow their work via Twitter @BBCCape. And it's really fantastic to see two people who have created something from the ground up.

Sean and Leena don't necessarily come from where we may expect diversity and inclusion initiatives like this to come from. Generally, they haven't been led by facets of HR or by D&I leaders or even through the recruitment team.

Sean is a UX principal for cognitive design at the BBC. He works in the user experience and design team in Salford in the northwest. He's also one of the BBC's neurodiversity leads working on the BBC Cape initiative, which stands for 'Creating **A** **P**ositive **E**nvironment'.

Leena works alongside Sean on the BBC's diversity initiative. She's also a user experience designer for the BBC's user experience and design team. Leena describes herself as on the autism spectrum and is also ADHD and identifies as being neurodivergent.

They recall that at the beginning of their journey, no one really knew much about neurodiversity. It was a relatively new concept at the time, especially when Leena started at the BBC: 'When I started talking to Sean about it, who was my line manager, he wasn't familiar with it himself.'

They just started having a conversation together about what it means to have a differently wired brain. Not just to discuss the challenges, in terms of accessing certain things within the workplace; they also wanted to share the fact that there's a pool of talent that is, unfortunately not being tapped into. They wanted to highlight that neurodiversity was about differently wired brains, and that these diverse perspectives could bring additional value to their teams. The fact that this could potentially lead to original insights, solutions, innovation, and people contributing in creative ways was also very appealing.

Leena, as an example, is a visual thinker and you can see this in some of the beautifully expressive images and videos she's produced and shared across social channels like Twitter @L1LHulk. Pictures are her first language. In contrast, she can find that verbalizing what she's thinking can be quite challenging. Ultimately, what they both wanted to show is that if you communicate in a different way, that doesn't mean it's less, it's just another form of communication. It can be equally valuable, if not more so, and how you communicate may often be dependent on the context.

What we love about this, and what we find fascinating is what change happens when this is led by two individuals coming together and having a mutually respectful conversation. Firstly a manager, trying to understand their colleague and then looking at what can be done to support them. But then beyond that, what can be done for the individual, how this can then take the learning gained out across the organization and beyond, which is exactly what they've done.

This is a positively disruptive staff network from the ground up, but then they were also successful because they gained support at a senior level to help fund and support the grassroots work:

It was a really interesting kind of time at the beginning there talking to Leena and listening to her experiences, because I'd been at the BBC for probably around eight years at the time, and it was the first time I'd met anybody who identified as autistic or had them explain this to me. It was something I'd heard of, but I didn't really understand (Sean).

Certainly when they first started off Sean found it difficult to know how to support somebody who is neurodivergent as he couldn't find any information. Leena's experiences were also that people didn't really know much about it.

So it was an opportunity for them, as a result of their conversations, to think about how they could change the experiences for other people because it couldn't just be them who had experienced this. This had got to be a wider issue across the organization.

We had a really supportive finance director. We took this idea to him and said, look, we'd love to do a little bit of work around this to see what we can explore and how we can improve this situation. He said yeah, absolutely fine, you go and do it (Sean).

So something really important that Sean and Leena have achieved is that as a manager and a colleague it doesn't cost a thing to open up the dialogue and have that conversation. However, showing the potential positive impact for the wider business can clearly help to gain senior stakeholder support.

It's like an inverted funnel, and the higher up the leadership chain it starts the better chance it has of reaching all managers and therefore the entire workforce. Sean had the support from his manager that allowed him to help Leena. With that overall support this then led to further opportunities of going out and talking to other people and collaborating on ideas so that they were able to develop some of the content they ultimately produced to raise awareness.

They created films that you can watch via the BBC Cape YouTube channel and they wanted to focus on the environment that people come into when they join the organization.

The reality is that they were in fact only two employees and not in charge of any recruitment. So for them the focus wasn't about how to go out and find talent and bring it in. It was more to raise awareness, so people could start to have the conversations to address some of the stigma in the workplace around being a neuro-minority. The impact of this can result in creating that positive environment that enables people to come in and thrive and to pursue a meaningful career.

In their words, they wanted to get their own house in order before they invited people to tea! Not only have they taken the BBC, the wider employees, and their colleagues on a journey, but actually allowing other people to tap into that content as well is the biggest gift of all.

We're positive we could all take a leaf out of that idea from Sean and Leena and we can see that change can start anywhere within an organization.

One of their fantastic pieces of shared content is a 360-degree virtual reality experience, where you can see the working world from a neurodivergent individual's perspective.[6] A lot of it firstly involved talking to people with different neurodivergent conditions and getting their stories. The reality is that some traits are shared between the different conditions whether it's autism, dyslexia, ADHD or dyspraxia. How people communicate, how people have sensory issues in terms of their environment, and also some of the challenges that come with being on the neurodivergent spectrum – each person will have their own tale to tell.

How did they go about making it and what was the idea behind it?

We worked with a producer, and we gathered information and stories. I explained to him how we wanted it to be from the individual's perspective, because a lot of the content out there is very much documentary style, or it's like a talking heads interview, which a lot of people on the spectrum may feel not so comfortable with. Like a camera pointing at them, and then someone firing questions at them saying 'How does this make you feel?', 'How do you process information?', 'What are the challenges you're feeling?'

It becomes quite invasive. So I thought, well, why not create a film where you get to see from the person's perspective almost like you put this lens on.

This was a brilliant way not just to help people generally understand the potential physiological and psychological impact of the working environment on those who are neurodivergent, but also to help those who are neurodivergent to know they are not alone and also offer a chance to see how they feel from another perspective.

When Theo shared these videos with employees at National Institute for Health and Clinical Excellence, he had people approach him to thank him for sharing them, and also to express their joy/relief/amazement at somebody capturing the way they feel and the experiences they have on a daily basis. Let's not forget that some people are so used to feeling uncomfortable, anxious and/or stressed in the working environment due to their neurological differences, that they become unaware or forget or just don't know that this is not the way most people feel.

When they started along this journey about four years ago or so, Sean and Leena knew maybe a couple of individuals within the BBC who were openly neurodiverse and spoke about it, but not really much more than that. They have seen a positive change in the last 24 months, and they modestly suggest that it's probably been helped by the external conversation around neurodiversity, and the fact that an awful lot more people, certainly on social media, are starting to talk about it and open up that conversation.

We'd say the BBC's recent coverage and their ability to positively project this message potentially to the four corners of this earth, means that the work two individuals have done in raising awareness on the subject of neurodiversity is more important and impactful than they would ever dare to believe or suggest themselves.

This is why the potential power of one manager having a conversation can never be ignored. And when we consider what it takes to break down walls consider this! 'Many people, who in many small places, do many small things, that can alter the face of the world.'[7]

Anybody reading this must believe in the power of the individual and the impact you can make on another person's life. Leena and Sean are the proof...

KEY POINTS
Line management

- Value each member in your team. They will think and communicate differently but will offer new ideas and perspectives.

- No conversation = no conversation.

- Shared understanding and improved communication between line managers and the team will result in better collaboration.

- Listen and ask what support each person requires and if there are training needs. You don't have to have all the answers. A line manager is not an expert in all things!

- Good conversations end up in better and more lasting relationships and can create lasting change.

Notes

1 Scholte, R H J *et al* (2007) Longitudinal stability in bullying and victimisation in childhood and adolescence, *Journal of Abnormal Child Psychology*, https://link.springer.com/article/10.1007%2Fs10802-006-9074-3 (archived at https://perma.cc/3NTM-DHWC)

2 Conti-Ramsden, G and Botting, N (2004) Social difficulties and victimization in children with SLI at 11 years of age, *Journal of Speech, Language, and Hearing Research*, https://doi.org/10.1044/1092-4388(2004/013) (archived at https://perma.cc/AXU6-JFP2)

3 Kumpulainen, K, Räsänen, E and Puura, K (2001) Psychiatric disorders and the use of mental health services among children involved in bullying, *Aggressive Behaviour*, https://doi.org/10.1002/ab.3 (archived at https://perma.cc/W4VD-9WT8)

4 Piek, J P *et al* (2005) The relationship between bullying and self-worth in children with movement coordination problems, *The British Journal of Educational Psychology*, https://doi.org/10.1348/000709904X24573 (archived at https://perma.cc/QUY6-5GY6)

5 Smith, T (2020) *Neurodiversity: Eliminating Kryptonite and Enabling Superheroes*, Ep 9: Leena & Sean – Enabling Superheroes at The BBC [Podcast] 6 January, https://podcasts.apple.com/gb/podcast/ep-9-leena-sean-enabling-superheroes-at-the-bbc/id1480239272?i=1000461718771 (archived at https://perma.cc/R5SW-Y9YS)

6 BBC Careers (2016) Project Cape Neurodiverse Immersive 360VR experience [Online Video] https://www.youtube.com/watch?v=ZLyGuVTH8sA (archived at https://perma.cc/6NFB-RTDK)

7 Raoux, M and Alavi, K (1990) East Side Gallery, Berlin, Germany, https://artsandculture.google.com/asset/untitled-kani-alavi-muriel-raoux/6gGWuEnyb4G50Q?hl=en (archived at https://perma.cc/UL9X-69CR)

13

Everyday meetings, conferences and seminars

Planning to be neuro-inclusive

Introduction

How often are we really thinking about the meetings we organize and the experience for those attending as a participant or a speaker? What's it like to be getting to or arriving at an unfamiliar setting? How does it feel when you are in a round-table meeting and expected to take your turn and hear what someone has said as you are preparing the words to speak? Amanda often has to travel across the UK taking trains, buses and walking into unfamiliar settings. She is often meeting people she has never spoken to before and finds small talk really hard. It's not that she can't do it but she finds it exhausting. Travelling and meeting takes huge amounts of energy. This is on top of planning to get to the place on time and ensuring you have yourself, your talk and your kit all with you. She remembers years ago going to deliver a talk on stress, in the days of using acetates and overhead projectors (yes, she is that old!). She was so stressed that she spilled water over the acetates and they all fell to the floor with the ink disappearing into a mess! She can still recall it vividly today.

We can all think of conferences where we know nobody there and stand in the coffee room thinking we need to make polite conversation with someone but not sure who to approach.

One really simple trick that normally works is to remember that everybody is there for the same purpose, so approaching someone and saying hi is OK. But a very simple method if you can't see anybody else standing alone to approach, is to approach a group of three people, as often the dynamic of a three-way conversation is that one of the three people is less engaged and therefore happy to divert their attention to another person for a two-way conversation.

This still takes some courage and won't solve the anxiety that you may have at attending an event, but it does work and we need as many hints and tips as we can take to help with meetings and events where we don't know anybody.

For conference organizers, just remember the positive impact you can have by making some adjustments that will stretch beyond those you think they will help, to a much wider audience. This can include creating collaborative spaces to help and facilitate conversations between attendees, as well as assistive technology and quiet spaces.

Theo, for example, has benefited from events that have live transcribers with the words projected onto screens or TVs. As he is dyslexic and ADHD he often finds it difficult to remember some of the details and key points of a presentation. Having a live script where he can take pictures to review after the event has been really helpful. Or if his mind races off for a second and he finds he's lost the speaker's train of thought he can quickly catch up by reviewing the screen.

So adjustments for those who may be hard of hearing have in fact helped Theo and others, creating a better overall experience for attendees. This technology can be utilized at both in-person events and online, so there really is no excuse not to.

The future of events has to be around attendee experience and that includes the speakers! Representation is also vital and if the event is not accessible you are cutting out very important and valuable voices.

Conferences

If you are planning a conference, start by thinking of your own biases or lack of knowledge. Depending on the form and content of the conference, are you aiming for inclusion and how do you ensure true representation? If we fail to acknowledge our implicit biases it will result in a meeting environment where underrepresented groups will continue to be marginalized and majority groups will continue to dominate. We exclude some people's voices because of where the meeting takes place, the cost and the delivery mode.

If we have learned anything from Covid-19 it is that we can deliver conferences remotely as well as face to face. Can we move to a blended option that widens the potential to engage? This offers choices for those who want to actually be in the room and for others who want to listen and ask questions from their sofa at home and still have a lot to contribute.

This blended approach also helps with capacity. How many times have you attended a conference to see a popular speaker or a speaker on a particularly interesting topic, and the room is packed full? For most people this is an uncomfortable feeling, but for some the bright lights and noisy, packed environment are just too much to take and a good reason to leave. Making better use of the space and the way we share and distribute the content has to be a focus for future event organizers.

Who are your speakers?

Whoever talks has the power. Equity is about access and power. Do we need to consider a range of ways to communicate with each other and not just through the spoken word? Do we rely on this form because that's the way it has always been delivered? For some people pre-recording their talk and then taking questions can be easier, for others having a dialogue with someone can be perfect. We need to consider different options rather than relying on the way we have always done it before.

Listening is as important as speaking. Can we ensure there are appropriate pauses in presentation and wait for others to process information before moving on?

Amanda recognizes she talks too fast. She has to consciously check to slow her pace and remind herself not to always feel that she needs to fill in the gaps. We can sometimes misinterpret slow responses as disinterest when they may be as a result of linguistic or cultural differences, or perhaps the need to cognitively process the information before considering a response.

In a live face-to-face conference setting we may have different ways of someone asking questions or seeking clarification. Accommodating different communication preferences can be provided through using different means, eg using low-tech approaches such as putting your questions on Post-it notes and placing them in a box or on a whiteboard or using voting apps that allow for polling and engagement from wherever you are.

We can all do better and we can learn from our challenges as well as our successes and share this with each other. If we can all write about what we have tried and describe any challenges and how we have overcome them (or didn't) we can all benefit. This is work in progress.

Planning the conference

- Ask the delegates for ideas: 'We want to provide an inclusive, diverse conference experience, but we need help. Can you help us?'
- Consider the information to be sent out before and after the event.
- Provide clear information about where it will take place and timings.
- Ensure there is information on how to get to the place with transport options – identifiable buildings are often helpful (eg near the shop with the orange sign; past Hotel X).
- Ask specifically if people have special dietary requirements.
- Make it explicit how to ask for adjustments. You could say for example, 'We strive to host inclusive, accessible events that enable all individuals, including individuals with disabilities, to engage fully. To be respectful of those with allergies and environmental sensitivities, we ask that you please refrain from wearing strong fragrances. To request an accommodation or for inquiries about accessibility, please contact (name, email, phone).'

Alternatively, you could offer a checklist for people to tick if they need any adjustments or specific support, for example:

I will need the following accommodations in order to participate:

- assistive listening device;
- captioning;
- reserved front-row seat;
- large-print handouts;
- advance copy of slides being projected;
- wheelchair access;
- wheelchair access to working tables throughout room;
- scent-free room;
- lactation room;

- gender neutral bathroom;
- diet restrictions – list: _____
- other: _____

_____

Ask permission to collect data about people's preferences and neurodiverse styles but ensure confidentiality. Establishing baseline data now and monitoring future progress is critical to show progress is being made.

For presenters

Provide presenters with a checklist requesting that they:

- submit materials in advance (but be reasonable with timeframes) so that they can be forwarded to individuals who may not be able to view screens or flip charts;
- verbally describe visual materials (eg slides, charts, etc);
- have printed copies available (in larger font);
- avoid using small print on presentations that can't be seen from a distance;
- ensure speakers (including those asking questions) always use a microphone;
- activate captions on any video used in the presentation;
- encourage hourly breaks;
- organize breakout group activities to maximize distance between groups (eg each group going to a corner of the room or side rooms).

It can be stressful and tiring presenting so ensure they know they have a quiet space they can go to before and after presentations as well.

The space and the place

Design for universal access. Universal Design is the notion that if you make a meeting accessible to people who have the biggest challenges, everyone benefits. How accessible is the venue? Sometimes it may be a challenge in terms of the choices you have as you may have a specific budget and need to use a certain location.

On the day

- Put up clear signage to show where the meeting or conference is being held.

- Consider breakout rooms and/or a quiet space for coffee/tea breaks so that people can choose to move away from the group and the need to have to make conversation.

- Offer name badges to be worn if wanted. Also consider whether participants could indicate their preferred pronouns (eg she/her/hers, they/them/theirs) at time of registration and add them to name tags or provide stickers.

- Background noises – music playing switched off.

- Consider the layout and set-up of rooms so that visual presentations are accessible to all and can be heard at all times. Do they have to be seated in rows?

- Consider if some people may need electrical outlets in accessible seating areas to accommodate devices, laptops, etc; extra space or work surface.

- At the end of each presentation do you think everyone should clap or not?[1] Firstly in Manchester University in 2018 and then Oxford University in 2019 they decided to substitute a clap at the end of the conference/ performance with using the British Sign Language equivalent – a wave of both hands. Consider if you want to do the same to reduce the sensory overload that may be uncomfortable for some.

Content and form of the day

- Check microphones are working and offer different types where possible. Some people find it hard to stand still and need to walk, and/or to have to remember to stay near a 'stick microphone'.

- Check if there is a hearing loop available.

- Can you provide notes in pdf format beforehand or afterwards? Either way do let your participants know what's happening.

- Can you provide closed captioning on speakers' slides?

- If you can, ensure someone is available for signing if this is required.

- Have some tables to sit at for note taking – especially useful if handwriting/ taking notes is difficult for someone.

- Make it known that participants can stand at the back of the room if they find it hard to sit still for long.

- Make sure to repeat questions posted by the audience before the speaker responds, especially if there is not a roving microphone available. Presenters or audience members may express confidence that they are loud enough and do not need a microphone. Regardless, encourage them to speak into one.

- Could you provide an alternative space to hear the lecture (a TV monitor set up in another room with headphones) for someone who may find it uncomfortable being in a setting with many people?

- Remote delivery of live conferences to widen engagement is now a far easier option. It opens up the potential for more people to attend but at the same time be in their own surroundings.

Break and lunch times

- Food choices – can people let you know beforehand if they have specific dietary requirements?

- Provide a quiet space to be able to take drinks/food if people need less noise and require a break away from having to make conversation.

- Provide a place to sit down at a table with their food. For some people balancing a drink and a plate is really difficult and stressful.

- Some conferences have some tables with topics cards on or to direct people who come from similar geographic or work areas to meet up so they know they have something in common. This can be used to help start a conversation.

After the event

Reflect on what has worked and what hasn't for next time. Ask attendees for honest feedback. Sharing your data creates accountability for yourself, and also for other groups and events around you. However, remember your role in collecting, storing, and sharing data responsibly. Unless strictly necessary to do otherwise, maintain demographic and other information related to diversity as de-identified data sets to limit the risk of exposure of confidential or sensitive information.

Meetings

Face to face

Start off by making a simple statement that inclusion is important. If people don't know each other, put some thought into how you can introduce yourself or ask people to complete something about themselves beforehand. Sometimes having to speak out and be interesting when you are feeling anxious can make it really difficult to listen to others at the same time! You could ask for each person to say their name and perhaps say 'something interesting about me you couldn't tell from just looking at me.'

Verbally acknowledge and draw attention to a 'Code of Conduct' if you have one. Making welcoming statements can enable participants to build a shared language and understanding of terms and definitions. Describe how moderation will happen and clearly identify the moderator. Provide name cards so that everyone can write on them how they want to be addressed (if they have a nickname for example) and their preferred pronoun.

Consider group dynamics and power dynamics of who speaks and who moderates.

Structure decision-making to include everyone. Put a system in place so that important conversations and decisions occur during the meeting, where everyone can have a voice and a vote. Important decisions made at meetings often happen adjacent to the meeting itself, over lunch, in bars, hallways, restrooms, etc; be aware that this may preclude some people who find this type of interaction uncomfortable and distracting. They also often take place in a noisier setting, making it harder for some people to focus.

Clearly note time constraints and stick to them.

Moderate Q&A sessions with awareness of inclusion to make sure more junior and less vocal attendees can get a word in. Moderators of Q&As play an important role in making sure discussions aren't dominated by a small number of vocal participants.

Invite those who may not speak right away to share their views or ask questions. Intentionally elicit multiple perspectives from multiple types of meeting participants. Questions could be posed before and after the meeting so they can be followed up at the next meeting for those who find it harder to vocalize in the meetings themselves. Consider letting the audience or participants prioritize the questions they want to be answered such as by using apps (eg sli.do).[2]

Provide written information to all participants in an email so that it can be read by text-to-speech software if necessary or printed out.

Online meetings

In online meetings it can be exhausting trying to get everyone to engage. Being a facilitator can be a bit like being the conductor of an orchestra all playing different tunes and starting off at different times. Many of the same principles you use for a face-to-face meeting can be used when planning online meetings. However, there are some differences which you will all be familiar with.

The person needs the added skills of engaging online with the technology as well as participating in the meeting. This can make it harder to pick up the nuances of physical communication, movements and eye-to-eye contact that would be present in a live setting around a table.

How you see someone on your computer screen may be different from others depending on your set-up. You can't say 'let's go around the room and ask everyone' in the same way as in a face-to-face meeting and no one can look anyone directly in the eye. Micro-gestures are missed altogether.

You have some control over your actions such as choosing to mute yourself, turning the camera off (and doing something else at the same time), or even finding out mysteriously at an inconvenient point in the meeting that your internet has gone down! Turn-taking and knowing just when you can speak can be particularly difficult sometimes in a web meeting and it often ends up that you seem to be talking over one another.

We can sometimes assume that someone is less interested if their camera is off but it may be a way of staying focused as you can move around or take notes, close your eyes, or think without being judged for doing this. So don't assume a camera off means someone is having a nap or making a cuppa!

When planning web meetings, do consider the size of the group and the length of the meeting. If the group is too big it will reduce the chance of participation or any meaningful discussions and some people may feel uncomfortable speaking up about something they disagree about. You may want to consider using breakout rooms to allow everyone to have their voice. Someone in each group can then volunteer to give feedback to the whole group and this allows for more voices to be heard.

What can you do?

Start by thinking of the length of the meeting. Who says it should always last an hour? Can you meet for 20 minutes, have a break, and then meet for another 20 minutes when everyone has had time to think about what is being discussed and can feed back?

DO HAVE A FACILITATOR

Having someone 'directing' or facilitating the meeting like a conductor in an orchestra is important. Their role is to both mediate and facilitate and, importantly, to keep track of who's talking – and who's not. The first thing is to watch closely for someone who is dominating the discussion and those who interrupt others. If someone tries to control the dialogue, interject and redirect the conversation back to the broader group. It is important that everyone has the opportunity to speak. For some, the group setting is really hard, especially if they are more introverted or have a speech and language challenge, or require longer to process information.

PROVIDE INFORMATION BEFORE THE MEETING

Information beforehand always helps everyone. Provide an outline of the meeting, who will be attending, the length and format of the meeting, and expectations and outcomes (if possible). Not all meetings have to last an hour so consider actually how long someone can remain focused in this setting.

SET THE GROUND RULES

At the start of the meeting set the rules and reiterate the purpose and length of the meeting. Anyone should be able to edit their name they want others to address them by and if necessary spell it phonetically, as well as giving their preferred pronouns. Check if anyone needs any additional support. You could ask a general question after a meeting such as 'Are there practices we are using in our meetings that are not working for you?' rather than saying 'Do you need adjustments?' as not everyone knows what specifically may help and you may need to problem-solve.

An anonymous group poll at the start of the meeting allows you to gain a feel of the room.

OFFER DIFFERENT WAYS TO ASK QUESTIONS

Be explicit about how people can ask questions (eg put hands up or type into chat any questions). State how they will be responded to – either in order or using an app so questions can be prioritized. Demonstrate how to do this. Using the chat facility and allowing people to post anonymously can be a way of really getting all people's views without fear of retribution, giving the ability to be honest. Have someone read out the chat and questions so everyone can respond and participate and encourage discussion.

GAIN FEEDBACK ABOUT BEING INCLUSIVE

There is no doubt facilitating a meeting takes practice. After meetings do try and find out what is working well and what isn't by asking your team members for feedback – either at the end of your meetings or with an email or app that allows anonymity.

CONSIDER WHO HAS NOT PARTICIPATED AND CONSIDER THE REASONS WHY

Keep in mind those who have not participated in the meeting and follow up to ensure everyone has an opportunity to contribute. Some people need to have time to reflect before responding. They may disagree with what is being said but feel uncomfortable confronting someone in an open forum. This can result in conformity bias which occurs when people feel pressured to agree with everyone else in the room. Creating a space where employees feel comfortable sharing opposing viewpoints will lead to better decision-making and more engagement from employees.

RECORD MEETINGS

Consider recording meetings (but be sure everyone is aware of this) so that attendees can review and reflect on the discussion if they need a longer time to process the information.

OFFER CLOSED CAPTIONING EVERY TIME

Some platforms offer automatic closed captioning so it runs all the time.

MEETING NOTES OR PRESENTATIONS

Where possible provide accessible copies of the entire presentation, including handouts, before the webinar. This enables webinar participants to review the information ahead of time so they can focus on listening to the presenters.

KEY POINTS

Everyday meetings, conferences and seminars

- Preparation is key. Ask for feedback and guidance from staff and also people who have attended events and see how you could do better next time.

- Up-front information helps – knowing what is happening and when can make a real difference to participation.

- Imagine each step of the journey of a meeting or conference and put yourself in the shoes of other people.

- Most adjustments don't cost a lot of money or time to put in place and allow everyone to be able to participate fully.

Notes

1 Weale, S and Perraudin, F (2018) Jazz hands at Manchester University: the calm behind the storm, *Guardian*, 5 Oct, https://www.theguardian.com/society/2018/oct/05/jazz-hands-at-manchester-university-the-calm-behind-the-storm (archived at https://perma.cc/NM5C-GY25)
2 Slido (2021) https://www.sli.do/ (archived at https://perma.cc/HA87-2QHP)

14

Champions, staff networks and communities

How to succeed in being an inclusive workplace

Introduction

In this chapter we discuss the ways organizations can put structure and processes in place to create neuro-inclusive work settings. While it is wonderful that organizations speak of diversity and inclusion, there remains a need to establish inclusive processes. To do so we also need to understand some of the keywords that are used. Sometimes we may assume that when we speak to each other we mean the same thing, but this may not actually be true!

To begin this chapter, we will outline some of the key terms we often use and what they mean to us such as equality, diversity and inclusion, and consider them in the workplace and then go on to discuss...

What is inclusion?

We talk a lot about inclusion but what does it really mean to you? Inclusion is fundamentally not just about being present. It is not tokenistic. It is being able to contribute to and feel a part of that group or organization and be valued.

In a workplace setting this means ensuring there are ways for all to contribute, and ensuring that others can access your communication styles.

It means being able to talk and share ideas without fear of saying the wrong thing or it being taken out of context. It also means having the skills or knowledge of key people in an organization to know how to make adjustments to all phases of employment and ensure they are put in place, not just talked about. Inclusion does not mean doing the same thing for and to everyone, eg having a standard practice for people who are dyslexic, as this will not achieve equality. It means doing the right thing for *each* person. That is equity. Successful inclusion happens when we can all feel valued and don't have to 'fit in' but we are integral and a valued team member. It is not easy and cannot be achieved in one step as there are elements including different people's attitudes and knowledge to address.

What is the difference between equality and equity?

We have talked in a previous chapter about the differences between equality and equity but we think it's important to repeat it here. When we talk about equality, we think about how everyone has the same opportunities to showcase their talents and skills and can make the most of who they are. Sometimes equality and equity are confused. Our society is continuing to make steps towards equality but being equal and fair is not always straightforward. Equity means we may need to differentiate what we do to ensure inclusion and sometimes people may need differing support to make their opportunities the same as others'. This is equity and is essential to consider when we are talking about neurodiversity and where our brains differ and our support needs will be different.

What is diversity?

Diversity can be seen as any differences between individuals on any attribute that might lead to the perception that another person is different from oneself.[1] It is socially constructed and can be 'othering'.

The diversity of individuals means that inclusion has to mean understanding how each person can contribute. This means understanding that each individual is unique and recognizing our individual differences and valuing them. These can be along the dimensions of race, ethnicity, gender, sexual orientation, socio-economic status, age, physical abilities, religious beliefs, political beliefs, or other ideologies. It is about each person. Cognitive diversity is the differences in the way we think, act and communicate.

If we cut up diversity into slices, such as delivering a campaign relating to neurodiversity alone, we run a risk of resulting in a 'them and us' situation.

*

Amanda has recently read documentation referring to 'the neurotypicals' and 'the neurodivergents' as if there are distinct groupings that separate us from them. The positive effects of diversity will be undermined if groups perceive dissimilar others as a threat. When the advantages of diversity are highlighted to the majority as well as the minority, interventions/support programmes are less likely to be viewed with resentment. We need to value intergroup differences rather than create factions.

A successful approach to achieving inclusion and diversity means actions need to be part of an ecosystem approach, not a one-off campaign. It needs to be embedded in all that we do. Embracing diversity of thinking can lead to better communication, improved understanding of how teams interact, less conflict and greater wellbeing. It's likely that when we consciously consider our differences (both strengths and challenges) we can assume our roles within the group dynamic more naturally and so teams become more cohesive and more productive.

Taking an all-inclusive approach

Ensuring workplace diversity is far more than just a moral issue but has key business benefits. Creating an inclusive approach and celebrating diversity in all aspects of business means everyone is a part of this and it is 'business as usual'. One way to achieve this is to frame programmes as all-inclusive, explicitly including majority groups and recognizing differences in us all so that we can hear and learn from different experiences and gain insight. We all gain from learning and integrating information about each other and this stimulates deeper information processing and complex thinking.

Researchers such as Galinsky *et al* in 2015[2] found that promoting diversity led to a reduction in bias and better intergroup interactions. Positive beliefs about diversity have also been found to positively impact whether diversity leads to greater social integration and innovation. PwC in 2016[3] found that educating their workforce led to staff feeling greater inclusivity where differences were valued and respected. The contrast to this is wanting everyone to be homogeneous in thoughts, feelings and actions. In reality each person is the opposite of this; we are all a sum of our parts and intersectionality is the reality.

Successful inclusion leads to feelings of belonging. In order to belong we need to have trust and openness. When we respect differences in us all we can then create a sense of belonging and open up the dialogue. In a culture where 'disclosure' has negative connotations and certain neurodivergent conditions still have a stigma attached to them (employers generally know less about ADHD and Tourette's) then belonging remains an elusive thing.

Inclusion means ensuring the doors are open

The amount of actual diversity in organizations is affected by recruitment, selection and promotion procedures. The first stage, recruitment, is critical because underrepresented individuals often forgo opportunities with organizations they deem unwelcoming. An ecosystem approach considers all points of the journey for the employee.

Inclusion is central to belonging

Belonging is a sense of fitting in or feeling like you are an important member of a group. Fitting in is when we feel connected or have an affinity with a particular person or group. A sense of belonging is not only innately human, but it is also important in building high-performing teams and is associated with strong performance in the workplace.

Affinity is a liking or feelings of empathy for someone especially because there are shared characteristics, but the opposite of affinity is feelings of dissimilarity, dislike, hatred or lack of empathy. When we consider the opposite, we see why affinity is so important. It certainly doesn't mean we need to all be the same but it does mean we need to have shared values. Good companies have values that are known by their employees so they can engage and be a part of living them.

In order to fit in and have an affinity with our team members we need to be empathic. Empathy is sometimes confused with sympathy. Empathy is our ability to read and understand another person's emotions, needs, and thoughts. It is considered to be one of the core competencies of emotional intelligence. It has been seen as one of the critical leadership skills. Good leaders need empathy as it ensures that they can influence, inspire, and help other people achieve their dreams and goals. Empathy is the stuff that enables us to connect with others in a real and meaningful way, which in turn makes us happier and more effective at work. Empathy is important for effective team working. In order to be empathetic we also need to recognize that we all communicate differently and what we say and what we mean may be very different from each other. We need to ask others and not assume. We need to check in with the person to see if we are correct.

What you can see from this is that equity, diversity and inclusion are integrally connected with belonging and wellbeing in the workplace.

Caring has currency

There is a real currency for organizations who care about their employees (and their customers). Fostering a sense of belonging is one of the most responsible and important things organizations can do to empower their teams to be at their best. Organizations that embrace a diverse and inclusive workforce see the value in hiring and nurturing professionals who are willing to challenge the status quo and coming up with new ways to solve important problems. Academics have also suggested that financial benefits for organizations flow from this. More diverse discussions can lead to better decision-making, more complex thinking and ultimately being better equipped for unforeseen challenges.

How do we succeed in being an inclusive workplace?

It is wonderful that organizations are speaking more about the imperative for diversity and inclusion in the workplace. There is even growing evidence of the impact for businesses that make this a primary focus. 'Diversity Wins',[4] published in 2020, is the third report in a McKinsey series, following 'Why Diversity Matters' (2015)[5] and 'Delivering Through Diversity' (2018).[6] The series investigates the business case for diversity. They have focused very much on gender diversity and ethnic and cultural diversity in corporate leadership – and have shown the business case strengthening from report to report; the most diverse companies are now more likely than ever to outperform less diverse peers on profitability.

We are seeing organizations making statements about their future plans and intent and describing some of their actions. Establishing inclusive processes, we all need to first understand the words we speak. Sometimes we assume that we mean the same thing, but this may not actually be true! In relation to neurodiversity most of the focus has been more on developing programmes for hiring those with autism or dyslexia rather than considering a wider spectrum of different talents. It is sometimes extremely specific rather than being neuro-inclusive.

Becoming an inclusive work setting is not easy and cannot be achieved in one step as there are elements to creating an environment for change,

FIGURE 14.1   Steps to create a neuro-inclusive workplace

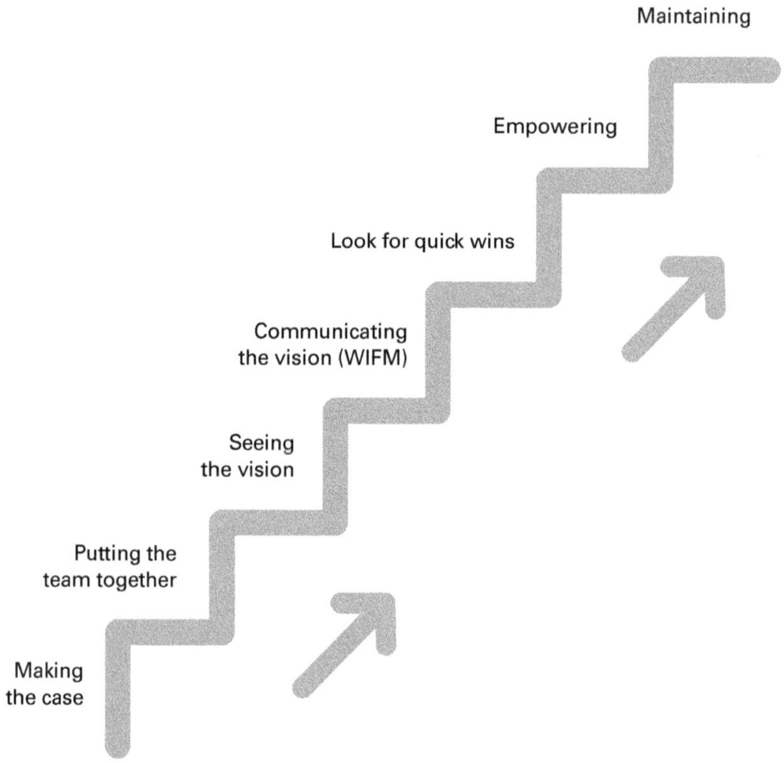

requiring that different people's attitudes and knowledge are addressed (see Figure 14.1). We need to move away from stereotypes, myths, misinformation and biases. Sometimes the language we use creates a barrier to communicating. We can use terms like disorder, disability and impairment. We use different words by different professionals such as specific learning difficulties in education and developmental disorders by health professionals. These differences can create misunderstanding and confusion.

Everyone involved must share a commitment to the philosophy of inclusion and a belief in the equal value of all. Inclusion requires all participants to be equal partners in the process.

> Diversity means understanding that each individual is unique and recognizes our individual differences. These can be along intersecting dimensions of race, ethnicity, gender, sexual orientation, socio-economic status, age, physical abilities, religious beliefs, political beliefs, or other ideologies.[7]

It is about each person.

How can we be inclusive?

- By gaining greater understanding.
- Being compassionate.
- Making sustained efforts rather than one-off initiatives.
- Recognizing where there is discrimination.
- Identifying and measuring where there is inequity.
- Being reflective and being humble to our mistakes.
- Not making neurodiversity this year's thing!
- Avoiding being tokenistic.
- Thinking about people and not campaigns.

At NICE, Theo set up a 'lunch and learn' session on neurodiversity. Soon he had over 30 employees in an email list who were happy to share thoughts and ideas on neurodiversity. This organically led to members of the group organizing events and writing interesting articles they wanted to share. This group included some senior members of the organization who had a personal interest in this area.

Before long, the organization would request advice and input from the group on things such as workplace layout and practices such as redesigning the office space or how to create accessible designs for the background to a Zoom call. The group grew informally and quietly into a network of like-minded individuals who were happy to help and support each other as well as the organization on the concept and practical implications of neuro-diversity in the workplace and beyond.

It was because of this work and Theo's reputation as a neurodiversity champion that people would feel empowered to quietly approach him with their own stories: 'Hey I'm dyslexic'… or 'I'm autistic'… or sometimes just, 'I always felt different and what you've been sharing really resonates with me.' So as an employee, don't always feel you need to wait for permission to do the big launch.

If you don't feel your organization or team is a safe place to do this or hasn't sufficient bandwidth or representation, then begin with external support groups. There are many that are based online and some local support groups which meet up in person. This can be a fantastic way of engaging with others and starting to test your thoughts and ideas whilst gaining insight from people with shared experiences. You can then take some of this dialogue and debate back to your organization to initiate meaningful change by helping them to understand where positive interventions can be made and what the potential benefits are to both the employee and the employer.

From an employer's perspective it is worth noting that many employees (particularly from underrepresented groups including neurodiverse employees) value the ability 'to bring your whole self to work'. Being able to openly express one's self in a pluralist inclusive work culture leads to retention of staff, good team morale and increased productivity. However, bringing 'your whole self to work' doesn't mean you need to reveal everything about yourself but choosing and knowing you can.

This is not our novel concept and has been given close attention by Mike Robbins in his book *Bring Your Whole Self to Work: How vulnerability unlocks creativity, connection, and performance.*[8]

> Google conducted an in-depth research project between 2012 and 2014 called Project Aristotle, aimed at determining the key factors that contribute to high-performing teams. It involved gathering and assessing data from 180 teams across the company, as well as looking at some of the most recent studies in the fields of organizational psychology and team effectiveness. According to the findings, the most significant element of team success is what's known as psychological safety: a culture of trust where people feel safe to speak up, take risks, and know that they won't be ridiculed for making mistakes or dissenting.
>
> When these actions – speaking up, taking risks, and owning mistakes – are modeled and celebrated, especially by those in leadership positions, it allows the team and the environment to be as psychologically safe as possible.[9]

CASE STUDY
The Admiral approach

One organization that is doing well in creating an inclusive culture is Admiral Insurance in the UK. Paul Billington from Admiral describes their processes and the steps they have taken over the past few years in building a more diverse and neuro-inclusive workforce. They have done this in stages building from awareness to providing a clear pathway of support and have included the training of a team of professionals within the business.

'At Admiral, we recognized that there was a growing, almost newfound awareness of neurodiversity beginning to show itself – it was no longer an understanding comparable to "dyslexics are just bad spellers" and other blanket judgements. Internally we had staff that had already told us of traits and struggles here and there, but we recognized that there was no centralized and consistent approach on how we supported people. Not that there wasn't support – there was, and it was certainly "doing a job", but there was no formalized route for staff, no signposting and little awareness on how to access guidance or assistance. There were some tools to aid people, but knowledge was sometimes weak and therefore, how did we know we were doing the best we could for staff? And more importantly, did all our staff know where to go to receive any guidance or support should they need it? How would managers understand how their teams best operate, respectful of those who could be neurodivergent?'

Amanda has been working with Admiral for several years in an iterative way to build a lasting, sustainable and inclusive system. Paul goes on to describe some of their actions.

'One of the first things we did was to reach out to experts in the field – and luckily, Prof Kirby has been a vocal champion in this area, so she was not hard to find! Understanding the current thinking, avoiding common pitfalls and misunderstandings in this area alongside building a strong through-line for staff, from the recruitment stage across their entire employment, was at the core of what we wanted to achieve.

'Education was prominent in those early days. Ensuring that we knew how to assist future staff to apply for roles with Admiral and verify that adjustments were made through the recruitment process, was key. In turn, creating training sessions to drive a solid knowledge base for managers and staff alike across the company that would help them to understand the changing world of neurodiversity – how traits can be missed, why someone isn't "just dyspraxic" and how a person's profile is not one thing or another – there was lots to communicate and absorb.'

They developed a stepped process and considered how mental health and wellbeing fitted into this framework: 'We centralized the support structure in a new "Workplace Support" team within the HR dept. Made up of staff that had previous experience of supporting disabilities and health conditions, workplace adjustments and a grounding in health, safety and wellbeing, one of the new core functions would be to understand neurodiversity as it stands, and how to assist anyone with, or without, a confirmed diagnosis. Linking in that with the effects on mental health, wellbeing and the barriers neurodivergent staff might face was incredibly important in developing strategies that would succeed for the person and the business.'

They carried out a series of actions: 'Creating awareness via wellbeing discussions, neurodiversity training sessions and articles on our internal intranet, the new team sought to establish connections and commonality of purpose within the business. To better support those with needs meant involving departments such as recruitment (potential and new staff), IT (software and hardware provision), and then gaining advice from outside the business too using Do-IT Profiler (for screening tools and recommendations), talking for example with the British Dyslexia Association and Autism Spectrum Connections Cymru. Additional to that we undertook neurodiversity awareness training for the team, accredited to OCN level 4 for "Supporting a Neurodiverse Workforce". This was vital to ensuring the right conversations took place, the correct thinking went into adjustments and fundamental ongoing support was in place.'

Paul importantly showed that this was a plan that started over one year but has now been continued for several years. They could see a business advantage in making these commitments: 'Celebrating diverse talents and bringing about understanding of an area that is unfortunately somewhat unrecognized as being a valuable and important asset to any business was important to us. Seeking to employ talented people with traits which oftentimes provide skill sets that, when provided the opportunity, flourish and deliver needed talents in so many areas of the workplace has been something that more businesses need to grasp. We are still developing our approaches in this area and will continue to explore how we respect and develop talents in our neurodivergent colleagues.'

This stepped process is evolving for Admiral and this is key to becoming an inclusive organization. Admiral have developed their own ideas and some central areas of work. Paul describes these:

- Wellbeing in the Workplace assessments and signposting etc (mental health)/all team trained as Mental Health First Aiders/making reasonable adjustments.
- DSE/musculoskeletal – working with disability, long-term health conditions and reasonable adjustments.
- Neurodiversity – we got a team trained on the accredited Neurodiversity Awareness course and also selected some staff from this to become Workplace Needs assessors. We are using Do-IT Profiler as a part of the screening process and then providing one-to-one support alongside the support of managers who oversee the individual and the team.

Admiral have taken a holistic approach to all these strands as they recognize that neurodiversity links to physical and mental health and needs a complete and overarching view. They are continuing to develop next steps in this process so there are pathways in place. Paul goes on to describe this in a little more detail: 'The recruitment team has direct contact with anyone who has said they are neurodiverse who has difficulties with the interview process or questions about office working based on needs. Contact is made and the team works with the Recruitment Officer and Recruiting Manager. The team also reviews any medical forms that indicate needs or some support.'

Admiral have staff that have been appropriately trained and train others within Admiral. Paul says, 'Training is conducted on neurodiversity awareness by our initial training teams. This often prompts some staff who have been having challenges and have not been diagnosed to speak to "Workplace Support", where we confidentially meet and talk about their circumstances, offer support, use the Do-IT Profiler, make any adjustments (environment, software, hardware, targets, day-to-day role etc), educate their manager and deliver whatever is needed at that point in time.'

Admiral have created a Tailored Adjustments Plan (TAP) that follows the person to each department allowing them freedom to explain to each new manager what they need. There are Workplace Support (WPS) follow-up meetings on the plan with the manager and staff member so that continuing support follows a staff member wherever they go in the business. Regular check-ins with staff on their adjustments are made as often as the person is comfortable.

What is key about this approach?

Admiral are continuing to build awareness in the organization through a number of actions including:

- intranet articles on work done, help offered, 'offer rather than declare';
- internal training course for teams on what neurodiversity is, held across the business – mentioning Workplace Support;
- specific training on core areas for speciality and correct advice;
- 1-2-1 confidential support sessions with staff; disability forum awareness.

They also have had HR buy-in so that if topics come up within performance management meetings etc, staff are signposted to Workplace Support. We think this is a great example of an embedded system that has been built up over time and is creating a culture of inclusion.

Setting up networks

We hear from Jennifer Offord, Senior Planning and Enabling Manager from 'Homes England' about her first-hand experience of neurodiversity networks and what has been achieved.

'For me, being in a neurodiversity network means I am not alone within my organization. On projects, I have felt the odd one out, conscious that I approach tasks differently to most. It is tiring having to explain why I am interested in connections that others don't see or feel relevant. In our network discussions, I find I don't have to justify myself so much.

'I have heard the sense of belonging that the network offers described as "finding your tribe". I can understand for some the comfort in that. But I think what brings our network members together is that we realize we are not the same. We notice and respect our unique "spiky profiles". We talk a lot about the limitations and frustrations of "one size fits all" processes that put people into boxes.

'In the network there is no expectation to communicate a certain way. Some, like me, interrupt a lot to present ideas, while others find this distracting and disruptive. Finding a balance is a work in progress and our Chair plays a key role. We are open about our conflicting needs and try to ensure everyone has their say, in their own way. Being valued and accepted as an individual means I feel more relaxed, and less on my guard.

'Through other network members, I have discovered a lot about different communication styles and the way I work best. This means I am more confident about what I can do well, and what strategies work for me. Based on what others have said, I realize now that having a clear "mission" or brief before starting tasks is necessary for me to work effectively. The network is gaining momentum, and we are starting to put our experience into practice through an informal buddy system, offering support to new starters and also their managers.

'Beyond supporting individuals, insight from our network is creating practical changes throughout the organization from recruitment, to training and procurement. Many of our suggestions have been simple and the benefits extend far beyond network members. For example, our network has demonstrated that mini-videos can communicate news more effectively than relying on long emails. We have also explained why setting out what will happen in advance of interviews will enable many candidates to feel at ease and present their strengths more clearly than being taken by surprise.'

So what has Jennifer learned from her experiences, that she can share? 'A neurodiversity network can begin as an informal group, on WhatsApp or Teams, or it can take a more formal structure with a committee and designated roles. A clear vision is important to give the network a purpose. Aligning objectives to the organization's goals can help target network activity to have the most impact.

'While a network can help drive change, buy-in from all in the organization is important and there need to be clear boundaries for what the network is and is not responsible for. Strong support from senior leadership and a sponsor helps networks to thrive. By reinforcing the message that everyone has a role in creating a neuro-inclusive culture, senior leadership and managers can involve the whole organization in driving change.'

Jennifer goes on to say: 'I am encouraged to see neurodiversity networks increasingly visible within different organizations, and across professions. It is great to see connections across networks too, uniting in the message that being neuro-inclusive is vital for organizations to support all employees to work at their best. Together our neurodiverse voices can help shape the future of work, to support collaboration and innovation, and ensure that no one feels alone due to neurodiversity.'

In an ideal world, a staff network will have the support and backing of the organization, and where possible it will be established and led by the senior leadership!

The benefits of staff networks go way beyond the inclusion of your staff. They can bring creativity and innovation to your people strategy and can help challenge the status quo, ensuring managers and employees are supported. Staff networks often serve to engender a feeling of belonging amongst your current employees, whilst also helping to attract new talent to the organization with new ways of thinking and new approaches to tackling the work you do.

Furthermore, it allows people to bring a 'more genuine' rather than a 'curated' version of themselves to work, as mentioned previously. They don't need to mask their personal traits, or the fact they have a child who's autistic or dyslexic. They don't need to feel ashamed of the fact that they have panic attacks or struggle to deal with change in their hyper-focused, structured world. Knowing that there are other people in their organization willing to share their experiences and offer support and advice, can help people open up, break down stigma, and educate those who've not had the opportunity to understand why somebody may feel or act in a particular way.

Key things to consider when looking to set up staff networks

1 Establish clearly the purpose of the group and why it is needed.
2 Gaining senior leadership buy-in.
3 Inclusion is everybody, try to make sure all are welcome.
4 Capture learnings to feed back into the business and empower positive action.

WHAT IS THE PURPOSE OF THE GROUP AND WHY IS IT NEEDED?

If you have no women in your organization, it may be sensible to first undertake due diligence before starting a women's network, to understand why the organization is failing so significantly at being diverse on the most basic of levels.

Looking for support externally to challenge the status quo may be your best bet, on the basis that the organization's issues and challenges may be as wide as they are deep.

Theo's example at NICE is a good place to start. Do some research, get some internal or external speakers in on the subject and see what the take-up is and how engaged people are with the subject. You may find that once you start talking about neurodiversity the debate will grow exponentially from that point forward.

GET SENIOR LEADERSHIP BUY-IN

The organization eventually has to get behind staff networks from the top down. It's not enough to have it on today's agenda, as tomorrow it will be all but forgotten. Too often we witness organizations get excited by the idea of neurodiversity, but then this initial enthusiasm stagnates, and moves little beyond awareness raising, essentially becoming nothing more than a bureaucratic tick-box activity. Senior leadership needs to see the value for their organization in how having a neurodiverse and inclusive workforce brings in new talents, and aids productivity and wellbeing.

Having a senior leader as part of the overall initiative can pay real dividends. Often you won't have to dig too deep to find somebody at senior level who either identifies as being a neuro minority or has a family member who does.

INCLUSION IS EVERYBODY, TRY TO MAKE SURE ALL ARE WELCOME

For a staff network focused on neurodiversity to work, we cannot exclude others. Who are we to define how somebody is impacted, and why they may want to be a part of this network? We must not underestimate how creative ideas, positive action and change can come from a wide variety of people. Having a group composed solely of those who identify as autistic or dyslexic could create its own 'groupthink' challenges. You could inadvertently create a group subculture, which is in its own way just as monolithic and singular as the wider work culture it is trying to influence.

And, on a practical note, think about the logistics of the network meeting up: when, where and how. For example, try not to organize the first meet-up in a busy space with bright lights and poor noise reduction. Be considerate of those attending; you may want to offer different ways of engaging that suit different styles of communication. You will also need to consider the difference in conducting virtual meetings compared with a face-to-face one. In a virtual meeting you may need to explicitly provide the rules of engagement, provide an agenda and say how communication works, such as use of chat, how to ask a question and contribute.

CAPTURE LEARNINGS TO FEED BACK INTO THE BUSINESS AND EMPOWER POSITIVE ACTION

Everybody benefits from successful staff networks, not just those that form the groups and attend the meetings. The learning and experiences shared in these networks can be utilized to improve the working environment for everybody and ultimately show others that this is a good company to join. It can also help feed into wider staff learning and development to ensure the workforce are adapting and changing with the times.

If there is a forum for representation, people who are neurodiverse can be empowered to have their voice and be in a safe space to speak up in a way they may not feel is possible if speaking to their line manager or to HR. This collective voice may be used to discuss support for themselves and their colleagues at work, as well as their children and wider family. Either way, people are talking, which is great! There are some caveats though. In any group rules of engagement need to be expressly stated. For example, someone may share something that should stay within the group. It's important there is a discussion around 'duty of care' in case someone says they feel very depressed for example.

Do remember (and it seems such an obvious statement) that people do not fit into neat boxes; intersectionality is the rule rather than the exception. Hence, an employee can be gay and dyslexic; black, female and autistic. As much as groups for specific groups with shared interests can be valuable, they should not be seen as an exclusive club but be open to others who may want to learn more too or who are not quite sure whether they fit into a neurodivergent paradigm.

In writing this book, Amanda was speaking to someone who recently gained a diagnosis of ADHD in her forties. She is a parent, now in her fifties, and is also a carer, and had been seen by numerous mental health services and diagnosed with anxiety but ADHD had never been considered or discussed. Ten years ago she would have joined one employee support group in an organization, but today she could potentially join four or five.

Building and engaging with communities

Another illuminating example of building and engaging with communities can be found in the recent publication by Universal called *Creative Differences: A handbook for embracing neurodiversity in the creative industries.*[10]

The creative industry is by nature a highly neurologically diverse place. In the words of High Contrast (who we met in Chapter 4): 'You only have to take a look around to see that there are many more music artists like me.'

There are incredible people who have said they are neurodivergent, like Florence Welch, lead singer of Florence and the Machine, and this encourages the external influencers within the neurodiverse community like Lucy Hobbs in the UK who runs a group called The Future is ND who meet and share ideas. This helps in the creative sector, especially where people are often working alone and need to feel connected. It has a dual benefit in terms of gaining support but also acts as a catalyst to work together.

This is another great way to embrace the power of neurodiversity.

Given the musical stars associated with Universal and their deep resourcing pockets and media platforms, it is not surprising that, as an organization, they have the time and budgets to foreground and support neurodiversity so visibly. However, before we become too cynical, it's not all about who you know!

A visible commitment by organizations to embrace neurodiversity can manifest in a number of ways, as we have described. A company can firmly plant a stake in the ground to show that neurodiversity is important, not only to current employees, but also to the external communities that exist around neurodiversity and more broadly around diversity and inclusion. They can do this by having awareness sessions, for example. This will help attract neurodiverse talent and fundamentally change hiring processes (for the better).

Building and engaging with communities is about value. Universal has created a valuable and shareable handbook that can be used by individuals and organizations alike. They are speaking loudly and passionately to those they would potentially like to attract to the organization in the future. Hence, the focus and structure of the handbook's content ensures it gives immediate value to people working within the creative industries, but arguably its weight and relevance can be felt much further than this.

There is also the undeniable fact that Universal have just created a whole new level of interest as a commercial organization and producer of music.

Not only did we love some of their artists before, we now also hold the organization in high regard. This can be a powerful move by any organization.

Now building a community from scratch may not be something you want to do; it takes some thought, consideration and planning to get it right. You also have to go back to the point at the beginning of this section around the 'why'. Similarly to a staff network, you should only be building something where you can offer value and where there is a specific need. However, it is worthwhile understanding the methodology used in building engaged communities as there is a mutual benefit and, if there is the time and budget available, it is often an advantageous venture.

Somebody who knows a thing or two about building highly engaged communities in targeted group demographics is Milimo Banji. He was the guy who sat with Theo at Recfest (the leading recruitment festival conference) and within the space of minutes was able to engage with the student population on the subject of neurodiversity.

Mils founded an organization, TapIn, which specializes in effectively building communities of students and graduates for organizations. These groups often have a very specific focus around careers support and advice, but the key element to his communities is that they are engaged and responsive. Why is this? It is because he speaks to the group's bespoke needs and demands; he provides the community with tailored hints, tips and advice on how to compete for jobs in niche or very specific markets like management consultancies.

Mils answers some key questions on the reasons why you would build an online community, who can do it and how you do it.

Why build an online community?

Social communities are some of the most vibrant and thriving ecosystems created in recent times. Platforms like Instagram, Facebook, LinkedIn and Twitter have become some of the most engaged channels for talent to reside in. During the Covid-19 pandemic, we've seen an increase in social media usage of over 40 per cent, with the majority of people flocking to social for entertainment, education and escape whilst living restricted lives at home. These social channels have become key avenues for the exchange of ideas and more than ever before, we're seeing talent go to social media before the web to learn more about their next job and engage with employers. With so many candidates now on social media, there's a need now more than ever for employers to build online communities and adapt their strategies by finding unique ways to engage with talent in this ever-changing candidate landscape.

Who can build a community?
Building social communities isn't unique to select employers, it's not an exclusive activity that is allocated to a select few. Any employer who wants to engage with talent and adapt their attraction and engagement strategy should be creating online social communities. The best way to attract talent to an organization is organically. When employers focus on building real brand affinity and deepen their relationships with candidates, what you'll find is that candidates start to become intertwined with your employer brand, share your content and engage authentically with you. Long-term investment in your community will reduce the cost of hiring whilst increasing the time each employee stays at the organization. You're not just hiring anyone, you're hiring loyal and passionate people that share your values – this will have positive impacts on everything from their happiness in the workplace to their overall performance and output.

Building an engaged community
The key thing to remember when building your community is that you are not the centre of the story, you are not the protagonist – rather you are the guide. The guide refers to your position in supporting candidates in learning more about your organization; you're essentially taking them on a journey of exploration and deepening their relationship with your brand whilst getting them closer to achieving their goals.

Building communities begins with value. Before posting anything on social media, you've got to understand the concept of value and how to create content that provides benefits to those in your community. When building your community, begin by really understanding your audience. Speak directly to them and find out what sort of content they'd find useful in learning more about you and advancing their career (Instagram Stories' interactive stickers are great for collecting insights like this in a fun way). You can then use the results you get to create value-driven content designed to serve your community, answer their questions and support them.

Value-driven content is the key to cutting through the noise on social media and earning the attention and trust of top talent. The typical content consumer in the UK now sees well over 5,000 advertisements every day, compared to just 500 in the 1970s; meanwhile, over 500 hours' worth of YouTube videos are uploaded per minute, and every day we send 350 million tweets and 294 billion emails, and post 95 million photos and videos to Instagram. With so much content and information swirling around cyberspace, you've got to show up consistently and frequently with value that warrants talent's time and attention. In a digital world where businesses are all trying to 'take, take, take', what can you give?

How can you educate, entertain and inspire your audience? How can you speak to them instead of at them?

Now what Mils has shared with us here is a very high overview of the importance of connecting with your fellow human beings in a meaningful way and at a place and time that suits them.

Let's not underestimate the skill that's required to build and engage with such communities; that's why we need to ensure the right tone of voice is used. A comment that is often used – 'Nothing About Us Without Us' – highlights the importance that when building communities we do not exclude those we are trying to serve. We can provide the platform, but the conversation is not ours to own.

Creating neurodiversity champions

We think it is wonderful to see neurodiversity groups and champions beginning and growing in many workplaces. It can be amazingly energizing to have people who 'get you'. They have great value and can provide a safe space to discuss ideas and views and learn from each other.

In addition, change champions are important for moving new innovations through the phases of initiation, development and implementation, and if you are a champion then you can have a big impact on your organization.

The concept of champions in other sectors has highlighted a series of core elements for success that are useful to consider in this space and include:

1 actively and enthusiastically promoting the specific area of interest;

2 making connections between different people in the organization;

3 mobilizing resources;

4 navigating the socio-political environment inside the organization;

5 building support for neurodiversity by expressing a compelling vision and boosting organizational members' skills and confidence;

6 ensuring that the awareness programme is implemented in the face of organizational inertia or resistance by, for example, gaining buy-in at board level.

Often the person who chooses to put themselves forward to become a champion is passionate about making change and will certainly have had experiences in the workplace that are valuable not only to those they are championing – here, people who are neurodivergent – but also to HR line managers in the organization itself. Sometimes people are chosen for the role because they are known as the one who is dyslexic or dyspraxic and are put forward. They may not want to be a leader or instigate running a group but just be happy to participate. We need to be sensitive to this too.

Defining the role of a neurodiversity champion

- This is a signposting role – Amanda often describes this as a bit like being a Special Educational Needs Coordinator (SENCO) in a school. The role is to signpost people to resources or processes within or outside your organization, and to be a listening ear.

- It is important there is clarity about roles and boundaries and what the limitations of the role are. The person is not an expert in other people's conditions, only their own. They are not a counsellor or a coach (unless trained in this).

- A champion can be empathetic, but it is not about sympathy. There is a big difference between the two. Usually neurodiversity champions are cognitively diverse themselves and will have had their own experiences which they may want to share, but it is important that they do not see themselves as THE expert in neurodiversity.

- The champion needs to have a basic understanding of neurodiversity but should avoid commenting about the person and their circumstances at home or work. It is not a diagnostic or an assessor role.

- Confidentiality frameworks are important to define and are key, but there should be conditions where if the champion is genuinely concerned about someone's wellbeing, they should be able to have a process in place about what to do and who to speak to.

- Some people who are champions provide awareness sessions for staff but the information they are providing needs to be both accurate and robust.

When setting up a Neurodiversity Champions programme, consider determining if the role is a project-related and time-bound role. It helps to have clear aims and an end goal. Alternatively, is the role part of a number of processes of organizational change? It can have elements of both but it is useful to consider this. Organizational change for sustainability requires champions and leaders to make and sustain improvement in their systems and processes. Any intervention needs to consider ways to enhance communication, trust and teamwork so there is a long-term plan. It is important, therefore, that this is not put on 'a' champion, but the work is undertaken as part of a group. No single neurodivergent person can offer everything required for success. It also requires an iterative process as each organization will be at a different stage and readiness for change.

When working with champions, particularly when they are neurodivergent, there can be significant impacts on self-confidence and self-esteem if there is a lack of support for their role, especially if things do not go as expected. We have spoken to some wonderful people who are feeling tired and burned out despite being passionate about being part of the change. They may soon feel that it is unsustainable.

Some people may end up being champions for all the best reasons in the world but we think we also need to be mindful of the choice to do it, maybe because it can be seen as the quick route to getting adjustments in place for their own job. Alternatively some might see the role as a means of settling grievances because of injustice and lose sight of the aims of the group. Some people end up doing it because they find it hard to say no or don't want to let people down once they have made a commitment.

Being a champion while presenting many positives including bonding with others in your organization and providing mutual support may also create a tipping point in someone's wellbeing if they are trying to balance job and home life when already at near full capacity.

Some people want to do good and may become really committed to doing the role well and even maybe over-enthusiastic, taking it all on their shoulders as well as continuing their day job. For some, as Amanda has seen, this may then result in becoming exhausted.

Be careful that there is not the assumption that someone has the technical or emotional skills to support others. For example, Amanda met Bob, who has dyslexia. He was often referred to by people in his organization as the 'expert' in dyslexia and was advising others about specialist software, equipment and guidance based on his own experiences without actually having any training. It is essential that boundaries are set at the start to define what the role is. This reiterates the need for appropriate training and supervision.

Amanda always works on the 'do no harm' approach and we need to be careful that someone doesn't end up becoming over-involved with someone else's challenges and not having adequate supervision or a clear pathway for referral. One example of this is Jan. She describes herself as autistic. She has been an amazing listener for some of her colleagues with mental health and anxiety challenges. She has not had any personal supervision or training in how to deal with some really raw stuff (one of her colleagues ended up taking an overdose) and didn't know where to signpost the person for more help. She blamed herself and felt she had failed the person she had been talking to and only resolved how she was feeling after having counselling herself. We need to be careful when we are trying to do good that we do not harm anyone in the process.

Interestingly, the evidence around the role of Mental Health First Aiders (MHFAs) has been varied. A report, published by the UK Health and Safety Executive in 2018,[11] concluded that while the approach raises awareness, the impact on mental health is inconclusive. Their findings concluded that there is consistent evidence that MHFA training raises employees' awareness of mental ill-health conditions, including signs and symptoms. However, there is limited evidence that MHFA training leads to sustained improvement in the ability of those trained to help colleagues experiencing mental ill-health. Finally it reported there was no evidence that the introduction of MHFA training has improved the organizational management of mental health in workplaces.

Big companies and small companies

It is easier to have processes and people to manage these in larger companies. Small and medium companies who are interested in creating a neurodiverse workforce may not have the structures in place, nor have Employee Assistance Programmes (EAPs), counselling services or HR departments for example. So this may mean there are not clear pathways for support and in reality one person may be taking on several roles around recruitment and support.

Amanda has been running accredited courses relating to neurodiversity awareness for organizations in the UK. One of the courses she delivers is with Janette Beetham, who runs Right Resources. The training they have been delivering together has been attended by people from a wide range of types and sizes of organizations including the police, large-scale employers, educational establishments, and unions.

Janette has had extensive experience delivering workplace assessor courses in the UK and being a workplace assessor herself and providing coaching. She has developed an accredited dyslexia and neurodiversity champions course and has worked in a wide range of settings. She is a great person to offer insight on what is gained by organizations taking this approach.

'Some of the more proactive employing organizations have dedicated "Staff Networks" and these provide neurodivergent staff with the opportunity to come together in a "safe" and supportive environment. However, while valuable in talking about their experiences, unless these networks benefit from training and support and have a structure to them, these tend to take the shape of social gatherings and so often end up being little more than "talking shops".'

She goes on to say that developing a framework can be more beneficial to the organization. 'By adopting a "champions approach" the network is more able to capitalize on the opportunity their employer has given to them (in terms of time and resources) and use this to take a more proactive approach to neuro-inclusion in the workplace. While the training for champions is sometimes provided using "in-house resources" (and this can work well if there are suitably trained professionals within the organization), if choosing external trainers it is recommended to "shop around" and choose carefully... as this is something that is far too important to get wrong.'

She describes some of the benefits that having training provides organizations. 'Champions training, when delivered by a specialist organization, should help ensure actions are founded on accurate awareness of neurodivergent conditions as well as providing clarity on what workplace support is available for staff. (Ideally this should look at what is available "in-house" and what individuals should expect to be able to access in national terms... including understanding the legal perspective.) Also, rather than focusing purely on their shared challenges, with this type of training neurodivergent individuals are more aware of the many commonly associated strengths – and often untapped potential. For many there will also be the realization that this is not a "one size fits all" situation and, though in the early discussion their challenges may be seemingly similar, each person's challenges will be unique to them.'

Janette explains her personal and professional reasons for developing and delivering the 'Dyslexia Champions' (which has been broadened more recently to encompass neurodiversity) training and accreditation. 'The numbers of people approaching me for impartial advice and guidance – many of whom had delayed seeking support due to fear of discrimination and the impact it might have on their career in the longer term. This was something I could empathize with having suffered in silence myself years ago – feeling like I had nowhere to turn (and experiencing the negative impact on my own mental health). Having insight and self-knowledge is so important and I am keen to ensure people feel safe to talk. No one should be struggling in silence. When someone reaches out for the first time, they need to know there are impartial, knowledgeable people they can talk to, who understand and can really listen… and then provide information to enable them to make informed decisions about whether to seek support, or not.'

This point she makes about being informed and impartial is important and we have emphasized the need to set boundaries on what the role is and is not. Janette describes how there is a need for good-quality and comprehensive training. 'It's great to see a number of specialist organizations now delivering champions training as those I have personally trained have said it is a really positive experience. Ideally the training should include not only awareness training (neurodivergent conditions) but also listening skills, mental wellbeing, awareness of common workplace challenges and how to access workplace-related support.'

KEY POINTS
Champions, staff networks and communities

- Get buy-in from the top of the organization so there is a commitment and it is not seen as a one-off activity but part of an inclusive approach taken by the organization.

- Networks can start informally and can aid collaboration and communication.

- Establish the rules, boundaries and purposes of a network. Revisit these regularly.

- Ensure that champions are not a substitute for professional guidance or support and don't 'burn out' with pressures and needs of others.

- Mutual values and respect for each other will aid collaboration.

Notes

1 Van Knippenberg, D, De Dreu, C K W and Homan, A C (2004) Work group diversity and group performance: An integrative model and research agenda, *Journal of Applied Psychology*, p 1008, https://doi.org/10.1037/0021-9010.89.6.1008 (archived at https://perma.cc/QLV3-QKR4)

2 Galinsky, A D *et al* (2015) Maximizing the gains and minimizing the pains of diversity: a policy perspective, *Perspectives on Psychological Science*, https://doi.org/10.1177/1745691615598513 (archived at https://perma.cc/SVX3-ANQJ)

3 PwC (2021) The PwC diversity journey Creating impact, achieving results, https://www.pwc.com/gx/en/about/diversity/global-diversity-week.html (archived at https://perma.cc/87L8-NE5G)

4 McKinsey (2020) Diversity wins: How Inclusion Matters, https://www.mckinsey.com/featured-insights/diversity-and-inclusion/diversity-wins-how-inclusion-matters# (archived at https://perma.cc/KF67-BVWB)

5 McKinsey (2015) Why diversity matters. McKinsey – Our Insights, 1 January. https://www.mckinsey.com/business-functions/organization/our-insights/why-diversity-matters# (archived at https://perma.cc/5F37-3K9V)

6 McKinsey (2018) Delivering Through Diversity, https://www.mckinsey.com/~/media/mckinsey/business%20functions/organization/our%20insights/delivering%20through%20diversity/delivering-through-diversity_full-report.ashx (archived at https://perma.cc/J7U7-Q6YP)

7 University of California, San Francisco (2021) Diversity. https://epibiostat.ucsf.edu/diversity#:~:text=Diversity%20means%20understanding%20that%20each,political%20beliefs%20or%20other%20ideologies (archived at https://perma.cc/3XZE-UPU8)

8 Robbins, M (2018) *Bring Your Whole Self to Work: How vulnerability unlocks creativity, connection, and performance*, Hay House Business, London

9 Robbins, M (2018) How to bring your whole self to work, *Greater Good Magazine*, 19 September, https://greatergood.berkeley.edu/article/item/how_to_bring_your_whole_self_to_work (archived at https://perma.cc/2GUJ-E4R3)

10 Universal (2020) *Creative Differences: A handbook for embracing neurodiversity in the creative industries*, https://umusic.co.uk/Creative-Differences-Handbook.pdf (archived at https://perma.cc/9BN2-H5SP)

11 HSE, (2018) Summary of the evidence on the effectiveness of Mental Health First Aid (MHFA) training in the workplace, https://www.hse.gov.uk/research/rrpdf/rr1135.pdf (archived at https://perma.cc/C75C-E35U)

Further reading

ACAS (nd) Employers: Changing your workplace to better support neurodiversity, https://archive.acas.org.uk/index.aspx?articleid=6679 (archived at https://perma.cc/7GHJ-PLNK)

15

Future workspaces and workplaces

Introduction: So what is the future for workplaces?

What will an ideal neuro-inclusive workplace look like in the next 25 years or even the next five? The major shift to home working in 2020 has opened up the floodgates to flexible working. It has seen us Zooming from call to call dressed in track pants, joggers and slippers mixed with professional attire up top.

A real mindset change has happened that could have taken years to achieve, yet in reality took months. This has had some clear advantages for some people and real challenges for others working from home.

As fun and exciting as this rapid change might have been for some in the early days, over time the reality of working, living, playing, relaxing, stressing all in a single space can and has taken its toll.

It's true that you can choose your friends, but you can't choose your family and often the place where you live. The reality of the situation is that many people find the journey to and time spent in a workplace an escape from their daily lives.

Just as some children may only receive their single main hot meal a day at school, there will be adults who find refuge in their workspace. Those people escaping abusive relationships, family members who are addicts or environments that are negative to their health and wellbeing, have been thrust into the dark depths of despair.

So when we look at the explosion of working from home, remote working, working from potentially anywhere in the world, for a few that might be a beautifully furnished purpose-built office in the house or garden, or even more extravagant a yacht in Mauritius. However, for most it will be a space in a bedsit, a hole underneath the stairs, the kitchen table, the coffee table, a shared office space that could be high end, but could be a shared box!

So the future workspace isn't just about what, it's very much about where, when and why!

As we've shared throughout this book, there is no single truth. Each of us is an individual and as complex as our brains are, our needs around workplaces and workspaces will need to be considered from an organizational perspective, but also on a micro (team) and macro (employee) level, to ensure we empower our people to perform at their best in a safe and accessible environment.

Working from home neurodiverse advantages noted

- Choice over when to work.
- Choice over where to work.
- Ability to break tasks into smaller chunks and take short breaks.
- Ability to move around when you don't want to be disrupted or to disrupt others.
- Creating the right environment without having to conform to social or unwritten office rules.
- Reduced interruptions such as random enquiries from colleagues, phone calls.
- Some sensory triggers can be reduced, such as noise from others around, and lighting can be determined.
- Specific seating and desks can be set up and a constant work station established.
- The individual can determine when to take a break or stretch their legs or walk and talk on a call.

Working from home neurodiverse disadvantages noted

- Sharing the space socially with others can lead to interruptions and distractions.

- Dealing with other unforeseen interruptions, such as deliveries and personal phone calls, dogs barking and children!

- Opportunity for procrastination. It can be easy to drift off to do other tasks such as household tasks, playing on games consoles, reading books etc.

- Routine can easily slip, particularly if there are demands from others such as trying to work around a partner's shifts.

- Internet access may vary, especially if being shared with others working from home.

- Gaining the accessible tools, seating and specialist equipment that are present in the workplace may not be possible because of cost, assessment and availability.

- Loneliness and isolation. Development of secondary issues such as stress and depression as a result of a lack of an adequate work environment and control over the ability to change it, can result in a performance drop.

- Constant need to demonstrate productivity to others can be problematic as informal guidance and communication can be missed.

- The person can develop habits of extending the work day such as starting earlier and ending later, checking emails on days off and being constantly 'on call'.

The future will probably see a swing from the necessity for working from home all the time, which had to happen for so many, to working from home some of the time. This will mean establishing new rules. With some consideration and planning, it can result in creating the best workplace solution for each person.

The moral of the tale is to take a person-centred approach.

Inclusive environments and accessibility

Jean Hewitt is part of Buro Happold's inclusive design team in London, one of the leading practices in the field. She has specialized in inclusive environments and accessibility since 2001, ensuring that client facilities are safe, accessible and inclusive for everyone. Her work specializes in access, inclusion and wellbeing in the built environment and includes auditing of existing places, appraisals of new designs (buildings and external environments), stakeholder engagement, co-design and advisory services. She is excited to be technical author for a new BSI guide, PAS 6463: 'Design for the Mind: Neurodiversity and the built environment'[1] informed by a steering group of experts from across the UK.

The PAS guide will provide information for designers, planners, specifiers, facilities managers and decision-makers on particular design features (such as lighting, acoustics, and finishes) which can make public and mainstream environments more inclusive for everyone. The content of the PAS guidance focuses on sensory processing differences and, in particular, design measures that may reduce the potential for sensory overload, anxiety or distress. Key beneficiaries will be anyone who has heightened sensory sensitivity including many people with, ASD, ADHD, SPS, Parkinson's, dementia, vestibular and other neurological conditions.

Jean says that, 'In addition to designing places to accommodate our diversity in form, size and physical ability, it should be a fundamental requirement to anticipate and design for neurological difference and mental wellbeing. This PAS is an exciting opportunity to ask designers to carefully consider the neurological diversity of humans so that places become comfortable for everyone to visit and use without encountering emotional distress or difficulty. We hope this will be an important first step in asking designers to regularly consider all neurocognitive profiles. I'm excited to have the opportunity to be involved in developing this guidance and thankful to the huge number of contributors (both professional experts and individuals with a range of conditions) who are helping to make this possible.

'We all hope to see a shift in approach by everyone in the built environment sector, so that neuro differences are seen in future as a fundamental everyday component considered as part of any good design, not an extra.'

So if this is about buildings and spaces in the future, what about learning and working practices? What will they look like? Is the future a really neurodiverse world? If this is the case, what do we need to do now in our education systems to be prepared?

CASE STUDY

Ravensbourne University: How do we prepare students for future working practices and ensure that we really attract neurodiverse teams?

Professor Gary Pritchard is Pro Vice-Chancellor Academic (Learning and Teaching and Student Experience) at Ravensbourne University in London. Amanda has been working with him and his team.

He talks about what he sees as the fundamental changes and the future from a university perspective preparing people for employment. 'Higher education has been transforming dramatically in the past 10 years due to factors such as Brexit, student expectations (now described as customers), technological change, the move to an aggressive competitive marketplace – and more recently Covid-19. Economic downturn, global lockdowns, a drive for remote and flexible working, demands for value for money, and a demand for greater connection between education and employment are just some of the forces that are dramatically disrupting the sector.'

He goes on to say: 'Students and their parents in the UK still see universities as the main means of securing future employment, and this means that employability and the student experience is more important than ever. Students expect to be taught and to learn using modern technology and methods and at a pace that they have chosen – not one that is mandated to them. They also demand an education that is tailored to their unique needs and acknowledges the diverse range of factors that need to be considered in nurturing deep learning in its cohorts.'

Gary describes one initiative he has been involved with. 'Ravensbourne is a small specialist design and media university based in London that attracts a broad and diverse student cohort that largely reflects the ethnic diversity of the capital itself (around 44 per cent). But it also welcomes neurodivergent creatives who require specialist support and an inclusive pedagogy. In 2019 Ravensbourne partnered with Professor Amanda Kirby's Do-IT Solutions organization with a project to screen all incoming first-year students using the Do-IT Profiler. The results revealed that a sizable minority of students have difficulties with learning skills, particularly reading. Those students are more likely than the average student to then also have difficulties with study skills and attention skills. Students who have reading or attention difficulties are also more likely than the average student to have at least one mental health diagnosis.'

Gary describes the value of understanding his students' neurodiverse patterns of strengths and challenges and how they used the data they gathered. 'This data allowed the university to identify support resources for all its students, but also enabled academic faculty at course level to have a richer picture of the learner needs in each cohort. Alongside this we were able to target the use of other specialist support resources such as coaching, mentoring and counselling to ensure that all our students were assisted in their learning journey and to prepare them for their working careers. We also used this intelligence to develop an inclusive curriculum (The Mindsets and Skillsets Manifesto). This includes our Digital Mindsets programme that seeks to prepare all students for the world of work. It was carefully designed to put so-called soft skills personal development on equal footing with skills acquisition and intellectual rigour. Traditionally such emotional intelligence, nurturing (if taught at all), is partitioned off into Student Services or "specialist workshops" outside of the core curriculum. By positioning this at the heart of the learning timetable, an intentional signal was being communicated: that nurturing the development of the whole individual – whatever that requires – has to be prioritized. By extending the norms of skills acquisition and competency-based approaches the Digital Mindsets programme seeks to nurture the creative individual beyond the academy, embracing the holistic notion of educating the whole person – with no student left behind. Here, critical life skills are investigated and multiple intelligences explored through a model that supports professional and personal development to create and support resilient and inclusive individuals prepared for work in the ever-changing creative industries and for living in the wider fast-changing societal and cultural flux in the 21st century.

'Digital Mindsets works to embed such modes into the curriculum in order to nurture rounded practitioners who are strong team players and self-reflective creatives who are fully prepared for the world of work. This model also rejects outmoded deficit-based pedagogies that rely on deficit remediation programmes that operate on the basis of encouraging students to work on perceived weaknesses as the basis for their academic and professional progression. Conversely, our strengths-based approach attempts to help students identify their own unique talents and then use them to develop a strategy for utilizing such gifts in negotiating their academic progression and careers.'

Gary and his team have a vision of how neurodiverse learning can operate for future students: 'By actively welcoming students who are neurodiverse into our community of learning, not only do we provide the personalized curriculum and support that our students deserve, but we also are developing a previously untapped rich source of talent that both higher education and the creative industries have missed out on historically. We owe it to ourselves and to this generation of massively gifted and unique students to ensure that they find their place, and flourish in this latest industrial revolution.'

We can look at education but what about ensuring that talent can be turned into employment?

Big new world is not all about big business

Amanda has been thinking a lot about the small businesses in the UK and worldwide and the link between innovation, entrepreneurship and neurodiversity.

Let's start by thinking of the 99.9 per cent of all businesses in the UK that are classed as small to medium-sized enterprises, ie employing between 1 and 249 employees:

- **0.6 per cent** are medium-sized businesses (50–249 employees);
- less than **4 per cent** are small businesses (10–49 employees);
- **96 per cent** are microbusinesses (0–9 employees).

This is similar in many countries globally. As we live in a post-Covid-19 world that has opened up options for an ideal mix of working from home and working flexibly, this offers opportunities for skilled workers to participate in their ideas even more, when they may have found a standard office setting too much.

Where is the wider conversation about neurodiversity and entrepreneurship?

Amanda has been talking with Rob Edwards as he has been very excitingly setting up the Neurodiversity and Entrepreneurship Association in the UK. Rob says: 'The pervading theme of conversations with academic researchers, charity leaders and business supporters about neurodiversity and entrepreneurship, is one of fragmentation.

'At the start of 2020, the UK had 5.94 million small businesses, equating to 99.9 per cent of the total business population, and yet, if we use that as a rough measure of entrepreneurship (probably as broad a term as neurodiversity), the data about how neurodiverse people contribute to this number is patchy, missing, and fragmented (Federation of Small Businesses).'[2]

Rob makes a very good point about the talent that's out there and how some businesses are working with individuals to get started. 'There are snapshots of great small to medium-sized businesses out there that have been created and are being led by, or employing, neurodiverse people. For example, the pioneering @geniuswithinCIC were showcasing fantastic small businesses on Twitter as part of a 12 Days of Xmas campaign.'

He goes on to say: 'Research also suggests that some of the skills that could be termed "entrepreneurial", like creativity, resilience and problem-solving, can play to neurodiverse strengths. And yet, where is the data about the number of these businesses? How many SMEs are being run by owners who might describe themselves as neurodiverse? Where does one go to get an overall picture of the wider landscape? Where are the comparative studies of the UK's progress against projects and initiatives in other countries? Where are the obstacles and issues recorded and aired, so that solutions can be discussed and created?'

He makes a good point that we need to have the data and to be able to search for the skills. 'Without an interconnected research base, shared knowledge and the pulling together of what information is available, it is a challenge to tackle the barriers that we do know about, like access to finance, education and training, implications for welfare benefit support, a lack of role models and mentors, and a robust and supportive business infrastructure.'

We are excited to see the setup of this new organization which will be '... focused on research, practice and policy, the Neurodiversity and Entrepreneurship Association is a new body that aims to gather the conversations about neurodiversity and entrepreneurship together, to connect academics, existing and prospective SME owners, and policymakers.'

We need to remember we have some way to go to be a really inclusive neurodiverse workplace and open conversations will only happen when people feel safe to do so in organizations of all sizes.

Ross Cooper, who is co-editor with Dr Katherine Hewlett, has been doing some wonderful work relating to Neurodiversity in the Workplace including curating the Westminster Achieve Ability Commission and Report (2017).[3] He says, 'The most consistent barrier we face is employers (and others) having so little understanding of neurodivergence. This means that disclosure is most frequently met with suspicion, distrust and opposition. This, in turn, means that our strengths are dismissed and our weaknesses become the focus of concern, rather than being valued for our ability to make innovative contributions.'

Jack of some trades and not master of all

We know that neurodivergent talent is often spiky with some amazing strengths but also often some challenges. It is balancing this out so the strengths can win. This may relate to everyday organization and time management tasks such as paying the bills on time and invoicing when you have done the work. Remembering to do this may be harder and may be not good time spent, reducing the time spent where the talent lies.

Amanda loves the work she does but can sometimes forget to invoice for it. Working as part of a team with other people who are much better at some of the day-to-day activities in a business can allow the business to thrive. No one is good at everything! The accounting, marketing and 'small stuff' are crucial to make a sustainable business. This is where working with a network or marketplace of people with different spiky profiles could offer some real shared solutions. We have the capability to do this. The future for neurodiversity in the workplace is a really exciting one.

KEY POINTS
Future workspaces and workplaces

- The future of workplaces will consider neurodiversity at the design stage of new spaces.

- The future of education needs to prepare children and young people for different workplaces that enable them to grow their talents.

- In the future we hope that those who are missed, misdiagnosed and misdirected get early support so they can travel their best pathway.

Notes

1 BSI (2020) Project launch: First building design standard for sensory and neurological needs, BSI, 6 October, https://www.bsigroup.com/en-GB/about-bsi/media-centre/press-releases/2020/october/project-launch-first-building-design-standard-for-sensory-and-neurological-needs/ (archived at https://perma.cc/7838-77K7)

2 FSB (2019) UK small business statistics business population estimates for the UK and regions in 2019, The Federation of Small Businesses, www.fsb.org.uk/uk-small-business-statistics.html (archived at https://perma.cc/96LA-2ZGN)

3 Achieve Ability (2017) Neurodiverse voices: Opening Doors to Employment, https://www.achieveability.org.uk/files/1518955206/wac-report_2017_interactive-2.pdf (archived at https://perma.cc/PAD2-4LTY)

16

Next Steps! Inclusion, equity and diversity = belonging

No one fits into one neat box

Introduction

In writing this book we have heard from some wonderful organizations that are making a real difference to people's lives in a tangible way. The companies who are taking on board the concept of neurodiversity and putting the policies and processes into place. Their passion and understanding is moving from rhetoric to real action.

We have also talked about missing people in pre-employment because of the silos we often operate. We may focus activity around disability, or gender, LGBTQ+ or Black, Asian or other minority ethnic groups. But the future is really about not considering neurodiversity as an isolated area of focus in an organization but instead really considering that everyone has merit, reducing bias and being truly inclusive. This may start in considering recruitment processes, it may be helping people to gain placements, and it may also require organizations to be assisted by companies with experience to guide them through the necessary changes.

When we started this book we were in a different place to where we are today and the concept of neurodiversity is changing. This is exciting.

In this chapter we hear from three amazing people talking about their personal and professional experiences and also about the organizations they run, where they are today and what their hopes are for the future.

Each person has written with a sense of passion and commitment in common, a theme that has run through our book. Many of us are here because we are neurodivergent or have family members who have struggled to gain the education and employment that they deserve. The first of these is a wonderful, impassioned story from Nancy.

Nancy Doyle

Nancy Doyle is the CEO of Genius Within, a community interest company specializing in supporting people who are neurodiverse to be successful. She stands up and champions neurodiversity in a sensitive and thoughtful way to make a real difference. She tells her personal story about why this is a passion for her.

'I have specialized in disability inclusion since my first job, which was as a support worker for adults with learning disabilities and mental health needs aged 18 years old. Having struggled with my own mental health as a teenager due to undiagnosed ADHD, I found both personal and professional interactions with the psychological profession unsatisfying. I decided to train as a psychologist, to understand the science-based approach, and planned to critique it from a position of knowledge. In the past 25 years, I have maintained my own personal journey of coming to understand my own psychology, and a professional one of learning more about others. My focus has been occupational psychology and the neurodiversity movement had an instant appeal to me early on due to the needless waste of human potential. Working as a trainee psychologist doing group work with marginalized young unemployed people in inner cities across the UK including London, South Tyneside, Hull, Leicester and Sheffield, I repeatedly came up against the same issue: bright, engaging, dynamic young minds who had no education and no self-belief. What caused this dissonance between potential and achievement? Neurominority status, intersecting with poverty, racism and sexism. Having also worked with individuals with developmental delay, learning disabilities and institutionalization I found it very frustrating that we were disabling an additional swathe of the population simply because our industrialized education system had excluded them. Literacy, numeracy, fine motor control, the ability to sit still and concentrate for lengthy periods, concentrating in noisy distracting environments – these skills should not define our working lives and yet they do. Not because you need those skills to be a painter, or a hairdresser, or a surgeon, or a paramedic, or a nurse or a publican or an entrepreneur, but because the entry points to all those careers rely on homogeneous, sausage machine education systems that few neurominorities can survive without having their souls crushed.

'So around 2003 I started developing a specialism in neurodiversity inclusion at work. I provided diagnosis, workplace needs assessments and coaching support to thousands of neurodivergent people, all of whom were either unemployed or at risk of unemployment. I qualified as a psychologist in 2005 and went on to conduct a research doctorate by evaluating the impact of disability adjustments for neurodiverse employees. I've studied management science, human resources and organizational theories as well as the neurobiology of neurodiversity, the emotional and social impact of marginalization and I am a qualified Expert Witness for discrimination tribunals. I also stand at the intersection of whiteness, a childhood in working-class schools but with undiagnosed, educated but poor parents and femaleness, having finally received a formal ADHD diagnosis at the age of 38. I situate myself both within and outside the paradigm, and my perspective is based on empirical observation, interpretative experience and critical review of the missing voices in the debate. I've been in this field for a long time, before it was popular, when people were routinely locked up in institutions and girls couldn't get an ADHD diagnosis at all.'

Nancy describes what she sees are her main priorities for the neurodiversity movement: elitism, bad science and amateurism. She goes on to say, 'I think the solutions are systemic, co-produced and well-evidenced in adjacent fields. We've been reinventing the wheel in neurodiversity and failing to learn from the right peers. I'm going to take each item one section at a time and outline the problem, and then the solution.'

Nancy talks about what she thinks is elitism. 'Neurodiversity is racist, sexist, classist and ableist. It has questionable LGBTQ credentials. Prevalence studies have reliably shown a demographic bias towards white, male, cis, heterosexual presentation. Girls are more likely to be diagnosed as anxious, or eating disordered, or to have personality disorders.[1] Black, brown and poor children are more likely to have conduct and personality disorder diagnoses and more likely to be criminalized.[2] Trans people suffer from diagnostic overshadowing and their gender issues are treated and supported before their autistic or dyslexic experiences. Is this because pale, male, well-resourced people are more likely to be neurodiverse? No. Genetic research has demonstrated that there are few differences between male and female ADHD markers, for example, yet the presentation differences are huge.

'The diagnostic criteria are based on behavioural observations, these are subjective, socially biased and, quite frankly, bad science. For years we've associated girls with empathy because that's how we name their behaviour, not because we can see inside their minds. We give them dolls to play with, we sing to them more and throw them around less as babies and then assume that the differences are biologically determined even though that is unlikely.[3] More contemporary research has debunked empathy deficits yet the machines of science and practice move slowly. Pejorative, pathologizing questionnaires are still a requirement for practitioners making diagnoses and they are still routinely excluded on the basis of insufficient evidence, asking the wrong questions.

'Elitism has very real consequences. Perceived "lack of empathy" or "lack of self-regulation" or tropes like "dyslexia is a middle-class condition" (only so because only middle-class families can afford diagnosis) give educators permission to withhold support, and ration it for the "kids who really need it" – the ones with disabilities we can see, or fit our stereotypes. In 2020 I had to critique an invitation to tender issued by a government security agency asking for autism training. It was issued on the basis that "autistic people don't experience empathy and therefore are more likely to be criminals. We need to know how to handle this". Actually, research indicates autistic people are less likely to commit crime! Twenty-five per cent of the prison population have ADHD[4] yet less than 1 per cent had a formal diagnosis and access to treatment. Autism, dyslexia, coordination and language disorders, intellectual disabilities all over are represented in unemployment, incarceration, poverty and poor long-term health outcomes,[5,6] yet the neurodiversity movement is laser focused on one area: white, male, autistic technologists. This is not what the neurodiversity paradigm promised to deliver. Without making a dent in standardization of education and entry-level work, the neurodiversity activism field is a commoditization, a greedy sell-out and the epitome of elitism. Those who make it through are supposed to hold the door open for others to follow, not slam it shut in their faces.'

Nancy talks about what she considers to be 'bad science': 'Biased research paradigms and asking the wrong questions have influenced our categorization process. We invested millions in scanning the brains of kids to find the bits that are broken. If they can't read, then there must be something wrong, we'll find it with our expensive clever systems of neuroimaging and genetic profiling. Traditional scientific paradigms have missed the most essential questions: Why? So what? WHY would human evolution continually throw up a sizable minority with specialist thinking skills? So what if we know the mechanism of what's happening on the inside? It helps us believe people when they tell us that they are struggling, and helps us to avoid character assassinations for those who literally don't have enough dopamine to sit still or sufficient sensory processing to find typing easy but what can we do about it? More than 60 per cent of neurodiversity research is neuroscience based.[7] Why? Are we going to operate? Use transcranial magnetic stimulation? What will all these millions achieve if we're not looking at ecological factors – environments that are conducive/restrictive, tools and processes that overcome barriers and unleash creativity? Alternatives to the sausage machine of education. While all the glory-seeking academics are rooting around for the pot of gold at the end of the rainbow, devising research questions that serve their own egos and finding mascot-type job roles in elitist businesses for a lucky few, 15–20 per cent of the population is struggling.'

Nancy goes on to describe an experience of one workplace needs assessment she was asked to review by a registered psychologist. 'My contact was concerned. She had been given a list of things she had to do differently at work in order to keep her job, things like setting goals at the start of the week to help with procrastination, colour-coding diaries – the list was basic, infantilizing and deeply insulting. The author of the report demonstrated a fundamental misunderstanding of human resources, disability legislation and the process of adjustments. Equality law worldwide indicates that organizations have to make accommodations. An assessment which sets a list of tasks on the to-do list of an already struggling employee is not legally compliant nor likely to work. The employee needs support, a coaching intervention to develop those habits or devise some that are achievable, personal, easy to adopt. The report should also have made recommendations for changes to working conditions, such as flexible hours or remote working to ensure quiet space for focusing, yet none were made. This is poor practice on the part of the psychologist; it is based on heuristics and an absence of scientific research. This is where our scientific efforts should be focused, not making up new rules about categories for diagnosis. Twenty-five years have passed since I became a psychologist in order to improve the profession. This sort of practice is exactly where my efforts lie – in the boring, back-office committee politics of writing best practice standards for practitioners, and generating research interest in practical field-based research to develop interventions that work.'

Nancy also talks about 'amateurism' and the risks of this. 'While we dithered with bad science and ill-informed practice, a large void has opened. Where can a neurodiverse/divergent person go for advice? Will they be offered Applied Behavioural Analysis (ABA) "treatment", which has deep, unaddressed flaws?[8] The neurodiversity self-advocacy movement has started to fill this space. My own sister reports that she gets more helpful information from parent networks on Facebook than from her daughter's speech and language therapist, who really wants her to try ABA to stimulate speech and is withholding funding for an AAC (Augmented and Alternative Communication) device until my sister has "tried it". All the while my three-year-old niece remains unable to communicate her needs effectively and is suffering needlessly. However, we have learned that fact and fiction are not easily discriminated against on social media and there is a huge risk to the system when the speediest, most caring responses are provided by those with the least training. Firstly, the advice might be wrong. Secondly, it is likely to be biased to anecdotal evidence – what worked for me rather than what has a good chance of working for you. Thirdly, it places a huge responsibility on the people who are giving it, who have their own traumas and exclusion to deal with. Lastly, it absolves the state, medics, educators, employers and psychologists of the obligation to deliver and improve.'

Nancy talks about her present work and the relevance of this and what she feels needs to be done. 'In the world of work, many HR teams have abdicated responsibility to in-house champions and lived-experience panels. Employees in need of adjustments are referred to Frank in finance, who has an autistic son, so must know everything. Kamini in marketing has a dyslexia diagnosis, and is now in charge of training managers in neurodiversity awareness. A group of in-house champions have determined that HR must issue a policy stating that no autistic people are invited to group socials in case it makes them feel pressured. In the group they are having a big argument as to whether autism can be caused by brain damage because one of them experienced birth trauma and says that it can, and the others find this discriminatory and want to ostracize him. These are real examples. From my experience as a trained expert legal witness I need to tell you that every single one of these cases could result in a disability discrimination claim. The employers are not doing due diligence and worse, their negligence means that employees are not getting the support they need and are risking their livelihoods. I have no doubt that Kamini will give advice on what works for her, that the autistic people who don't want to be invited to lunch mean well, but it is anecdotal. When I advise HR, don't do it on the basis of my personal diagnosis, I do it on the basis of my training in psychology, management science and knowledge of the law.'

Nancy's point is an important one we have reiterated in the chapter relating to misusing 'champions', and also the burden this can place on the person being given this role. She goes on to reiterate this point. 'And what of Frank in finance? How is he going to cope if someone reveals to him that they are so worried about losing their job they've been self-harming? Is it fair to ask him to take on this extra role, for which he is not paid or trained? What about the colleagues' privacy and confidentiality? Is their data being captured and stored safely by Frank? Does he know he has to do that? Employers are not asking these governance questions and have deferred responsibility to a vulnerable population. Outside the workplace, self-advocates are routinely responsible for each other's mental wellbeing and those who form a viable income stream in this field become conflicted – in order to earn a living they have to put their own raw trauma in the public domain, and handle that of other people. It is not fair or safe and we need a viable alternative.'

Nancy describes the actions she thinks should be taken to make an impact: 'I am arguing vociferously for my contact to complain about her workplace needs assessment report. I have personally written the professional practice guidelines that this professional has contravened. I know that if they are reported to their regulatory body there will be an investigation, perhaps a hearing, and a report that the whole profession sees, so that we can transparently learn from the mistake and update our practice. One example will be held up, often anonymously, to shine a light to others. This is how professional systems of practice are supposed to operate. We can't improve the support networks by circumventing them, we have to go in directly and give each other the opportunity to learn and improve. Chip chip away at poor practice and simultaneously build the evidence base of what does work, what is ethical, what services individuals find helpful.'

Nancy discusses what she thinks should happen and describes this as systemic inclusion. 'So what is the answer to all this? Well, in what Judy Singer calls the "feeding frenzy" around neurodiversity, we're currently stuck on compliance and tokenism. Employers hire and expect individuals to ask for the help they need, even when it is perfectly predictable that 20 per cent of the workforce will need some sort of adjustment. We've spent years focused on Autism at Work projects. Entire conferences are dedicated to business people from flashy large corporations doing 'show and tell' about how awesome they are for hiring 80 autists into their tech teams.

Does this work? They say yes. They say the autistic technologists are doing an awesome job. And from a simplified "if and then" level of analysis I guess they are right. The logic works: *if* we can't hire autistics via traditional recruitment *and* we create these special programmes *then* they can be included and they do a good job. *If* we create special programmes *and* they do a good job *then* it is working. *If* they do a good job *and* we have proved it works *then* we have increased inclusion. But from a critical perspective, *who* is on these programmes? Where are the poor, female, undiagnosed autistics? Do they have a job yet? What about dyslexics? What about the intellectually disabled? *If* you need a diagnosis to get on these programmes *and* that diagnosis is determined by your privilege *then* your programme is elitist. And further, *if* you can only join the programme if you are autistic *and* other people cannot apply *then* your programme is positive discrimination, which is illegal in the UK, Australia and many US states.'

Nancy's point relating to access to special programmes is important. If the route into a programme is by gaining a single diagnosis of autism, what does that actually mean when different people will have different patterns and strengths as well? Is the pass-card the diagnosis or that you have the skills for the job? Is the application process tilted towards males more than females and those 'lucky enough' to be formally diagnosed?

She goes on to say: 'Chris Argyris came up with a theory called "double-loop learning".[9] He asserts that in single-loop learning, we see a problem and fix it. You can't read? Have some software. Autistic people can't get a job? Have a special programme. Argyris' work points out that a lot of what we think of as sophisticated science falls into this trap. Paradigm shifts and scientific breakthroughs come when we shift our thinking to question the structures that created the problem in the first place. Ten per cent of you can't read? I wonder whether reading is really an essential human endeavour and what can you do instead? One per cent of you turn out to be excellent employees but can't get through recruitment processes? I wonder if we should change those recruitment processes and make them more focused on the eventual job performance, not heuristical HR practices that have poor predictive validity. When we zoom out a level, from the perspective of the square peg in the round hole to the number of pegs, and the variety of holes possible, and the frequency of the poor fit, we find that systemic pattern level, from which we can create systemic change.'

Nancy describes how her company works and what they do. 'In my company, Genius Within CIC, we've provided coaching interventions for more than 10,000 people. We measure success for individuals. We ask them and their managers to anonymously rate performance before and two months after coaching. We ask our coaches to record the topics they want to focus on. We ask them for their experience on the programme, qualitatively. We follow up after one year to ask what happened to their jobs which were at risk, and their career. We have a lot of data now, some of which I have had peer-reviewed and published in specific cohorts.[10,11,12,13] Ninety-two per cent of our clients want help with memory and concentration. That's nearly all, in a diverse group of neurominorities and hidden disabilities. Eighty-two per cent organizational skills, 78 per cent time management, 67 per cent stress management, 67 per cent communication. Our most common point of referrals is six months into promotion. Ninety-five per cent of clients keep their job. Twenty-five per cent of clients get promoted within a year. Managers report a 50 per cent increase in performance. Clients themselves report a reduction in stress and a 70 per cent increase in productivity. It works. But it is STILL single-loop learning. For it to be double-loop learning we need to zoom out. What these data show is that there are predictable trends in adjustment compliance. For a double-loop, systemic approach we need to plan for them and not react, one person at a time. We can build universal HR systems[14,15] and prevent distress and poor performance.'

Nancy and Professor Almuth McDowall in 2020 started to set up a Research Practice Alliance Centre at Birkbeck's School of Organizational Psychology to consider levelling up the neurodiversity toolkit in management science. So what does Nancy think about Diversity and Inclusion?

'In scientific training, you learn that when you have a new idea, the first port of call is to read widely around the subject and find adjacent fields from which you can port principles and theories. Neurodiversity at work is failing on this front, and so I'm going to introduce some relevant learning that I think will illuminate our practice. Firstly, diversity, equity and inclusion research more broadly. Many neurodiversity advocates and practitioners I know approach D&I like we have to teach them about us, but we should also note what they have to teach us. In racial equity work, terms like virtue signalling, performance activism and tokenism have become popular. These allude to an approach where racial diversity is tolerated, onboarded one person at a time, like a mascot or a few mascots, without actually changing any of the systems that caused the lack of representation in the first place. Sound familiar? It is considered incredibly poor practice to ask the single female board member or only black person in management to educate others about inclusion. Sound familiar? Racial diversity work has identified a tendency to "top slice" and lump all races and ethnicities into one BAME category. This tends to result in recruiters selecting east Asians over black Africans or Afro-Caribbeans but still "ticking the box" – this reminds me of the autism privilege over dyspraxia, for example.'

So what does she think makes a difference?

'In academic research, systematic reviews aggregating the results of tens of individual interventions have found that in-house champions and panels of lived experience are performative and do not increase representation. What works is coaching/mentoring programmes and holding managers to account for recruiting and promoting inclusively.[16] We are currently rein- venting the wheel and making all these mistakes again, when it is not neces- sary if we just took a professional, multi-disciplinary and evidence-informed approach to the work.

'However, the "neurodiversity at work" field is overrun with "experts" from education, or clinical practice, or marketing and MBAs, who have not spent enough time on their own training and research to see what has already been done. Knowing about neurodiversity is not enough. We need services that also know the law, human resources, can view the situation from individual and organizational perspectives, who can intervene when an individual idea should not be scaled because it is anecdotal.

'My first big intervention in psychology practice was getting the practice guidelines updated to firmly state that reports should go to the individual first, not their employer. This principle hasn't been considered because in clinical and educational practice the norms are professionals sharing infor- mation about a client, all with their own ethical guidelines. I pointed out that HR and managers are not regulated professionals and not able to decode reports, and that we should summarize the employer versions with "need to know" only information, not developmental history and IQ scores. It took me years to get that through, with many boring committee meetings in which I had to sit still and listen! I know that there are still instances where this slips through the net, and I urge all employers reading this not to ask for all the details in reports, it's confidential. Ask for what you need only! I urge all employees to complain to the Health Professionals Council or the British Psychological Society if your psychologist sends a confidential report to your employer before you have signed it off. You have the right to withdraw. Help improve practice.

'Secondly, involving communities of lived experience is not new. Self- advocacy was not invented by autistics, the internet, or the need to push back on institutionalized professions. There are a number of examples here, for example the failed token disability employment programmes of the

1980s and 1990s and their much more successful incubated social enterprise successors[17] as well as mental health and substance misuse recovery communities.[18,19] In recovery communities, people with lived experience become mentors, but not immediately on arrival, not on the basis of their social media activity, but on the basis of their own recovery. An individual will arrive and complete a self-discovery journey of healing, in a group so that they have exposure to other peoples' journeys, which may be different to theirs.'

We have discussed this in the chapter relating to neurodiversity champions and compared this to mental health first aiders and the need for appropriate supervision to support people and respecting the qualifications and training someone actually needs and supervision once someone is acting in a support role.

Nancy talks about the difference for someone with the appropriate professional training and the support they receive. 'As such, they get informal, client-centred training in breadth and depth of lived experience. They then become supervisors and mentors, whilst receiving their own supervision. If one of their clients has an experience that triggers them, they have a safe space to debrief. If one of their clients reveals abuse, suicidal intentions or self-harm, they have a safeguarding mechanism and support to enact it. They conference with professionals who are managing the service and designing the workshops. They contribute to materials and evaluation protocols. They are included and valued, without being overexposed or burdened. If they take a month off sick, someone will be there for their clients. It is a safe system.

'I've seen this work well in employment. One client I have employs 65 per cent neurominorities, of all flavours. They have an in-house champion group, but they don't ask these individuals to take responsibility for their colleagues. The panel is part of the procurement decision; when I pitched for the work to do assessments, coaching and training for this company I had to be interviewed by the in-house champions. They took great care to make sure I was the "right" kind of psychologist, that I wasn't going to train their HR team to believe they had no empathy, or make adjustment recommendations that foisted a long to-do list on their colleagues. They worked in partnership with the procurement team who checked that my company was registered with the Information Commissioner's Office and had a good data control record, that we were insured, etc. This is also a safe system. This organization is leading the way and the areas in which they now need support involve conflicts where two employees require competing adjustments (eg low and bright light) or where meltdown outbursts cannot be tolerated by colleagues with PTSD. Whose needs win? This is what I call the "sharp end" of neurodiversity, beyond the bright lights of skill and unusual talents, making it work on an everyday, team-based level, protecting employment but also protecting from discrimination. It is complex, holistic work that needs an ecological frame in which legal duties are balanced with personal experiences. It's exactly the right time for co-producing policy and processes.'

What does Nancy see as the future of neurodiversity? 'So as we move into this maturing phase in the neurodiversity field, my long-term hope is that we develop systemic, co-produced practice. I'd like to upend and redesign education, but I am a workplace psych not an educational psych so I guess I need to stay in my lane! For me personally, I love my work and I am proud of my neurodiverse, disabled, female-owned and led business. My own ADHD forms a massive part of my success as a human and it has also been disabling. I didn't attend school for two years in my teens and I was hospitalized for anxiety, depression and disordered eating. I am aware that my needs were simultaneously minimized and mistreated as a female, yet privileged due to my white skin. My parents were educated enough to fight my corner. I was diagnosed with school phobia and allowed to study from home, rather than labelled a school refuser or a talent. My parents were listened to, and argued with, but not dismissed. This experience was deeply scarring, but I emerged with solid GCSEs and a platform on which to build a career, rather than a criminal record or a crack habit.

'My granddad once took me for a G&T when I was about 18. I was living in bedsits and failing to achieve any A-Levels. I'd started eight so far, but hadn't finished any (*how* did they miss the ADHD)? He said that I needed to work. That education wasn't engaging me and that I should ignore my parents who were insisting that I go to uni and get a job. He told me that I shouldn't follow the trodden path, but go where there is no path and leave a trail, which I think is Emerson. He was right. All my work, with my company and Employable Me, advocating from practice to change, filling the gaps in the scientific literature, is aimed at social inclusion. When I took that job with disabled adults and young people I found my vocation, my passion and my motivation. Finding my own "Genius Within" transformed my life and this is the gift I wish to pass on. I still think that if we had that missing 15–20 per cent working at their best across all industries the world would change.

'We need to come together as a sector, avoid the us/them traps, professional versus lived experience, educator versus clinician, HR versus manager and develop communities of practice, amplifying the skill and value that each element brings. That, after all, was the original purpose of the Neurodiversity Movement.'

We also hear from another genuinely impactful organization with values that we all need to listen to. The voice of this case study is from Atif Choudhury, and was written with the heartfelt assistance of Raphaele von Koëttlitz, whose ongoing support helps bring so many of Atif's visions to life.

Atif Choudhury

Atif is a CEO and award-winning social entrepreneur, with a background in economic justice and disability inclusion projects. He set up Diversity and Ability (D&A), a multi-award-winning disabled-led social enterprise that exists to increase the social and economic participation of disabled people. They have supported over 20,000 disabled and neurodivergent people in education, the workplace and through social justice projects.

Atif describes their work. 'Ten years ago, D&A was created to fully promote and advocate a social model of disability by galvanizing the lived realities and assets of disabled people to fulfil the spirit of the then newly formed Equalities Act. As an end-user-led organization, 85 per cent of the team self-identify as disabled, myself included, and our work is guided by this wealth of varied lived experiences to ensure support is relevant and authentic.

'At D&A, it's not just about teaching tools to support neurodiversity, but about inclusion, belonging, and the safety of connecting with others that share similar experiences of disablement. The impacts of disability are all too often rooted in wider-reaching intersecting factors that, when piled up, create immense levels of inequality. Growing up on a council estate in Thamesmead, as a young dyslexic Bangladeshi, I know concretely what this means and how it can impact your life.

'Everyone deserves the opportunity to learn, work and thrive, but it's often not afforded to those navigating systemic marginalization. Exclusion does not happen in a vacuum, but is a product of many layers of intersecting societal barriers. That is why when we talk about disability, we must always think about wider disabling factors such as race, religion, gender and class etc, that compound socio-economic disadvantages.

'Effective support and societal change in terms of the inclusion of disabled people hinges on the recognition of these interlinked barriers. Disabled people do not have homogeneous identities, needs or backgrounds and when this is ignored it leads to powerlessness and loss of agency. Society suffers when we fail to recognize and harness the value in diversity.'

Atif talks about his own experiences and how this differs for so many. 'I was only diagnosed with dyslexia at university, at the point of dropping out. This was a pivotal turning point for me emotionally, educationally and professionally, and is a story that echoes millions of others, particularly those from poor, BAME backgrounds. Accessing support, particularly for those experiencing hidden disabilities, is a privilege. This support is often denied to those who need it the most, due to cultural understandings and financial means.

'This is particularly highlighted by our work with people impacted by homelessness, where it's estimated roughly 50 per cent have learning differences such as dyslexia, which more often than not are undiagnosed.[20] Mental health conditions are also rife, with about 44 per cent disclosing a mental health diagnosis (as opposed to 23 per cent of the general population).[21]

'There is a clear link between unsupported, undiagnosed learning differences and access to civil society in terms of baseline social welfare, education and employment opportunities and stable housing. This is often compounded by digital exclusion; statistics show that disabled and homeless people are among those with the lowest digital access in our society.[22] This is due to a variety of factors including financial means, physical access points to computers and charging points as well as barriers posed by learning differences and poor digital literacy skills.

'In our digital-by-default world, it's critical to be able to access and effectively use technology to benefit from online services, to maintain social connections and be included in the job market. To illustrate, one study by the House of Commons indicates that almost 90 per cent of jobs require some form of digital skill.[23] This being said, technology has the potential to be both enabling and disabling. When used as a tool to overcome day-to-day literacy barriers, for example through using built-in accessibility functions or assistive technology, technology can facilitate increased participation in society and access to information. However, usability and accessibility can equally be compromised by lack of fundamental digital literacy skills or challenges linked to a learning difference.'

Atif goes on to describe some of the work they have been doing in the past few years to make a difference. 'We have been working with anti-homelessness charities such as Crisis and St Mungo's since 2014, to tackle the issue of digital skills gaps, providing digital literacy and core skills training to enable service users to access the internet and use technology in their daily lives. One training recipient, who faces significant literacy barriers, shared his story of how discovering text-to-speech functionality on his smartphone enabled him to advocate for his rights when faced with eviction from his home. He was able to scan a letter that contained information confirming his payments were up to date and have it read out loud. He was then able to relay the information and calmly diffuse the situation with a bailiff. He explained how the use of technology in this way not only diverted what would have otherwise been an extremely stressful encounter but also, crucially, it allowed him to take control of the situation and make sure his housing wasn't jeopardized. Armed with new strategies and hope, the participant said he was finally able to start looking to the future and exploring employment opportunities that had previously been out of reach.

'Another participant, who moved to the UK from Somalia with child refugee status at the age of 14, spoke little English and only as a second language. She struggled with reading and writing at school and never learnt to read and write independently. She was diagnosed with dyslexia at the age of 28. The tailored digital skills training introduced her to various apps and assistive technology programs that allowed her to be more independent and confident in navigating essential services and day-to-day tasks. Through using voice recognition software she was able to get online and research universal income and housing benefits available to her. She also explained how she was emotionally dependent on having to get a neighbour or friends to read out her post until she started using text-to-speech software to read it out to her. This reduced the anxiety of not knowing what was contained in the letters (even medical ones) and having to rely on others, as well as granting her a level of personal privacy that she had previously been forced to sacrifice for so long.

'Providing tailored support and access to assistive technology can help break the cycle of homelessness. I draw on these examples to illustrate the very real knock-on effect and cyclical nature of social and economic marginalization when intertwined with disability.'

Atif concludes his thinking about considering what is the true value of diversity: 'D&A shines a light on the value diversity can bring; after all, we can achieve miraculous things when we all have a seat at the table. Every day I look at the organization and smile, knowing it's the organization I needed when I was younger. Cultivated by the powers of such lived experiences, I am truly convinced that when welcomed, the diversity of thought can change the world; perhaps it's the only thing that ever does.'

Alan Kriss

Alan is CEO of Specialisterne USA/Canada. 'Specialisterne began its journey focused on autism. But it did not take long for us to learn that in the employment context, diagnoses are less relevant than personal experience and the impacts of living outside the norm. Many persons who identify as neurodivergent face similar challenges obtaining and maintaining employment. Yet they have the skills and motivations to be an asset to an employer. Specialisterne is here to bring candidates and employers together and to help build successful careers. Specialisterne focuses on competitive employment and is not focusing on supported employment solutions.'

What do they think makes them different from other organizations?

'One of the things that makes us different from other organizations and makes us unique is our focus on the employer side of these employment issues. In many countries like the US and Canada, early interventions and supports are improving so that more young people are getting through high school and often getting post-secondary education. These are capable and motivated people who are looking to start their careers. But employers have not kept up with the evolution. They maintain the same recruitment methods that they were using at the beginning of the last century. So employers tend to systematically overlook autistic talent as well as other people with a range of neuro-differences. We do more than educate employers. We work with them to first begin to successfully recruit and manage neurodivergent persons, and then to work closely with them to help them implement changes that would systematically improve their diversity outcomes in recruitment and beyond into developing careers.

'Some organizations teach and some do what is needed for the employer. We teach and we do, depending on the need and the evolutionary stage or maturity of the employer with respect to inclusive cultures, policies and processes. In terms of candidates, our focus is on those who are employment ready, or at least quite close, and we work with employers to create social and physical environments for them to be themselves, a state in which they will be so much more productive.'

Alan describes Specialisterne's aims now and for the future. 'We're trying to be a lantern for propagating improved tools, methods and processes for

FIGURE 16.1   Specialisterne maturity curve

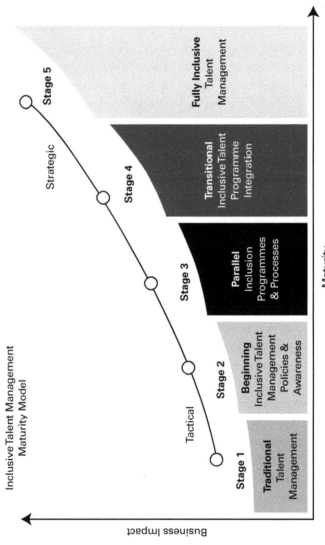

Employ Different Thinking

Inclusive Talent Management
Maturity Model

Business Impact

Stage 1
Traditional Talent Management

Stage 2
Beginning Inclusive Talent Management Policies & Awareness

Stage 3
Parallel Inclusion Programmes & Processes

Stage 4
Transitional Inclusive Talent Programme Integration

Stage 5
Fully Inclusive Talent Management

Tactical

Strategic

Maturity

© 2020. Specialisterne Canada Inc.

recruiting and onboarding people. We are forced to take an outlier's perspective because we work with outliers who have skills to do many jobs. Globally our objective is to generate meaningful employment for 1,000,000 people who are autistic or who are neurodivergent. This is about transformation in the employment market; ensuring there's an equal chance of attaining employment and of developing real careers. We want to change systems and have a transformational impact.

'We see the future as all about innovation and working with partners from a number of different perspectives and objectives including employers, post-secondary institutions, HR management and research, working with a wide range of diversity partners, recruitment providers, system providers and including industry-specific associations to leverage their expertise and match their emerging needs.

'We have a stepped approach (see Figure 16.1) working with employers where they are in their maturation, going from stage one which is traditional forms of placement to stage two beginning, stage three working in parallel, stage four transitional steps, and stage five delivering an inclusive solution.'

Paul Sesay

Finally we hear from Paul Sesay and his incredible journey and why he champions diversity and inclusion. Like the other case stories he is dedicated to the work he does. He is making a real difference in the UK diversity and inclusion space working with organizations from all sectors of employment, driving standards up year on year.

The story told above by Specialisterne is one of organizations embedding policy and practice in a completely inclusive manner, which aligns well to Paul's ambitions and the actions he has taken so far to encourage organizations to do so.

'As the proud founder and CEO of a number of Diversity and Inclusion initiatives including The National Diversity Awards, The Inclusive Companies Membership, The Inclusive Top 50 UK Employers List and the Inclusive Companies Awards, and most recently "The Precedent Group", my business acumen has mainly been with a social focus. With over 17 years' worth of experience within the Diversity, Equality and Inclusion sector, I have worked alongside some of the largest organizations in the world on their D&I profiles, helping to advance inclusion across each strand, across each level of employment. I am extremely proud to have created a national platform that allows me to work with diverse communities, helping inspirational individuals from various backgrounds to achieve and empower disadvantaged groups across the nation.'

Paul tells us about himself as a young man. 'My journey really began when I was a young lad, fostered from a very young age, growing up in inner-city areas and raised with no visible role models guiding me through life. Consequently, this meant I grew up with no ambition, no goals, and not many dreams that I can recall. It was a trip to Liverpool and a chance meeting that ignited that fire in my belly, and I knew then that I wanted to make a change, and not just a change for myself but also for the lives of others too.'

His story of someone believing in him and inspiring him is one that we all need to take on board as it can change lives. He goes on to say, 'Iconic Liverpool DJ and club MC James Klass took me under his wing when I arrived in Liverpool and gave me countless opportunities to build my own unique skill set and instilled the belief that I could become something, that I could make a difference and I could be successful. James was the inspiration behind me changing my entire outlook on life.

'I worked for various companies, primarily in a sales role and I found that I was actually really good at it! I got my head down and I worked hard, and I outsold all the other team members, by far. I could feel that fire in my belly once again, and I knew that I had what it took to set up my own business, I just had to take that plunge.

'And I did. Inclusive Companies was born and a team of four were working hard to break down barriers that individuals from disadvantaged backgrounds felt that they faced when applying for job opportunities in major organizations. We developed school workshops designed to inspire youngsters to raise their sights and believe in their abilities, as well as recruitment fairs and conferences.'

Paul also describes how he was able to revisit his vision even in challenging times. 'The recession hit, and whilst this had a detrimental impact on my business, I didn't want to lose sight of what was important; there was still work to be done across D and I and I wasn't about to give up so easily. I quickly identified that there was an urgent need to highlight role models across the UK for the contributions they provide across minority communities, and so the National Diversity Awards was born.

'Nine years later and the National Diversity Awards is a ceremony that the nation has truly taken to their hearts, with over 60,000 nominations and votes received in 2020 alone, highlighting the tremendous work of Positive Role Models, Community Organizations and Entrepreneurs up and down the country.'

Despite making a real difference, Paul certainly hasn't become complacent. 'My journey continued and I wanted to expand my portfolio of D&I initiatives and so set up the Inclusive Companies Awards and the Inclusive Top 50 UK Employers List, both of which recognize cross-industry organizations who are striving for an inclusive workforce across each level of employment and highlight the work that they carry out for D&I both internally and the contributions across their local communities.'

Paul has continued to drive forward what needs to be considered as inclusive practice and has recently taken this to the next step. 'The most recent initiative to develop a truly inclusive business is Precedent Group, which delivers a portfolio of recruitment services with particular focus on diversity and inclusion. We work with progressive, forward-thinking organizations to enable them to capitalize on the competitive advantage of building and maintaining a diverse workforce. We harness our expertise and network to create and deliver future-facing talent for the modern world.

'Thinking differently is in our DNA and we believe that all candidates, regardless of their background, ethnicity and gender, should be represented in a manner in line with their skills and abilities. We work with all our partners to fully understand their requirements and hiring practices to seamlessly match talent into their businesses.'

Paul is certainly not ready to stop what he is doing: 'Over the years we have seen slight progress across the inclusion spectrum, but I know there is still so much more work to be done, especially when we look at the levels of diverse representation within UK-based organizations. In 2017 I designed a support network that allowed me to work holistically with organizations on their unique D&I journey, providing them with the tools they need to become a fully inclusive employer. Inclusive Companies is now the premier cross-industry network harnessing best practices and innovation to drive inclusion for all. It was designed and exists to challenge the lack of diverse representation within UK-based organizations and to assist employers in fostering a truly inclusive environment within which they recognize and value the difference of each employee.

'It is through this network that we have been able to identify organizations who are ahead of the curve in the diversity arena.'

One thing he has achieved is that he has managed to engage all sectors of business in this initiative. 'University Hospitals of Morecambe Bay NHS Foundation Trust (UHMBT) were named the UK's most Inclusive Employer in 2020, taking the Number One position on the Inclusive Top 50 UK Employers List for the first time ever in recognition of their continued dedication to workplace diversity. They have made significant progress in striving to become "Effortlessly Inclusive". Ensuring the best possible experience for colleagues and patients is at the heart of their Inclusion and Diversity Strategy – understanding and learning from current lived experience, to make improvements that are far-reaching and make a real difference to people in their communities.'

It is interesting to see what Paul says has been great about this organization: 'UHMBT has a number of procedures to help staff understand the organization's commitments to equality of opportunity, which starts on the employee journey even before they begin in post. They have a public-facing web page for Inclusion and Diversity which enables staff and patients to understand how seriously they take equality and diversity. On that page are their annual reports for inclusion and various action plans together with their overall five-year "Towards Inclusion" strategy (2016–2021), as well as monthly inclusion newsletters and information about inclusion networks.

'Following on from the recruitment process, their corporate induction, which is mandatory for all staff, covers information and contact details for their inclusion networks for colleagues (covering BAME, LGBT+, Gender, Forces, Respect, Personal Fair and Diverse champions and Carers) and a Network for Inclusive Healthcare. In addition, they have a mandatory Equality and Diversity training course, which is essential to all roles, that staff complete every three years.'

Paul also describes a very different organization but one that is nevertheless a very well-known international brand. '2019 saw media giant Sky ranked as the UK's Most Inclusive Employer. Serving 24 million customers across seven different countries, Sky's 31,000 employees help connect customers with the very best of sports, news, the arts and to their own local, original content. Their technology allows customers to watch what they want, when they want, how they want, and as they connect millions of families to content they love, it is their responsibility to do it safely through services such as Sky Broadband Buddy and the Sky Kids app. And their online streaming service, NOW TV, brings viewers all the enjoyment of Sky with the flexibility of a contract-free service. Sky is also a proud employer – signed up to Disability Confident (a UK government scheme) and a "Race at work" signatory, as well as being recognized by *The Times*, Stonewall and also as the UK's most Inclusive Employer.'

Paul makes an important point that we have reiterated a number of times in this book that you can make a difference if you are one person, a small team or a small organization. Passion and commitment can go a long way. He says, 'You might think a big organization like Sky would have a large inclusion team, but they don't, because they believe a sustainable approach is empowering every team to understand any inequality and take action. It is evident that Sky are tapping into their own inherent sense of fairness and the times they've felt excluded, to connect their people with purpose and make the changes needed both today and in the future.'

Paul describes what Sky has set up: 'Sky has six thriving employee networks, each with an executive sponsor who guides them to focus on what matters most. These volunteer-led communities have the freedom to push boundaries and agitate for change through the creation of bottom-up pressure and a collective voice, to make life at Sky great for everyone both on screen and behind the scenes. At Sky, inclusion is everyone's responsibility.'

Paul speaks of where we are in considering inclusion, and why we cannot go back to where we were. 'In 2021, I have seen a shift in the inclusion approach of organizations participating in the Inclusive Top 50 UK Employers List. The disruption of Covid-19 followed by the impact of the Black Lives Matter movement has truly shone a light on the power of inclusive leadership and prompted employers to examine inadequacies internally. Companies featured on this year's list have felt the importance of ensuring individual voices are heard and standing up as responsible employers against inequality, injustice and intolerance.

'The topic of diversity, equity, and inclusion (DEI) has become a focal point for major organizations across the globe. The most prosperous employers understand the value of harnessing diverse talent and are taking action to ensure their company is not left behind in the quest to become fully inclusive. It is clear to see that a host of companies are making improvements across many areas, whilst some are falling behind in others.

'Since I began my business venture in 2006, my core values have remained consistent throughout the years, to enhance diversity and inclusion across each protected characteristic. As we move through 2021, companies should ask themselves new questions for a changed workplace. Leaders now have an opportunity to build a more equitable and inclusive workplace that will improve their organizations far beyond Covid-19. Companies that capture the moment will not only be better placed to support their employees but will also drive sustainable business performance.'

What is consistent among Paul, Atif, Alan and Nancy is considering how to embed their innovative and thoughtful practices.

Judy Singer, the Australian sociologist, seen by some as the 'mother of the concept of neurodiversity' reminds us in a blog she wrote in February 2021:[24]

> Don't be intimidated by the hefty word 'Neurodiversity'. It's simply a word that describes the incredible diversity of human minds, in which no two of the billions of us on the planet are exactly alike. We are all 'Neurodiverse'. There are not two groups of people in the word, 'normal people' and 'the neurodiverse'. There is only flawed humanity, all of us imperfect, all of us with needs, all of us interdependent.
>
> Neurodiversity is not a new name for 'Neurological Disability'. It is the name of a social movement by neurologically categorized outsiders with labels like autistic, ADHD, the dyses, etc to remind us of the wonder of the extraordinary diversity of the human mind, and to bring us back to our senses. It calls us to stop dividing people into 'the productive' and 'the unproductive', where the possession of 'a job' is the highest measure of virtue, while those who cannot win the gruelling race to get one, are punished by punitive welfare systems and grudgingly doled out the meanest portion to survive on.
>
> Despite the fancy name, the recognition of the value of neurodiversity changes nothing about human nature: it just gives us a 'rallying cry' – in the jargon of our age – to mobilize for what humans have strived towards throughout the ages: fairness, justice, a fair share of the riches of the world around them. That is, enough to have their basic needs met, and enough over to allow them to develop their potential, to care for each other and to enjoy the beauty and glory of our world.
>
> At such times, it will require courage to stand up for minorities, along with humility, patience, perseverance and work. And it must be real work in the service of the future of humanity, not 'busy work' as conscripts goaded by the carrot of consumer goodies and the stick of a punitive 'welfare' system. We must not buy into the belief that work, any paid work, is inherently a virtue. Not when it is used to pollute the planet for the sake of producing consumer junk for people in a perpetual dissatisfied state from the meaninglessness of their working lives.

What have we learned?

In the process of writing and completing this book, Theo and Amanda have changed. They have listened to and learned from many wonderful people and organizations striving (and in many cases succeeding) to create change. They all have one thing in common. They are driven and committed to an inclusive and equitable agenda and are not satisfied with the status quo. They are all saying we CAN do more. We have heard from people being a part of that change process and challenging the status quo.

This can be an exciting time if we can really make change and widen the opportunities for employment for all. It makes sense to harness and not lose the talent that we have in society. We are encouraged about the future if we can embrace the true concept of neurodiversity in that it is about the wonderful variety of strengths and skills in us all and is not an exclusive club that only some can join.

We need to be aware that in times of global challenges we don't resort to recruitment processes that continue to preclude groups of people in society because of the way we select or exclude talent. If we take on board the changes we need to make, we can hope for future workplaces that are truly inclusive. But it does require a change in both culture and practices.

Notes

1 Young, S *et al* (2018) The economic consequences of attention-deficit hyperactivity disorder in the Scottish prison system, *BMC Psychiatry*, https://bmcpsychiatry.biomedcentral.com/articles/10.1186/s12888-018-1792-x (archived at https://perma.cc/6KTP-EK3X)

2 Mandell, D S *et al* (2009) Racial/ethnic disparities in the identification of children with autism spectrum disorders, *American Journal of Public Health*, https://ajph.aphapublications.org/doi/10.2105/AJPH.2007.131243 (archived at https://perma.cc/G3LA-QDNN)

3 Rippon, G (2019) *Gendered Brain: The new neuroscience that shatters the myth of the female brain*, The Bodley Head Ltd, London

4 Young, S *et al* (2018) The economic consequences of attention-deficit hyperactivity disorder in the Scottish prison system, *BMC Psychiatry*, https://bmcpsychiatry.biomedcentral.com/articles/10.1186/s12888-018-1792-x (archived at https://perma.cc/6KTP-EK3X)

5 Fazel, S, Xenitidis, K and Powell, J (2008) The prevalence of intellectual disabilities among 12 000 prisoners – a systematic review, *International*

Journal of Law and Psychiatry, https://doi.org/10.1016/j.ijlp.2008.06.001 (archived at https://perma.cc/5UBH-7QXY)

6   Underwood, L *et al* (2016) Autism spectrum disorder traits among prisoners, *Advances in Autism*, https://www.emerald.com/insight/content/doi/10.1108/AIA-11-2015-0023/full/html (archived at https://perma.cc/79LX-YLGM)

7   Doyle, N and McDowall, A (2019) Context matters: A review to formulate a conceptual framework for coaching as a disability accommodation, *PLoS ONE*, https://doi.org/10.1371/journal.pone.0199408 (archived at https://perma.cc/R4ZU-6XE2)

8   Milton, D (2018) A critique of the use of Applied Behavioural Analysis (ABA): on behalf of the Neurodiversity Manifesto Steering Group, Kent Academic Repository, https://kar.kent.ac.uk/69268/1/Applied%20behaviour%20analysis.pdf (archived at https://perma.cc/5VYA-ZVKD)

9   Argyris, C (1977) Double loop learning in organizations, *Harvard Business Review*, hbr.org/1977/09/double-loop-learning-in-organizations (archived at https://perma.cc/SM93-ZE85)

10 Doyle, N (2021) Adapting other internal resources to a neurodiverse workforce. In S Bruyere and A Collela (eds), *Society of Industrial and Organizational Psychology: New Frontiers Series, Neurodiversity*, American Psychological Association

11 Doyle, N, Randall, R and Mcdowall, A (nd) Does it work? Assessing program effectiveness by Meta-impact from personalised development pathways. In prep and under review

12 Doyle, N and McDowall, A (in press). Diamond in the rough? An 'empty review' of research into 'neurodiversity' and a road map for developing the inclusion agenda, *Equality, Diversity and Inclusion: An International Journal*

13 Doyle, N and McDowall, A (2015). Is coaching an effective adjustment for dyslexic adults? *Coaching: An International Journal of Theory and Practice Coaching*, https://www.tandfonline.com/doi/full/10.1080/17521882.2015.1065894 (archived at https://perma.cc/64L5-VJD9)

14 Doyle, N (2021) Adapting Other Internal Resources to a Neurodiverse Workforce. In S Bruyere and A Collela (eds), *Society of Industrial and Organizational Psychology: New Frontiers Series, Neurodiversity*, American Psychological Association

15 Doyle, N and McDowall, A (in press) Diamond in the rough? An 'empty review' of research into 'neurodiversity' and a road map for developing the inclusion agenda, *Equality, Diversity and Inclusion: An International Journal*

16 Roberson, Q M (2018) Diversity in the workplace: a review, synthesis, and future research agenda, *Annual Review of Organizational Psychology and Organizational Behavior*, https://doi.org/10.1146/annurev-orgpsych-012218-015243 (archived at https://perma.cc/6UEW-PUQE)

17 Kalargyrou, V, Kalargiros, E and Kutz, D (2018) Social entrepreneurship and disability inclusion in the hospitality industry, *International Journal of Hospitality & Tourism Administration*, https://www.tandfonline.com/doi/full/1 0.1080/15256480.2018.1478356 (archived at https://perma.cc/XP7G-23PU)

18 Bassuk, E L *et al* (2016) Peer-delivered recovery support services for addictions in the United States: A systematic review, *Journal of Substance Abuse Treatment*, https://doi.org/10.1016/j.jsat.2016.01.003 (archived at https://perma.cc/E4W6-6XUJ)

19 Leamy, M *et al* (2011) Conceptual framework for personal recovery in mental health: systematic review and narrative synthesis, *British Journal of Psychiatry*, https://doi.org/10.1192/bjp.bp.110.083733 (archived at https://perma.cc/ VWF7-LR2J)

20 Thamesreach (2010) Homelessness Literacy Report, Turning the Key: Portraits of low literacy amongst people with experience of homelessness, https://thamesreach.org.uk/wp-content/uploads/2017/07/Turning-the-Key-Literacy-Report.pdf (archived at https://perma.cc/EVH5-NFZA)

21 Thamesreach (2010) Homelessness Literacy Report, Turning the Key: Portraits of low literacy amongst people with experience of homelessness, https://thamesreach.org.uk/wp-content/uploads/2017/07/Turning-the-Key-Literacy-Report.pdf (archived at https://perma.cc/EVH5-NFZA)

22 Office of National Statistics (2019) Exploring the UK's Digital Divide, 4 March, https://www.ons.gov.uk/peoplepopulationandcommunity/ householdcharacteristics/homeinternetandsocialmediausage/articles/exploringt heuksdigitaldivide/2019-03-04#what-are-the-barriers-to-digital-inclusion (archived at https://perma.cc/8WN8-C67W)

23 House of Commons Science and Technology Committee (2018) What digital skills do adults need to succeed in the workplace now and in the next 10 years? https://assets.publishing.service.gov.uk/government/uploads/system/uploads/ attachment_data/file/807831/What_digital_skills_do_adults_need_to_succeed_ in_the_workplace_now_and_in_the_next_10_years_.pdf (archived at https://perma.cc/6K7N-PQW4)

24 Singer, J (2021) Thoughts on Neurodiversity and the future [Blog] *NeuroDiversity 2.0*, 24 February, https://neurodiversity2.blogspot.com/ (archived at https://perma.cc/H56D-CUSK)

APPENDIX

What is ADHD?

Attention-deficit/hyperactivity disorder (ADHD) is a developmental condition that affects attention, impulsivity and activity levels. Some individuals may have a diagnosis of attention deficit disorder (ADD), the name used for this condition between 1980 and 1987.[1,2]

There are three types of ADHD: predominantly hyperactive, predominantly inattentive, and combined (which has both hyperactive and inattentive features).

How common is ADHD?

Studies suggest that between 2 and 7 per cent of children and adults have ADHD, with an average of around 5 per cent.[3,4] ADHD is still relatively under-recognized and underdiagnosed in most countries, particularly in girls and older children. ADHD often persists into adulthood and there are increased risks factor for other mental health disorders. There is evidence of negative outcomes, including educational underachievement, difficulties with employment and relationships, and criminality.

Common challenges described by adults with ADHD

IMPULSIVITY

- Speaking/acting before thinking.
- Interrupting others because of ideas and thoughts that can't wait to be shared.
- Jumping to a new topic of conversation without finishing the current one because of multiple ideas.
- Difficulty waiting turn.

HYPERACTIVITY (THIS IS MORE OBVIOUS IN CHILDHOOD)

- Difficulty sitting still and 'doing nothing'.
- Being restless and fidgety, eg tapping feet, playing with pen, being over-talkative, and doodling.
- Feeling restless internally – some people talk about having a 'busy brain'.

INATTENTION

- May be easily distracted; this may vary as some people find specific noises around them distracting or other people talking or movement.
- Losing concentration/daydreaming, especially for more boring tasks.
- Can hyper-focus on tasks of high interest.

ORGANIZATIONAL CHALLENGES

- Difficulty organizing selves and work without practising and having automated procedures in place.
- Can start tasks but finds it hard to finish them or misses out steps.
- Produces work of a variable quality depending on load of work, other distractions and level of anxiety.
- Feelings of frustration because the person wants to be organized and is often aware of their challenges.

Strengths associated with ADHD

- Creativity.
- Good initiator.
- Energy.
- Hyper-focused.
- Makes connections between things.
- Project oriented.
- An ideas person.

What is Autism Spectrum Disorder or Condition?

Definition

Autism Spectrum Disorder (ASD)/or Autism Spectrum Condition (ASC) is a developmental condition that affects communication and social inter-relatedness. Some people may have a diagnosis of autism or Asperger's syndrome depending when they were diagnosed. These were conditions that used to be diagnosed separately but are now considered to be part of ASD/ASC[5,6] Different people will have different challenges and strengths and not one person is similar to another.

In the autism community, many self-advocates and their allies prefer terminology such as 'autistic', 'autistic person', or 'autistic individual' because they consider that autism is an inherent part of an individual's identity. Identity-first language is also used such as 'person with'. Ask the person their preference.

How common is autism?

It used to be thought that autism was fairly uncommon. Rates vary worldwide and this may be because of the method of identification and awareness. The rates are around 0.5–1 per cent of populations. This has increased for several reasons in the past few years, partly because of increased awareness.

Challenges described by some adults with Autism

SOCIAL COMMUNICATION

- Autistic people may have difficulties with interpreting both verbal and non-verbal language like gestures people make or tone of voice.
- Language skills may vary, from some autistic people having no language to some having good language skills.
- May take things literally and not understand more abstract concepts or pick up on sarcasm.
- May need additional time to process information or respond to questions.
- May repeat what others have said to them.

SOCIAL INTERACTION

- Autistic people often have difficulty recognizing or understanding others' feelings and intentions and expressing their own emotions. This makes it harder going into new social or work situations, especially to start with.
- May have difficulties in some social interactions because of communication differences.
- The person may appear to others as insensitive or be direct.
- May find noisy or busy settings overwhelming and need to have time alone.
- May find it harder to make friends.
- May mask challenges they are having in order to conform to social stereotypes.
- May assume others already know they have some challenges, so may not inform others or wish to do so.
- May be reluctant to discuss challenges, which may be related to poor past experiences with others when they have disclosed they are autistic.
- May be very able in some aspects of employment (and may be very well qualified) yet may face real difficulties with tasks that appear simple to others, eg getting to appointments on time, mixing with a group of other people.
- Difficulty coping with change to routine if no time to prepare or understand what the change may be.
- May lack confidence when asking questions or asking for help.
- May be anxious when faced with unfamiliar situations, questions and/ or people and if anxiety is heightened may 'melt down' or 'shut down'. 'A meltdown happens when someone becomes completely overwhelmed by their current situation and temporarily loses behavioural control'; 'A shutdown appears less intense to the outside world but can be equally debilitating.'[7]
- May appear impatient/confrontational if they do not understand why they have been asked to do something.
- Are more likely to take language literally.
- Some people may have heightened sensitivity to certain sounds, touch, tastes, smells, light or colours and being exposed to them may cause them to feel more anxious.

- A changing or new environment may cause anxiety. Some people have repetitive behaviours (called stimming) and this may occur when the person is feeling more anxious and help them feel calmer.
- Many autistic people have intense and highly focused interests.

Strengths associated with autism

- Hyper-focused.
- Specific interests.
- Detail oriented.
- Retention of facts.
- Creative.
- Good analytical skills.

What is dyslexia?

Dyslexia (also called Developmental Dyslexia) is a developmental condition that specifically affects literacy (reading, writing and spelling). People who have dyslexia have poor literacy after taking into account the education and teaching support they have had.

How common is dyslexia?

It can be hard to be precise, as many studies don't look at people's history and therefore can't tell the difference between dyslexia, alexia and illiteracy due to lack of education. It's commonly stated that 10 per cent of the population have dyslexia.[8] Rates may vary from country to country dependent on awareness, definition used and the type of assessments undertaken.[9]

Challenges described by adults with dyslexia

- Challenges with filling in forms, especially if hand-written.
- Slower at reading information and needing to re-read it.
- Making spelling errors or missing out key words in written text, eg emails.

- Difficulty structuring written work, eg reports, assignments.
- Difficulty writing down information accurately while doing another task such as listening to someone on the phone.
- Challenges remembering things or a series of instructions, eg appointments, instructions, items to bring to meetings.
- Finding way around unfamiliar places.
- Reluctance to disclose dyslexia to others. This may be related to poor prior experiences of doing so.

Strengths associated with dyslexia

- Creative.
- Outgoing.
- Resourceful.
- Entrepreneurial.

What is dyscalculia?

Dyscalculia (also called Developmental Dyscalculia) is a developmental condition that specifically affects mathematic ability. People who have dyscalculia have poor mathematic ability after taking into account the education they have had.

Innumeracy due to absent, patchy or inadequate education is not the same as dyscalculia, even though it may result in similar difficulties with mathematics. (Innumeracy is poor mathematics skills due to a lack of education and/or skills practice, whereas dyscalculia occurs despite sufficient education and time to practise skills.) Some people may have had mathematics skills but then lost them, eg due to stroke or head injury. This is called acalculia.

How common is dyscalculia?

It's hard to say, as most studies don't look at people's history and therefore can't tell the difference between dyscalculia, acalculia and innumeracy due to lack of education. This varies from country to country depending on awareness of the condition. Studies of children vary from 3.6 per cent in the UK to 6.4 per cent in the US.[10,11,12,13]

Challenges described by adults with dyscalculia

- May avoid maths-related tasks, eg paying bills, checking change.
- Slower completing simple maths tasks.
- Confusion with mathematical operator symbols (+ − × ÷ etc).
- May have difficulties accurately recording numbers, eg telephone numbers, bank details.
- May make mistakes when dialling telephone numbers.
- May have challenges telling the time, especially with analogue clocks.
- Challenges with time management.
- Challenges when trying to estimate distance.
- May forget passwords, pin codes, etc.
- May feel anxious when undertaking maths-related tasks.

Strengths associated with dyscalculia

- Creative.
- Artistic.
- Thinker.
- Empathic.

What is developmental coordination disorder?

Developmental coordination disorder (DCD) is a developmental condition that affects motor (movement) skills, coordination and balance. In the UK, it's often known as dyspraxia.

DCD is distinct from other motor disorders such as cerebral palsy or stroke.

How common is DCD?

Studies suggest that between 1.8 and 4.9 per cent of UK children have DCD.[14]

Common challenges described by adults with DCD

- Challenges with everyday life skills, eg preparing a meal, ironing, DIY.
- Challenges with handwriting fast and neatly.
- Challenges with skills requiring balance.
- Challenges with organization and time management.
- Challenges with tasks that need fine and accurate movements.
- Slower at learning new skills requiring speed and accuracy, but once learnt can do them.
- Lack of confidence because of childhood/school challenges.
- Increased association with anxiety and depression.
- Frustration when others don't understand why they have some challenges.

Strengths associated with DCD

- Empathic.
- Caring.
- Persistent.
- Creative.

What is developmental language disorder?

Developmental language disorder (DLD) is a developmental condition that affects the understanding of and/or production of spoken language. Some individuals may have a diagnosis of specific language impairment (SLI), an older name for this condition, or SCLN (specific communication and language needs).

How common is DLD?

Studies suggest up to 7.6 per cent of UK children may have DLD. This may vary from country to country depending on definitions, awareness and assessment approaches.[15]

Common challenges described by adults with DLD

- Difficulties following a series of instructions.
- Needing information to be repeated.
- Anxiety going into an unfamiliar setting.
- Taking longer than others to respond to a question.
- Needing additional time to respond and process information.
- Not recognizing quickly the social nuances of a conversation.
- Substituting related words, even when they don't mean the same thing (says 'couch' instead of 'chair' or 'beef' instead of 'chicken').
- Difficulties finding words.
- May use substitute words or use word fillers.
- Not always picking up on the meanings of jokes; may take things literally.
- Finds it difficult to focus on what someone is saying, particularly if there is background noise such as in an office.
- Often seems disinterested in conversations, even with friends or loved ones.
- Finds it harder to answer questions about what was just discussed and may need additional time to process the information.
- Finds it harder to join in 'office talk'.
- May appear rude or direct to others.
- Trouble following multi-step verbal instructions.
- Difficult responding quickly in a group setting.

What are Tourette's syndrome (TS) and Tic disorders?

Tourette's syndrome (TS) was named after Dr Georges Gilles de la Tourette who described the condition in 1885, although it had been described earlier. It is the most common cause of tics. It is also sometimes known as multiple tic disorder or tic spectrum disorder. TS is also commonly associated with other disorders including ADHD and obsessional compulsive disorder. Tics are relatively brief, rapid, intermittent, purposeless, involuntary movements (motor tics) or sounds. The latter are called vocal or phonic tics.

How common are tic disorders?

The rate is somewhere between 0.3 and 1 per cent of the population. Up to 20 per cent of the childhood population can have transient tics which go away over time. It is three to four times more common in boys than girls.[16] About 0.05 per cent of adults are thought to have Tourette's syndrome.[17]

Common challenges reported

Most tics are abrupt in onset and duration (clonic tics), but may be slow and sustained, either dystonic (associated with a twisting type of movement), or tonic, if the muscle contractions are isometric and not associated with any movement (eg arm or abdominal tensing).

Tics may be:

- 'simple' and include sniffing and throat clearing;
- 'complex' (coordinated, sequential movements resembling normal motor acts/gestures but that are inappropriately intense and may be repetitive).

Complex vocal/phonic tics may include barking and animal noises.

There are wide variations in TS, from potentially not very obvious signs such as shaking of the head or tossing hair that may not interfere greatly in every day functioning, to severe, pervasive and impairing challenges.

Tics may fluctuate in severity and are also suppressible, and persist during sleep. Most patients describe a sensation before the tic begins. Other symptoms include:

- Echolalia (copying what others say).
- Echopraxia (copying what others do).
- Palilalia (repeating one's last word or part of sentence).
- Coprolalia (inappropriate, involuntary, and swearing) – this is uncommon, occurring only in about 10–15 per cent of patients. However, it has been misconceived by some to be the main presenting feature of Tourette's syndrome.

Challenges for some people

- Higher rates of anxiety and depression.
- Having to cope with others' (mis)perceptions in public and/or in the workplace; being stigmatized.

- Tics may worsen in situations when the person is under stress. Although the symptoms of TS are involuntary, some people can sometimes suppress, camouflage, or otherwise manage their tics in an effort to minimize their impact on functioning.

- People with TS often report a substantial build-up in tension when suppressing their tics to the point where they feel that the tic must be expressed (against their will).

- Tics in response to an environmental trigger can appear to be voluntary or purposeful but are not.

- Tics are often reduced in calm and more focused conditions.

Strengths associated with TS and Tic disorders

- Creativity.
- Sense of humour.
- Empathy.
- Persistence.

Notes

1   American Psychiatric Association (2013) *Diagnostic and Statistical Manual of Mental Disorders, 5th edition*, American Psychiatric Publishing, Washington, DC, USA

2   Russell, G *et al* (2014) The association of attention deficit hyperactivity disorder with socioeconomic disadvantage: alternative explanations and evidence, *The Journal of Child Psychology and Psychiatry*, 55 (5), pp 436–44, https://acamh.onlinelibrary.wiley.com/doi/10.1111/jcpp.12170 (archived at https://perma.cc/2UXB-W2RP)

3   American Psychiatric Association (2013) *Diagnostic and Statistical Manual of Mental Disorders, 5th edition*, American Psychiatric Publishing, Washington, DC, USA

4   Sayal, K *et al* (2018) ADHD in children and young people: prevalence, care pathways, and service provision, The Lancet Psychiatry, 5 (2), pp 175–86

5   American Psychiatric Association (2013) *Diagnostic and Statistical Manual of Mental Disorders, 5th edition*, American Psychiatric Publishing, Washington, DC, USA

6   Chiarotti, F and Venerosi, A (2020) Epidemiology of autism spectrum disorders: a review of worldwide Prevalence Estimates since 2014,

Brain Sciences, **10** (5), p 274, https://doi.org/10.3390/brainsci10050274 (archived at https://perma.cc/G47H-5X8W)

7 National Autistic Society (2021) https://www.autism.org.uk/advice-and-guidance/what-is-autism (archived at https://perma.cc/2WTL-ZHW4)

8 The British Dyslexia Association (2021) https://www.bdadyslexia.org.uk/about (archived at https://perma.cc/L3MF-VJX9)

9 Mather, N, White, J and Youman, M (2020) Dyslexia around the world: a snapshot, *Learning Disabilities: A Multidisciplinary Journal*, **25** (1), pp 1–17, 10.18666/LDMJ-2020-V25-I1-9552

10 Lewis, C *et al* (1994) The prevalence of specific arithmetic difficulties and specific reading difficulties in 9- to 10-year-old boys and girls, *Journal of Child Psychology & Psychiatry*, **35**, pp 283–92

11 Badian, N A (1983) Dyscalculia and nonverbal disorders of learning. In H R Mykelbust (ed), *Progress in Learning Disabilities*, Ulverscroft, New York, USA, pp 235–64

12 Badian, N A (1999) Persistent arithmetic, reading, or arithmetic and reading disability, *Annals of Dyslexia*, **49**, pp 43–70

13 Shalev, R S *et al* (2000) Developmental dyscalculia: prevalence and prognosis, *European Child & Adolescent Psychiatry*, **9** (Suppl 2), II58–II64, https://doi.org/10.1007/s007870070009 (archived at https://perma.cc/4TFV-Z6AS)

14 Lingam, R *et al* (2009) Prevalence of Developmental Coordination Disorder using the DSM-IV at 7 years of age: a UK population-based study, *Pediatrics*, **123**, e693–e700

15 Lindsay, G and Strand, S (2016) Children with language impairment: prevalence, associated difficulties, and ethnic disproportionality in an English population, *Frontiers in Education*, **1** (2)

16 Scahill, L, Specht, M and Page, C (2014) The prevalence of tic disorders and clinical characteristics in children, *Journal of Obsessive-Compulsive and Related Disorders*, **3** (4), pp 394–400. https://doi.org/10.1016/j.jocrd.2014.06.002 (archived at https://perma.cc/C77X-L3VA)

17 Knight, T *et al* (2012) Prevalence of tic disorders: a systematic review and meta-analysis, *Pediatric Neurology*, **47** (2), pp 77–90

GLOSSARY

ABI: This stands for Acquired Brain Injury.

Acquired Brain Injury: Any injury to the brain. This includes Traumatic Brain Injury but also stroke, encephalitis, brain cancer, hypoxia, poisoning, substance abuse and other brain injuries.

ADD: This stands for Attention Deficit Disorder.

ADHD: This stands for Attention-Deficit/Hyperactivity Disorder.

AS: This stands for Asperger's Syndrome.

ASD: This stands for Autism Spectrum Disorder also known as ASC.

Asperger's Syndrome: See Autism Spectrum Disorder. Asperger's Syndrome is a milder ASD which was not typically associated with low IQ. In 2013, Asperger's Syndrome was removed from DSM-5. It remains a diagnosis in ICD-10 but has been removed from ICD-11.

Attention Deficit Disorder: Attention Deficit Disorder is an old term for ADHD. ADD was introduced in DSM-III in 1980 but was changed to ADHD in the revised version (DSM-III-R) in 1987.

Attention-Deficit/Hyperactivity Disorder: A condition characterized by inattention and/or hyperactivity and impulsivity. Symptoms must have been present prior to age 12 years. There are three subtypes of ADHD: predominantly inattentive, predominantly hyperactive-impulsive and combined.

People with predominantly inattentive ADHD have severe inattentive behaviour, but do not have severe enough hyperactive or impulsive behaviour to meet a diagnosis of combined ADHD. People with predominantly hyperactive-impulsive ADHD have severe hyperactive and impulsive behaviour, but do not have severe enough inattentive behaviour to meet a diagnosis of combined ADHD. People with combined ADHD have severe inattentive, hyperactive and impulsive behaviour.

Auditory discrimination: The ability to hear differences and similarities in phonemes or words, eg that 'cat' and 'cot' sound similar but are distinct.

Autism Spectrum Disorder: A condition characterized by difficulties with social communication and interactions and restricted, repetitive patterns of behaviour, interests and activities. It is a developmental condition, so is present from early childhood.

The term ASD includes conditions formerly described as Autism, Asperger's Syndrome and PDD-NOS. Also known as Autism Spectrum Condition.

Biopsychosocial model: A theory about illness/disability. This theory states that people's experiences of illness/disability depend on the interaction between their health or disability (bio-), their mental health, emotions and feelings (psycho-) and the physical and social environment they live in (social). Therefore, to help someone with an illness or disability, you need to look at all three of these aspects.

Camouflaging: This may be seen in females with ASD who may 'cover up' the challenges they have by modelling their behaviour on others around them.

Chronic Tic Disorder: A condition characterized by motor (movement) *or* vocal tics that have lasted for more than one year.

Cognitive: Mental processing or thinking.

Comorbidity: When two or more medical conditions that are not related to each other are found in the same person at the same time. This term generally should not be used for Neurodiverse conditions as they are often related to each other in some way.

Compensating: This is described by adults with ASD as either 'shallow' (eg laughing or nodding at others' jokes) or 'deeper' compensation. Compensation requires executive function and requires the ability to consider what may happen and to be able to switch between social rules and think about the social niceties. It is much harder to do when distracted or feeling distressed and can lead to mental fatigue.

Co-occurrence: When two or more medical conditions are found in the same person at the same time. This term is the preferred one to use for Neurodiverse conditions as it does not imply that they are unrelated to each other.

CTD: This stands for Chronic Tic Disorder.

DCD: This stands for Developmental Coordination Disorder, also known as Dyspraxia in some countries.

Developmental Coordination Disorder (DCD): A condition characterized by difficulties with big (gross) and small (fine) movement and balance. It is a developmental condition, so is present from early childhood. In the UK, this is often called Dyspraxia.

Developmental Language Disorder (DLD): A condition characterized by difficulties with receptive and/or expressive language. It is a developmental condition, so is present from early childhood. This used to be also called Specific Language Impairment, Specific Communication Language Needs.

Diagnosis: A statement or conclusion that describes the reason for a disease, illness or problem.

DSM: This stands for the *Diagnostic and Statistical Manual of Mental Disorders*. This book is used by many professionals around the world to diagnose mental health conditions. It is the American Psychiatric Association diagnostic categorization.

The various DSM editions are referred to by number: DSM-I was published in 1952, DSM-II in 1968, DSM-III in 1980 and revised (DSM-III-R) in 1987, DSM-IV in 1994 and revised (DSM-IV-TR) in 2000 and, most recently, DSM-5 in 2013.

Dyscalculia: A condition characterized by difficulties with mathematics. These difficulties may extend into telling the time and estimating distances. It is a developmental condition, so is present from early childhood.

Dysgraphia: Difficulties with handwriting – can be related to content and production.

Dyslexia: A condition characterized by difficulties with reading, writing and spelling. It is a developmental condition, so is present from early childhood.

Dyspraxia: See Developmental Coordination Disorder. Originally came from the 'brain injury' literature.

Education, Health and Care Plan: A relatively new term, replacing Statements of SEN in England.

EHCP: This stands for Education, Health and Care Plan.

Empathy: The ability to read and understand others' emotions, needs, and thoughts.

Executive function: A set of mental skills that make sure things get done. They are used in planning, time management, problem-solving, emotional regulation and keeping track of what you're doing.

Executive function deficit: Difficulties with executive function skills. Someone with an executive function deficit may have a hard time planning or starting tasks and seeing them through.

Expressive language: How a person communicates, using facial expression, gestures, body language and aspects of spoken language including vocabulary, word/sentence meaning, grammar rules, etc.

Expressive Language Disorder: A type of Developmental Language Disorder characterized by difficulties with expressive language. It is a developmental condition, so is present from early childhood. It is listed in ICD-10 as

Expressive Language Disorder but is included in DSM-5 under Language Disorder.

Hyperactivity: Active movements seen more in children with ADHD. In adults this may be seen as drumming fingers, fiddling with jewellery, doodling, rocking on a chair.

ICD: This stands for the International Statistical Classification of Diseases and Related Health Problems. It is a medical list that classifies diseases. It is created by the World Health Organization and is used by doctors around the world.

The various ICD editions are referred to by number: ICD-6 was published in 1949, ICD-7 in 1955, ICD-8a in 1968, ICD-9 in 1978 and ICD-10 in 1993. ICD-11 has been written and accepted. It will start being used in 2022.

ID: This stands for Intellectual Disability.

IDP: This stands for Individual Development Plan.

Impulsive behaviours: In adults this may be acting without thinking, eg a tendency to express thoughts and emotions without any sort of censorship; acting without regard to how such behaviour may affect others, spending money or making key decisions without reflecting on the impact on yourself or others.

Intellectual Disability: A group of conditions characterized by significant difficulties with general intellect and everyday functioning. They are developmental conditions and are present from birth. This term includes conditions such as Down's Syndrome. In the UK, Intellectual Disability is called Learning Disability.

IQ: This stands for Intelligence Quotient. It is a widely used scale for measuring general intelligence.

Kinaesthesia: The awareness of the position and movement of the parts of the body by means of sensory organs (proprioceptors) in the muscles and joints.

LD: This stands for Learning Disability. It is a UK term. In the US it can refer to Dyslexia as well.

LDD: This stands for Learning Disabilities and Difficulties. It is a UK term.

Learning Difficulty: See Specific Learning Difficulty. Learning Difficulty is a UK term.

Learning Disability: See Intellectual Disability. Learning Disability is a UK term.

Medical model: A theory about illness/disability. This theory states that people's experiences of illness/disability depend predominantly or only on the symptoms of their physical or mental health/disability. Therefore, to help someone with an illness or disability, you just need to treat their illness or disability, eg with medicine, physical therapy, etc.

Mental Retardation: See Intellectual Disability. This historic term is no longer used as it is considered pejorative.

Misophonia: Select sound sensitivity syndrome, sound-rage. People who are sensitive to certain sounds sometimes cope by blocking them out. Misophonia, literally 'hatred of sound', was proposed in 2000 as a condition in which negative emotions, thoughts, and physical reactions are triggered by specific sounds.

Mixed Receptive-Expressive Language Disorder: A type of Developmental Language Disorder characterized by difficulties with both receptive and expressive language. It is a developmental condition, so is present from early childhood. It is listed in ICD-10 as Mixed Receptive-Expressive Language Disorder but is included in DSM-5 under Language Disorder.

Multisensory: Relating to multiple senses, eg hearing, sight and touch.

ND: This stands for Neurodisability.

NDD: This stands for Neurodevelopmental Disorder.

Neurodevelopmental Disorders: This term refers to a cluster of related conditions that affect the brain (neuro-) during development. It includes ADHD, ASD, DCD, DLD, Dyscalculia, Dyslexia, ID and Tic Disorders.

Neurodisability: This term refers to any disability that affects the brain (neuro-). It includes NDDs but also other conditions including brain injury, stroke, encephalitis, brain cancer, neurodegenerative conditions such as Alzheimer's Disease and neurometabolic conditions such as Phenylketonuria.

Neurodivergence: This refers to people whose brains (neuro-) diverge from the norm or the 'average'.

Neurodiversity: This term was originally coined by Judy Singer, an Australian social scientist, to refer to Autism and was also described around the same time by Harvey Blume. Its meaning has now expanded to include (but not exclusive to) conditions often relating to a number of conditions including ADHD, ASD, Dyslexia, Dyspraxia (DCD), Dyscalculia, DLD and Tic Disorders,

The term Neurodiversity moves away from considering specific conditions negatively, as 'disorders', 'disabilities', 'deficits' or 'difficulties', and instead as traits of strengths and challenges that are a part of human variation.

Neuroqueer: A newer term that considers Neurodiversity/Neurodivergence from the perspective of queer theory. It is defined as both an identity and an ethos, involving being Neurodiverse, approaching this as a form of queerness and actively choosing to embrace, embody and express one's own Neurodiversity.

Non-stimulants: A family of medicines that are sometimes used to treat the symptoms of ADHD. They work by decreasing impulsive behaviour and/or improving attention span.

Obsessive-Compulsive Disorder: A condition characterized by the need to repeatedly perform certain routines (compulsions) or the presence of repeated thoughts (obsessions). These cannot be controlled by the person for very long and are severe enough to negatively affect the person's life.

OCD: This stands for Obsessive-Compulsive Disorder.

PDD-NOS: This stands for Pervasive Developmental Disorder – Not Otherwise Specified.

Pervasive Developmental Disorder – Not Otherwise Specified: See Autism Spectrum Disorder. PDD-NOS is an Autism Spectrum Disorder which is often, but not always, milder than typical Autism but more severe than Asperger's Syndrome. PDD-NOS is sometimes referred to as Atypical Autism. In 2013, PDD-NOS was removed from DSM-5. It remains a diagnosis in ICD-10 but has been removed from ICD-11.

Phoneme: The smallest unit of sound, eg 'b', 't' or 'ch'.

Phonology: To do with the systems of sounds that make up a language.

Pragmatics: To do with language in use and the contexts in which it is used. This includes things such as taking turns in conversation and implied meaning.

Proprioception: Perception or awareness of the position and movement of the body.

Psychostimulants: A family of medicines that are often used to treat the symptoms of ADHD. They affect dopamine activity in the brain and can help with focusing thoughts and ignoring distractions.

Receptive language: How a person understands other people's communications including how they understand other people's facial expression, gestures, body language and aspects of spoken language including vocabulary, word/sentence meaning, grammar rules, etc.

Self-stimulatory behaviour: Making repetitive movements, sounds or words or observing repetitively moving objects. For example, hand flapping, rocking, head banging or watching spinning objects. Self-stimulatory behaviour is commonly carried out by people with ASD to relieve anxiety and other negative or heightened emotions, happiness, boredom and/or to block out unpredictable or unwanted environmental stimuli. In adults this may be seen as drumming fingers, rocking back and forth on a chair, or repetitive playing or fiddling with objects.

Semantics: To do with meaning in language, including words, phrases, signs and symbols.

Sensory: To do with the senses – touch, taste, smell, hearing and/or sight.

SLI: This stands for Specific Language Impairment.

Social model: A theory about illness/disability. This theory states that people's experiences of illness/disability depend predominantly or only on how they interact with their physical and social environment. Therefore, to treat someone with an illness or disability, you need to change their physical or social environment. For example, someone who uses a wheelchair would no longer be 'disabled' if the environment they lived in accommodated their needs by having ramps and lifts instead of stairs.

Specific Language Impairment: See Developmental Language Disorder. The term SLI was replaced with DLD in 2017.

SpLD: This stands for Specific Learning Difficulty.

Specific Learning Disability/Difficulty: This term includes conditions that affect specific aspects of learning rather than general intelligence or overall functioning. It includes Dyscalculia, Dyslexia and Developmental Coordination Disorder (Dyspraxia). The term tends to be used more in educational systems.

Stimming: See self-stimulatory behaviour.

Synaesthesia: When stimulation of one sensory or cognitive pathway results in involuntary (automatic) experiences of a second sensory or cognitive pathway. For example, someone might see numbers and automatically strongly feel that each number is associated with a particular colour or someone might hear a particular noise, such as a trumpet, and automatically see a green circle.

Tactile: To do with touch.

TBI: This stands for Traumatic Brain Injury.

Tic Disorders: A term which includes Chronic Tic Disorder and Tourette's Syndrome.

Tics: The production of sudden, repetitive, non-rhythmic involuntary (automatic) movements, sounds and/or words. These include clapping, blinking, head jerking, repeating/echoing words or involuntarily saying taboo words or phrases.

Tourette's Syndrome: A condition characterized by motor (movement) and vocal tics that have lasted for more than one year.

Traumatic Brain Injury: Any injury to the brain that is the result of physical trauma, eg a blow or fall. TBI is classified as mild, moderate or severe based on length of loss of consciousness and/or Glasgow Coma Score immediately after injury.

Working memory: The 'temporary storage' part of memory that is used, for example, to store numbers when doing sums in your head or for storing ideas when decision-making.

Working memory deficit: Difficulties with skills and tasks that use working memory. Someone with a working memory deficit may have a hard time with decision-making, following instructions with several steps, doing sums in their head and/or copying text.

INDEX

Note: Page numbers in **bold** indicate Glossary entries.

CPSIA information can be obtained
at www.ICGtesting.com
Printed in the USA
JSHW031605040522
25574JS00002B/27

9 781398 600249